An Awai Books Trade Paperback Original.

Drawings and original text found in Him Her That are © Wisut Ponnimit. All rights reserved.

English translation by Matthew Chozick © 2013 Awai Books/Awai LLC.
Publication rights for English edition arranged by Awai LLC New York/Tokyo

Published in the United States by Awai Books, an imprint of Awai LLC,
New York. 1133 Broadway, Suite 708, New York, NY 10010

ISBN : 978 1 937220 01 3
eISBN : 978 1 937220 02 0

First edition : 2013
Printed in the United States of America
Art Director : Takahiro Furuya
Editor : Sebastian Girner
Image Editor : Xiroh

Portions of this book have appeared in *Tamukun to ipun* (2006 Shinchosha Publishing Co.,
Ltd.), *Blanco* (2008 Shogakukan Inc.), *hesheit* (2009 Nanarokusha Publishing Inc.), and
Romance (2010 Ohta Publishing Co.). The stories in this book were selected by Matthew
Chozick with helpful feedback from Wisut Ponnimit, Kazuhiro Kimura, and Keisuke Tsubono.

www.awaimedia.com

HIM HER THAT WISUT PONNIMIT

**Translated from Japanese by
Matthew Chozick**

AWAI BOOKS
New York · Tokyo

CONTENTS

ROMANCE

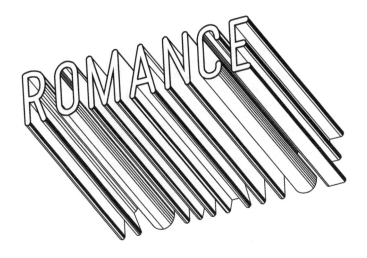

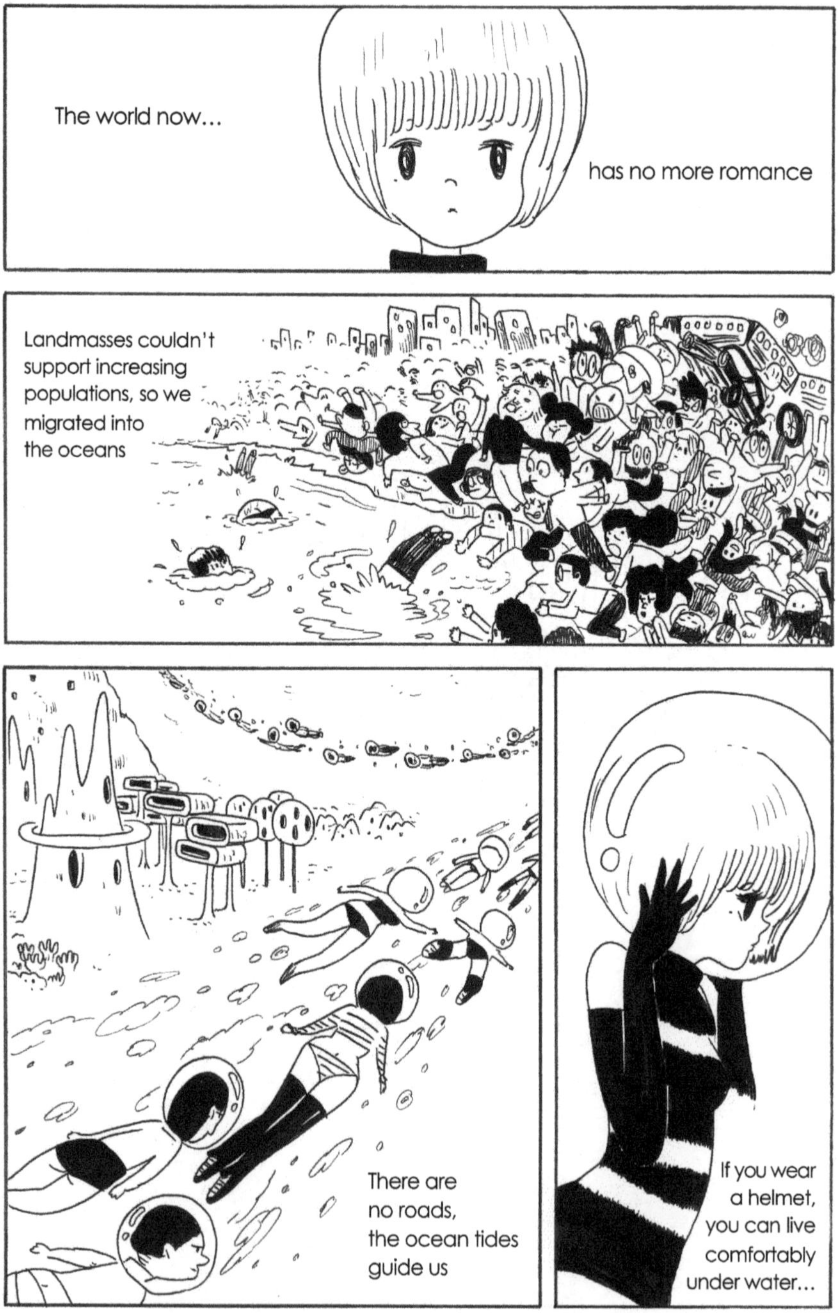
The world now...
has no more romance
Landmasses couldn't support increasing populations, so we migrated into the oceans
There are no roads, the ocean tides guide us
If you wear a helmet, you can live comfortably under water...

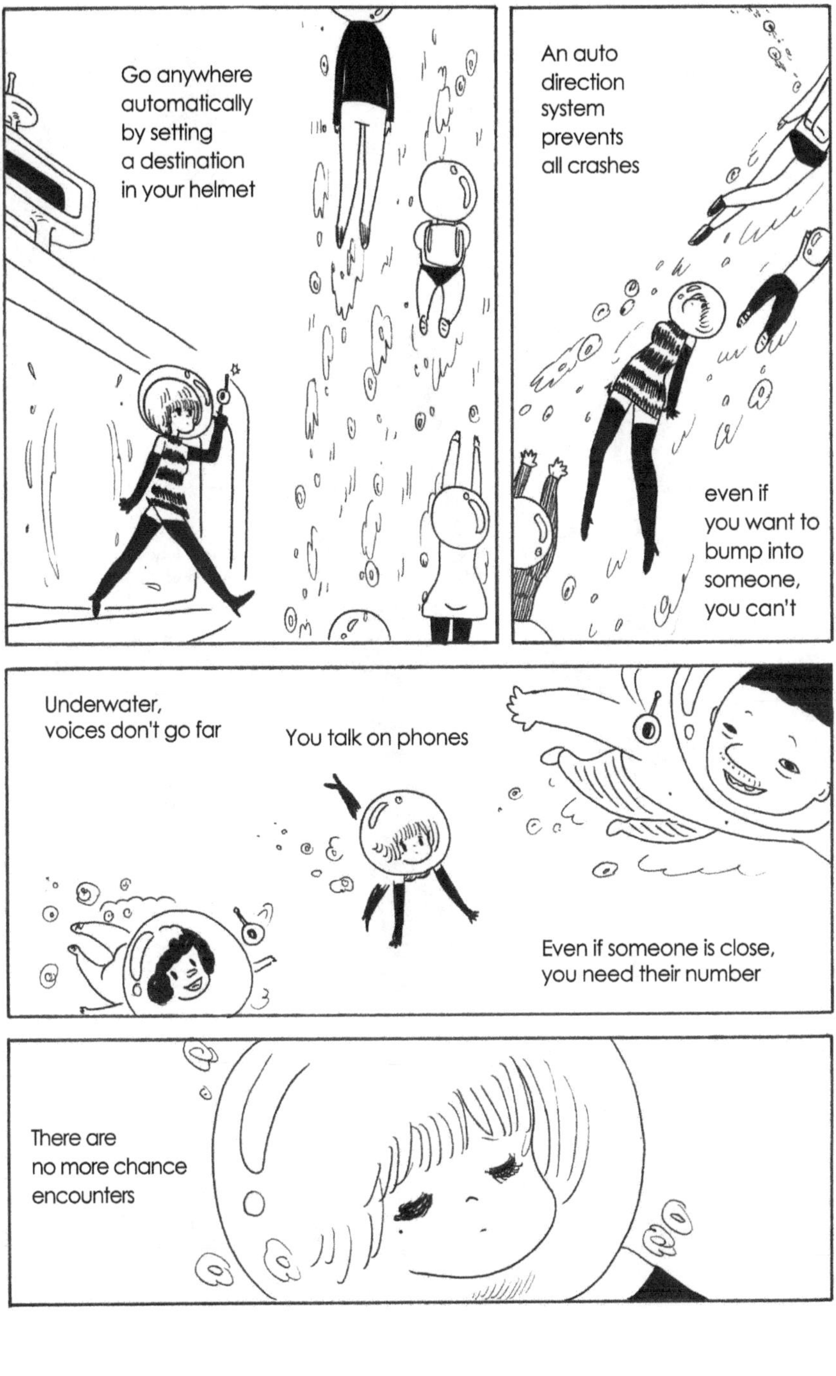
Go anywhere automatically by setting a destination in your helmet
An auto direction system prevents all crashes
even if you want to bump into someone, you can't
Underwater, voices don't go far
You talk on phones
Even if someone is close, you need their number
There are no more chance encounters

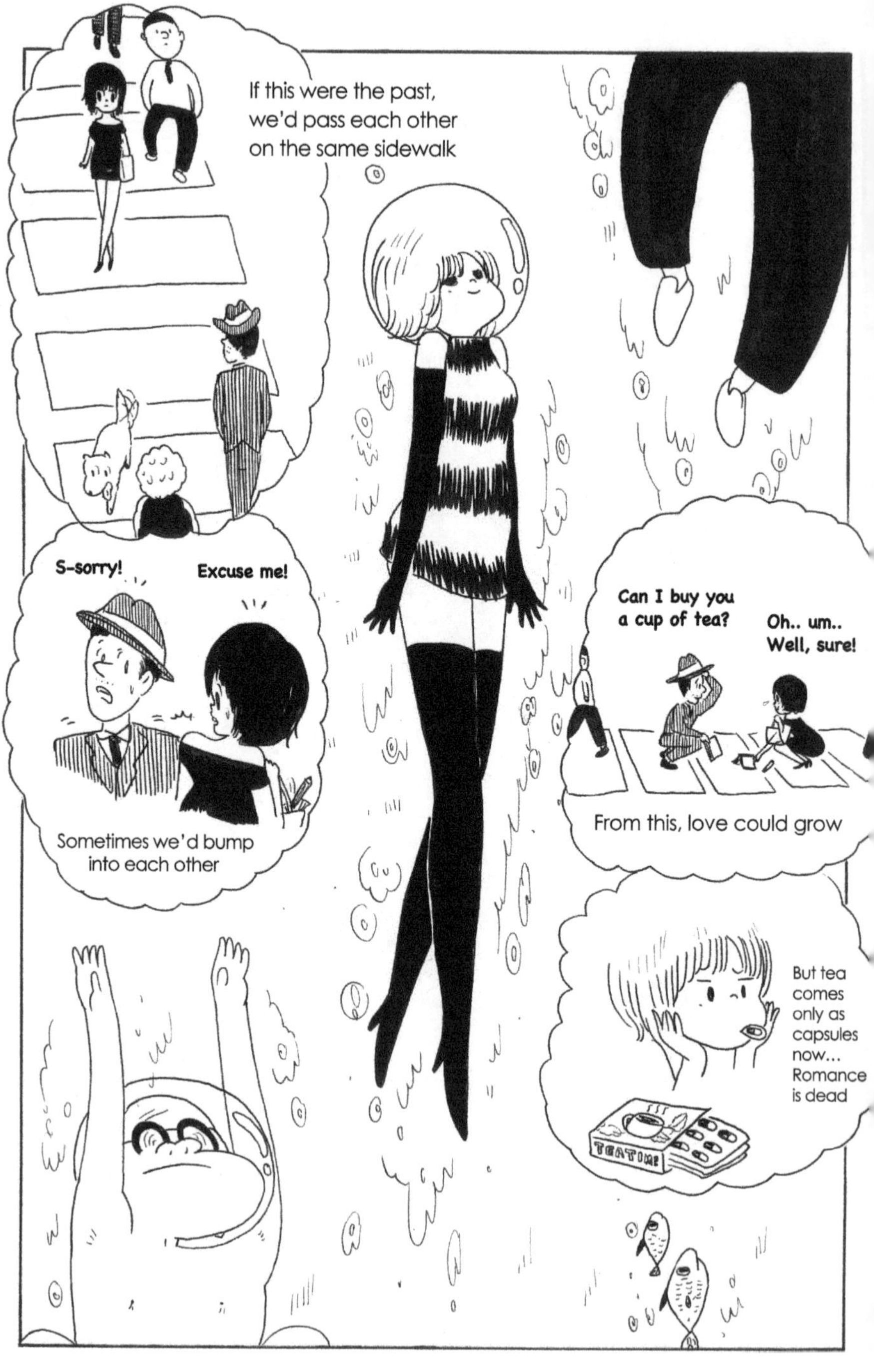

If this were the past, we'd pass each other on the same sidewalk
S-sorry!
Excuse me!
Sometimes we'd bump into each other
Can I buy you a cup of tea?
Oh.. um.. Well, sure!
From this, love could grow
But tea comes only as capsules now... Romance is dead

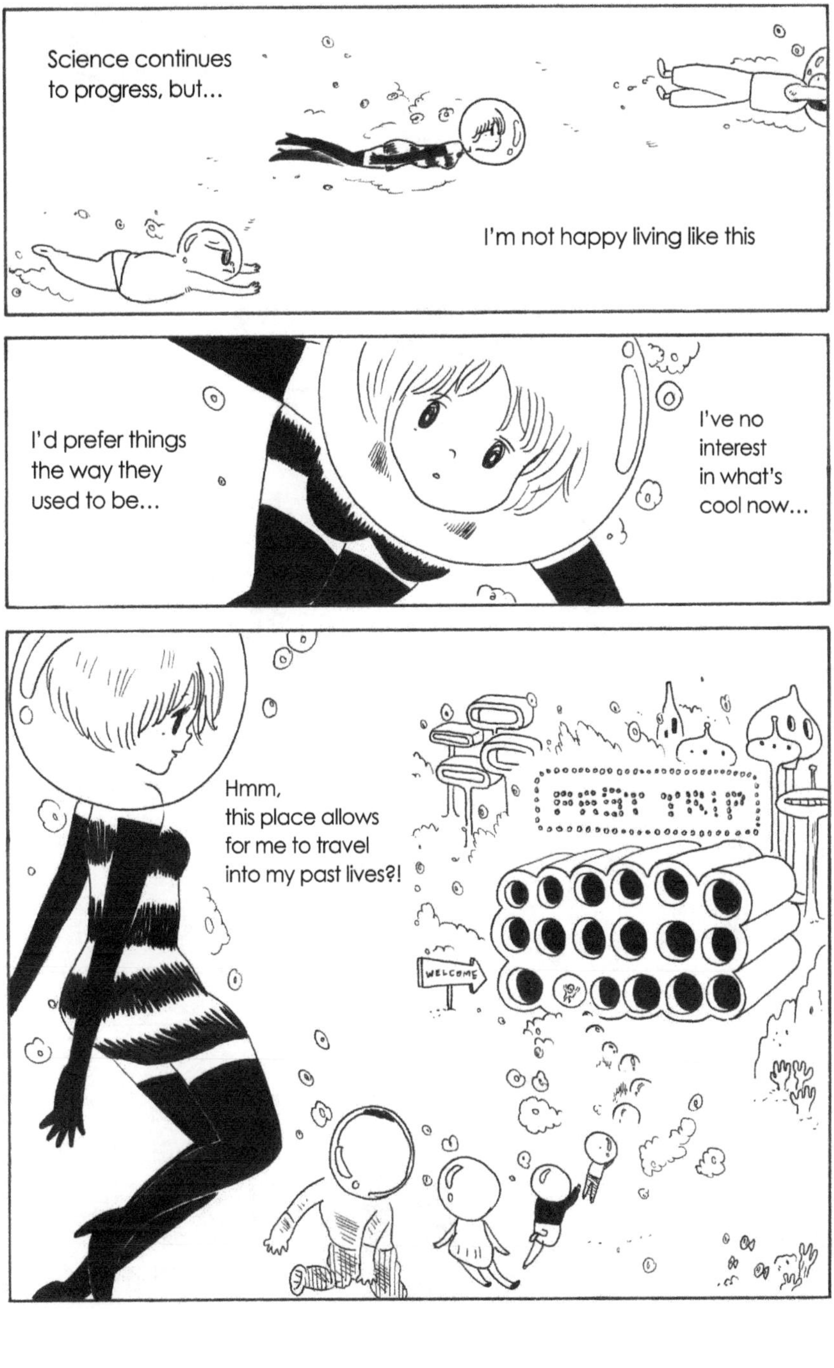
Science continues to progress, but...
I'm not happy living like this
I'd prefer things the way they used to be...
I've no interest in what's cool now...
Hmm, this place allows for me to travel into my past lives?!
WELCOME

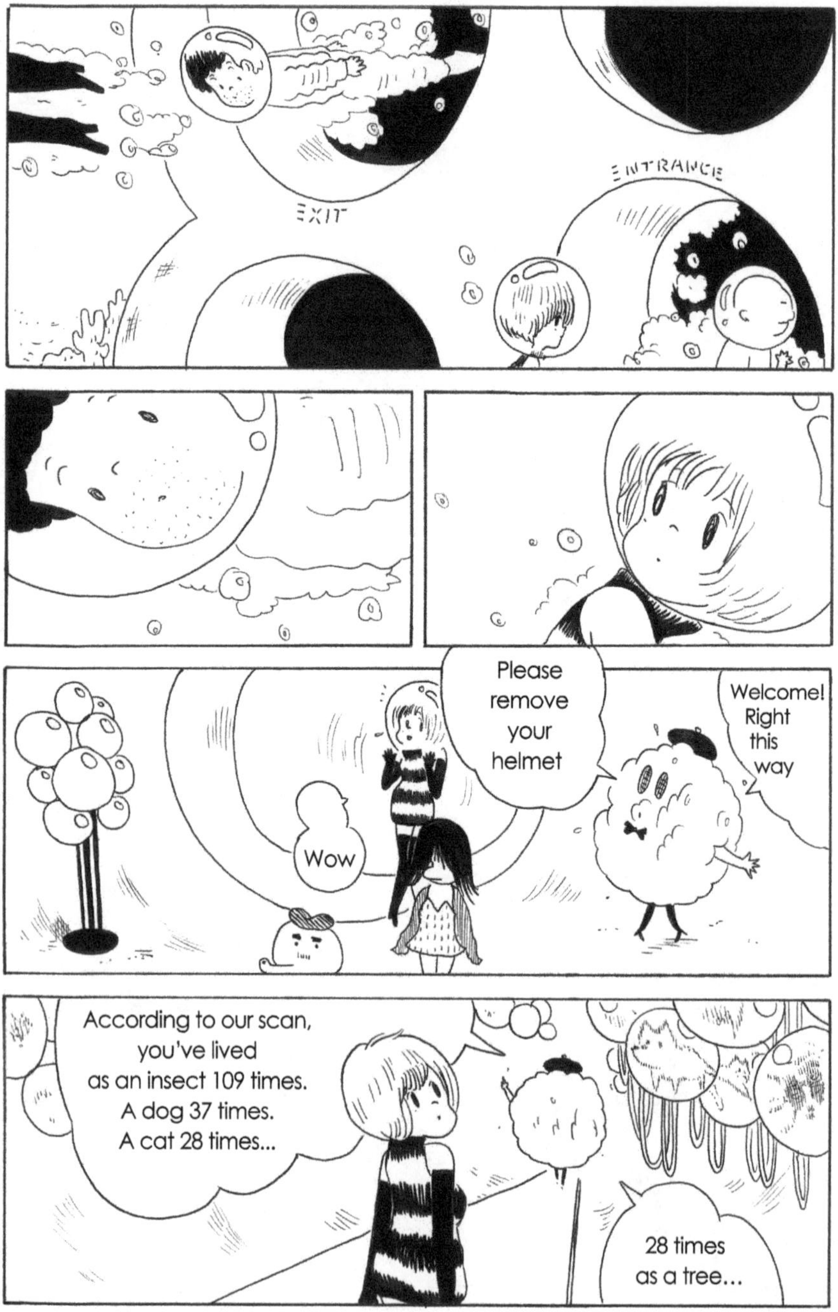
ENTRANCE
EXIT
Welcome! Right this way
Please remove your helmet
Wow
According to our scan, you've lived as an insect 109 times. A dog 37 times. A cat 28 times...
28 times as a tree...

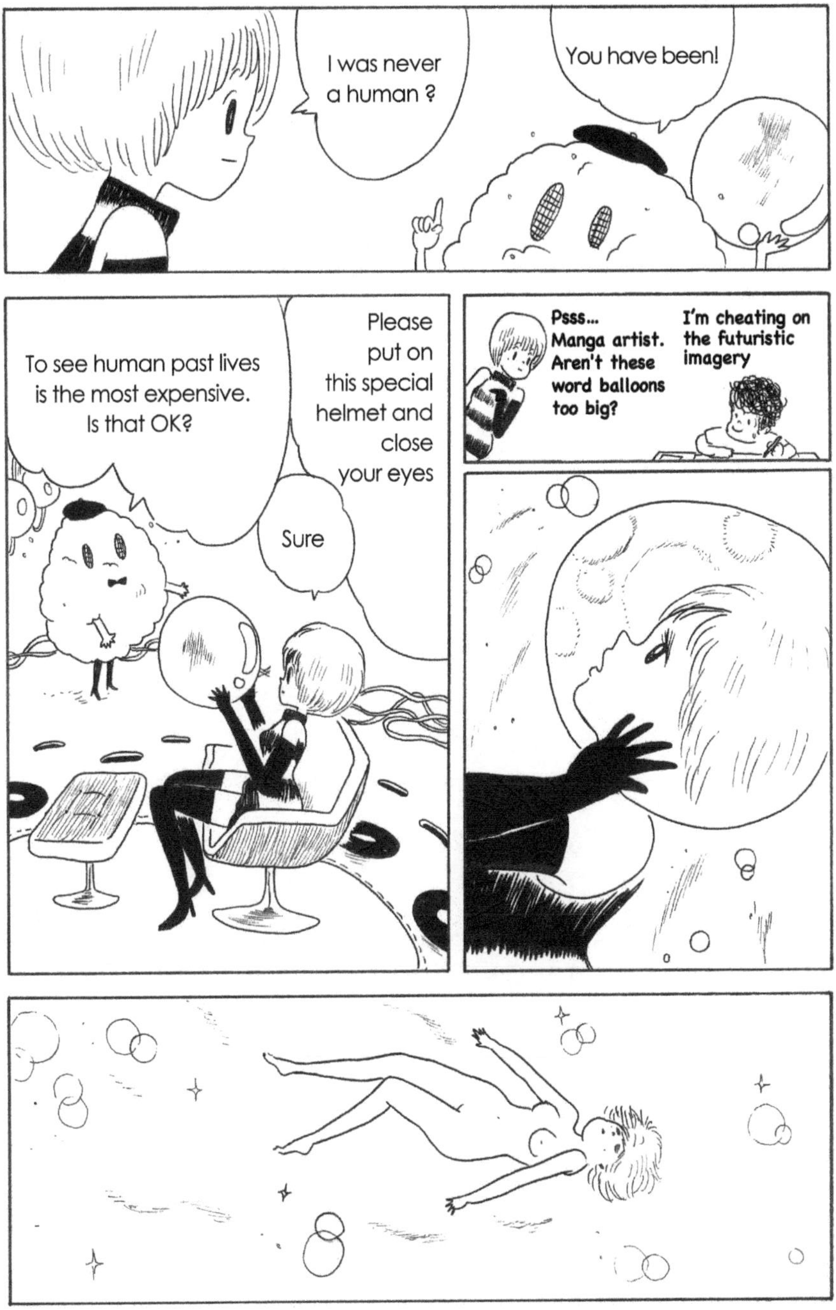
I was never a human ?
You have been!
To see human past lives is the most expensive. Is that OK?
Sure
Please put on this special helmet and close your eyes
Psss... Manga artist. Aren't these word balloons too big?
I'm cheating on the futuristic imagery

Forgetting

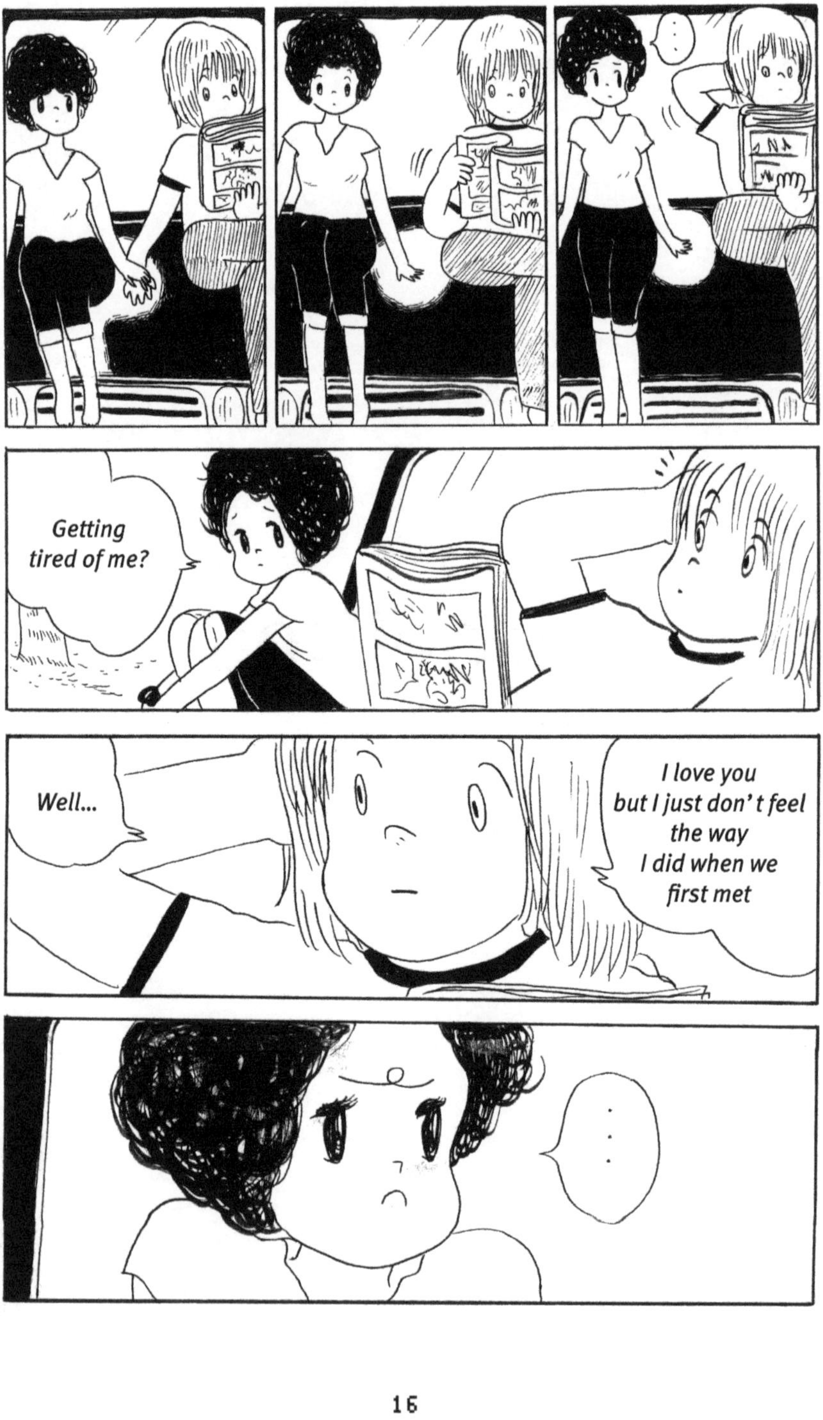
...
Getting tired of me?
Well...
I love you but I just don't feel the way I did when we first met
...

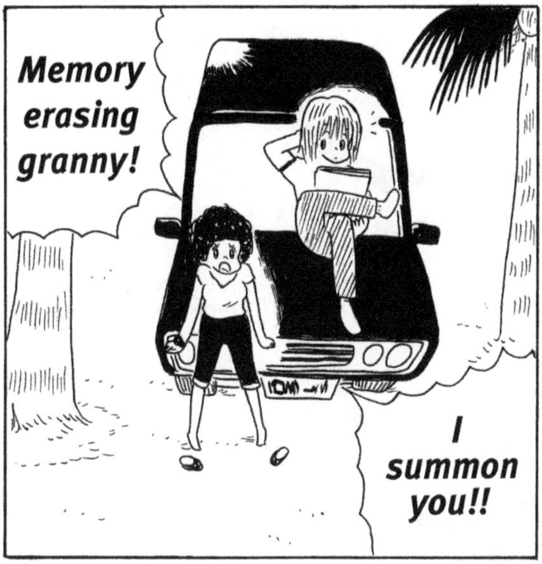
Memory erasing granny!
I summon you!!
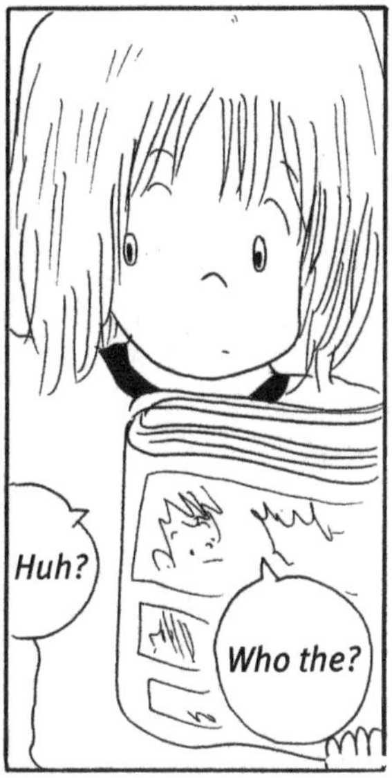
Huh?
Who the?
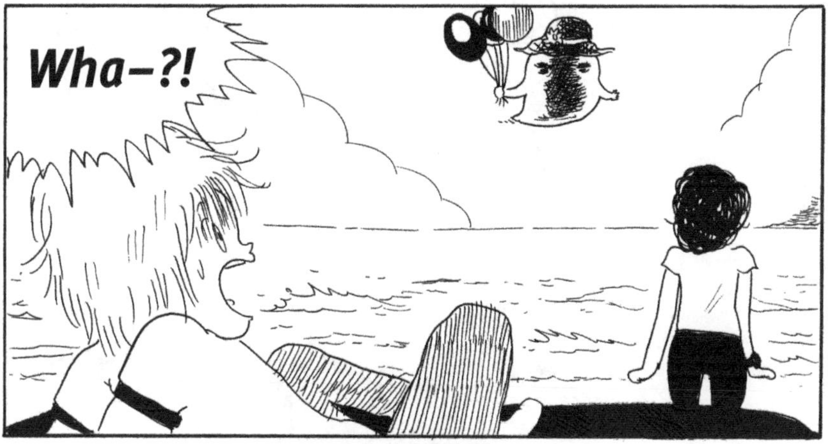
Wha–?!
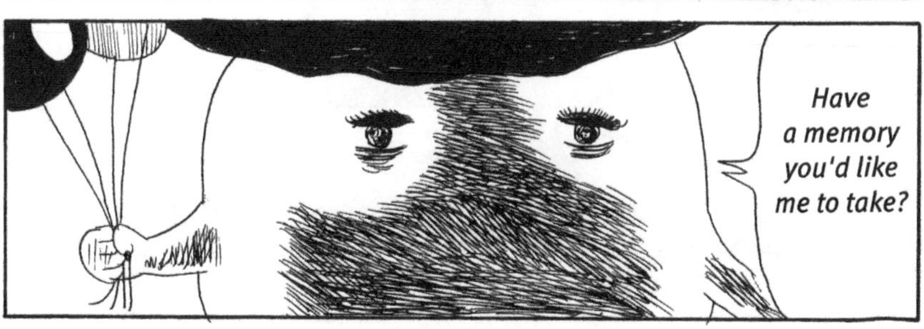
Have a memory you'd like me to take?

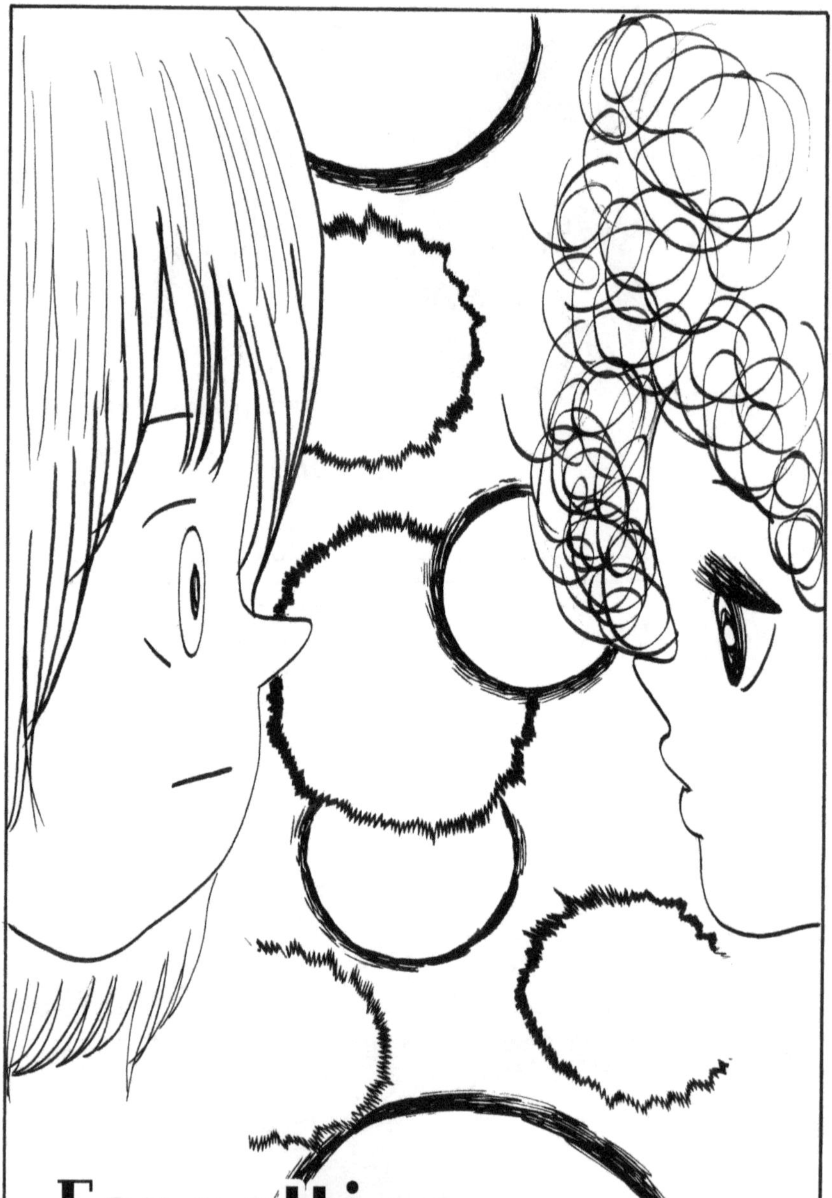
Forgetting

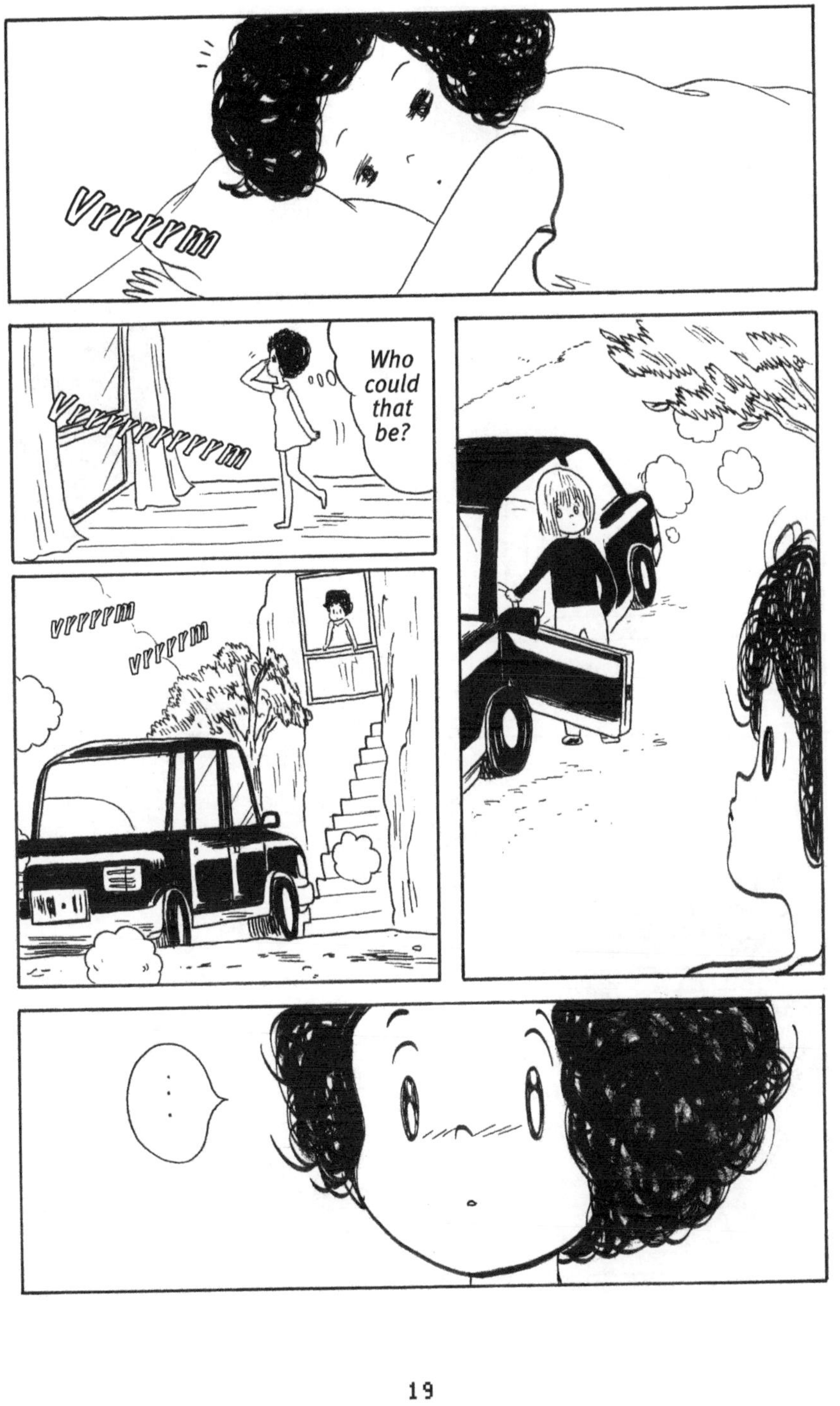
Vrrrrrm
Vrrrrrrrrrrrm
Who could that be?
vrrrrm
vrrrrm
. . .

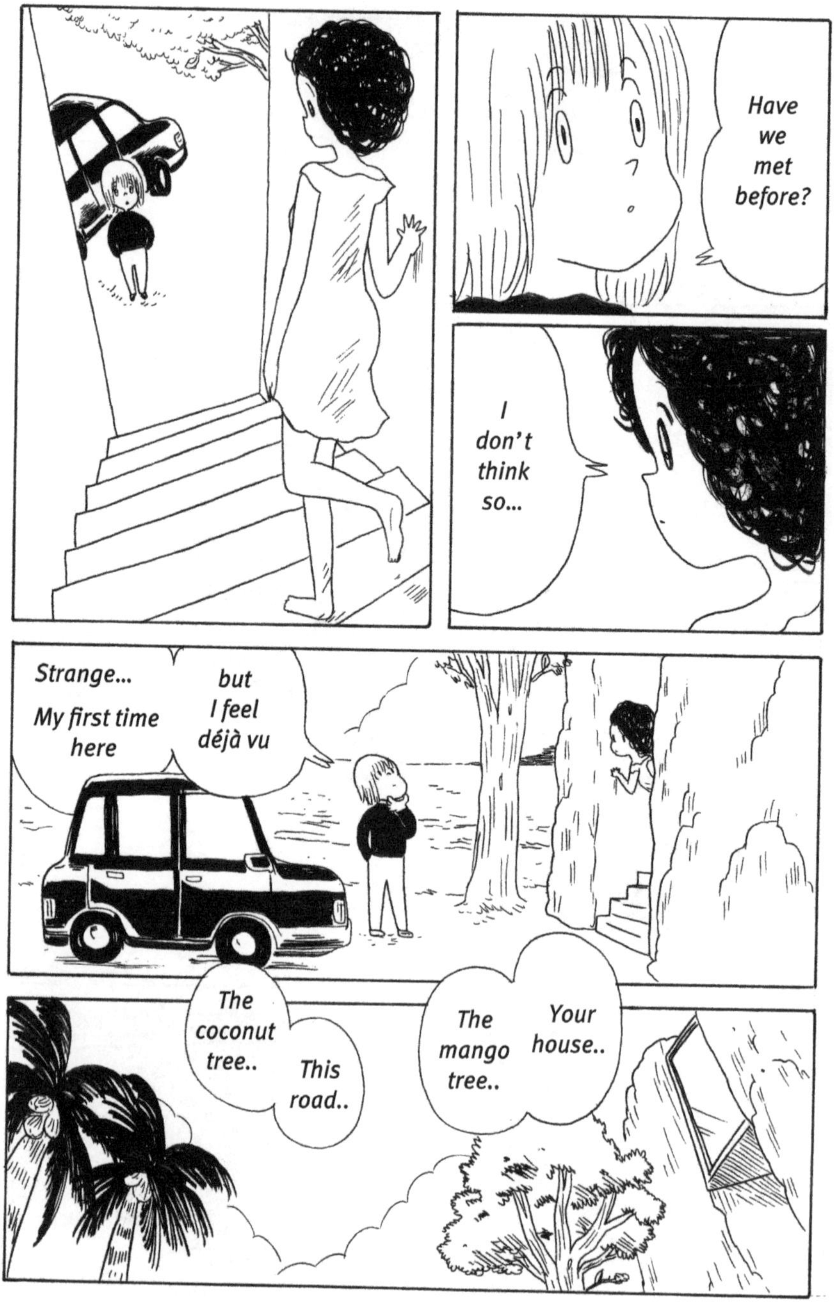
Have we met before?
I don't think so...
Strange... My first time here
but I feel déjà vu
The coconut tree..
This road..
The mango tree..
Your house..

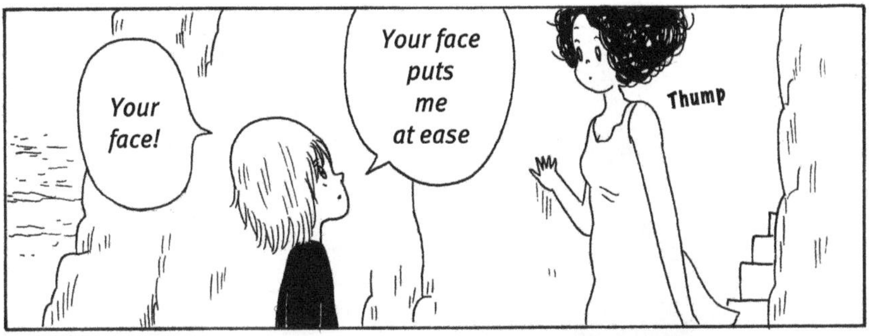
Your face!
Your face puts me at ease
Thump
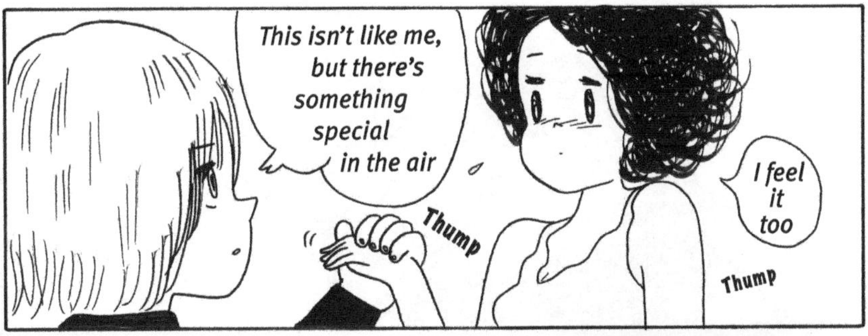
This isn't like me, but there's something special in the air
Thump
I feel it too
Thump
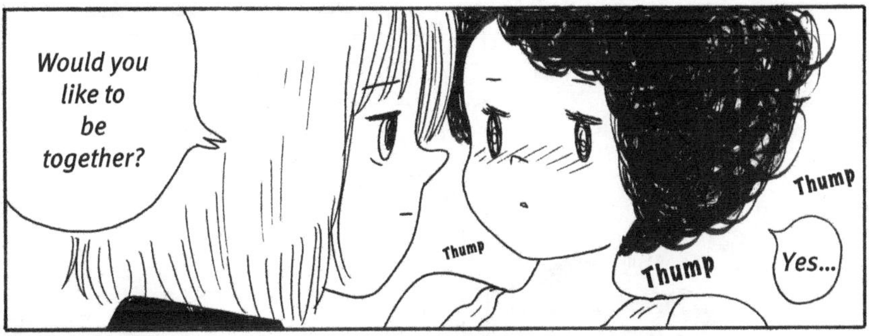
Would you like to be together?
Thump
Thump
Thump
Yes...
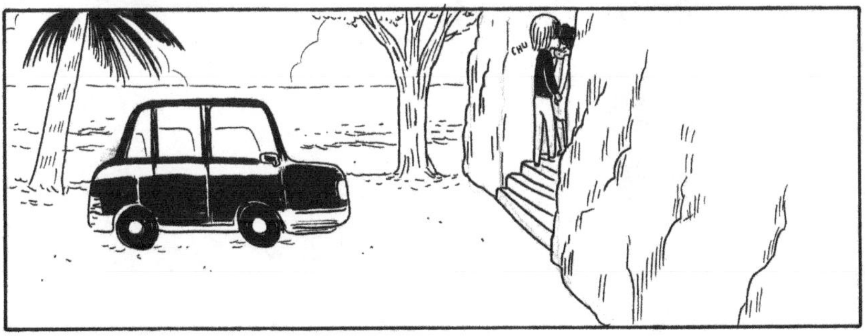

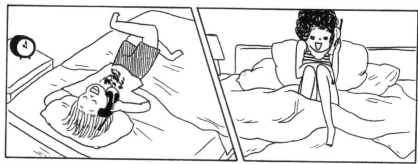

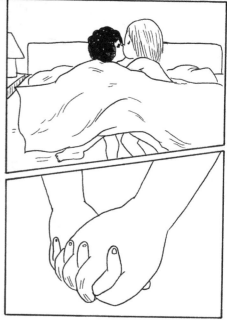

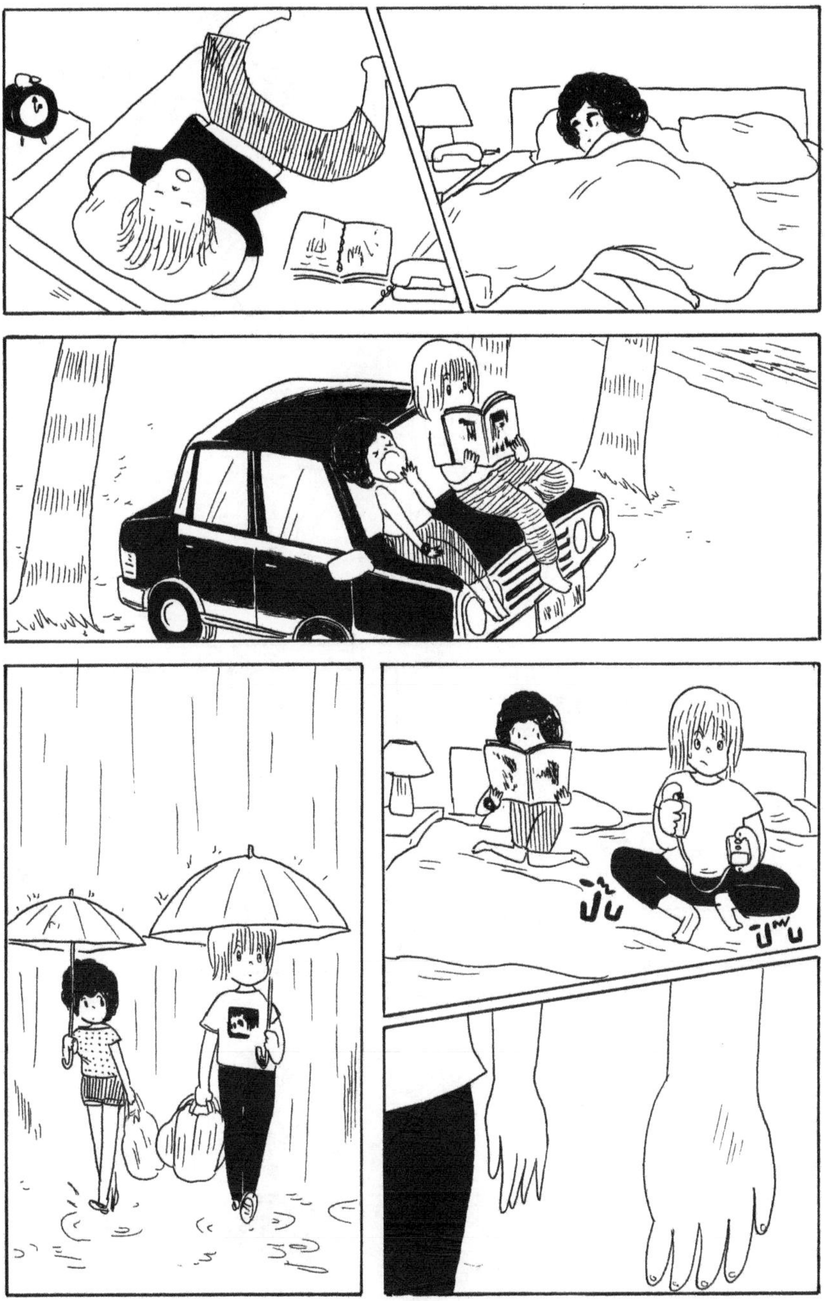
ปิ๊น
ปี๊น

RING
RING
Hello
How are you?
You eat already?
Yeah
You?
Yeah
...
...
...
...
OK, well I gotta go

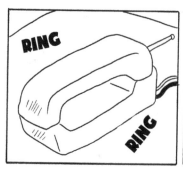

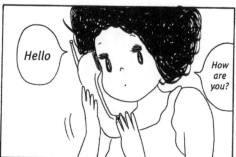

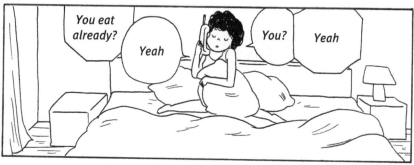

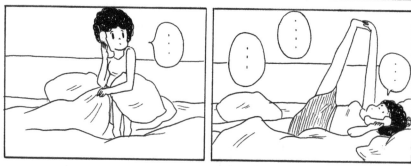

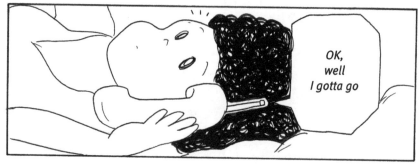

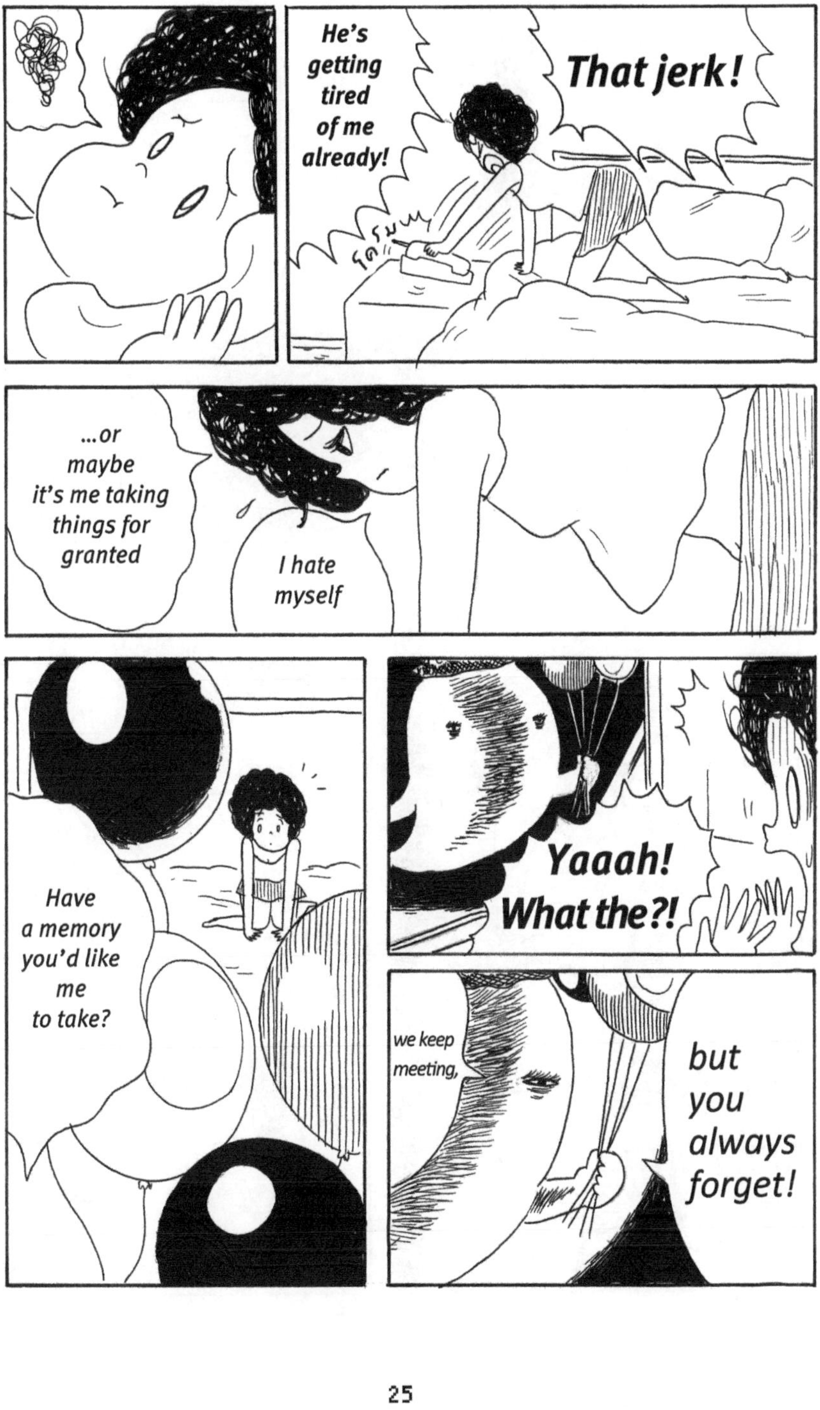
He's getting tired of me already!
That jerk!
โครม
...or maybe it's me taking things for granted
I hate myself
Have a memory you'd like me to take?
Yaaah! What the?!
we keep meeting,
but you always forget!

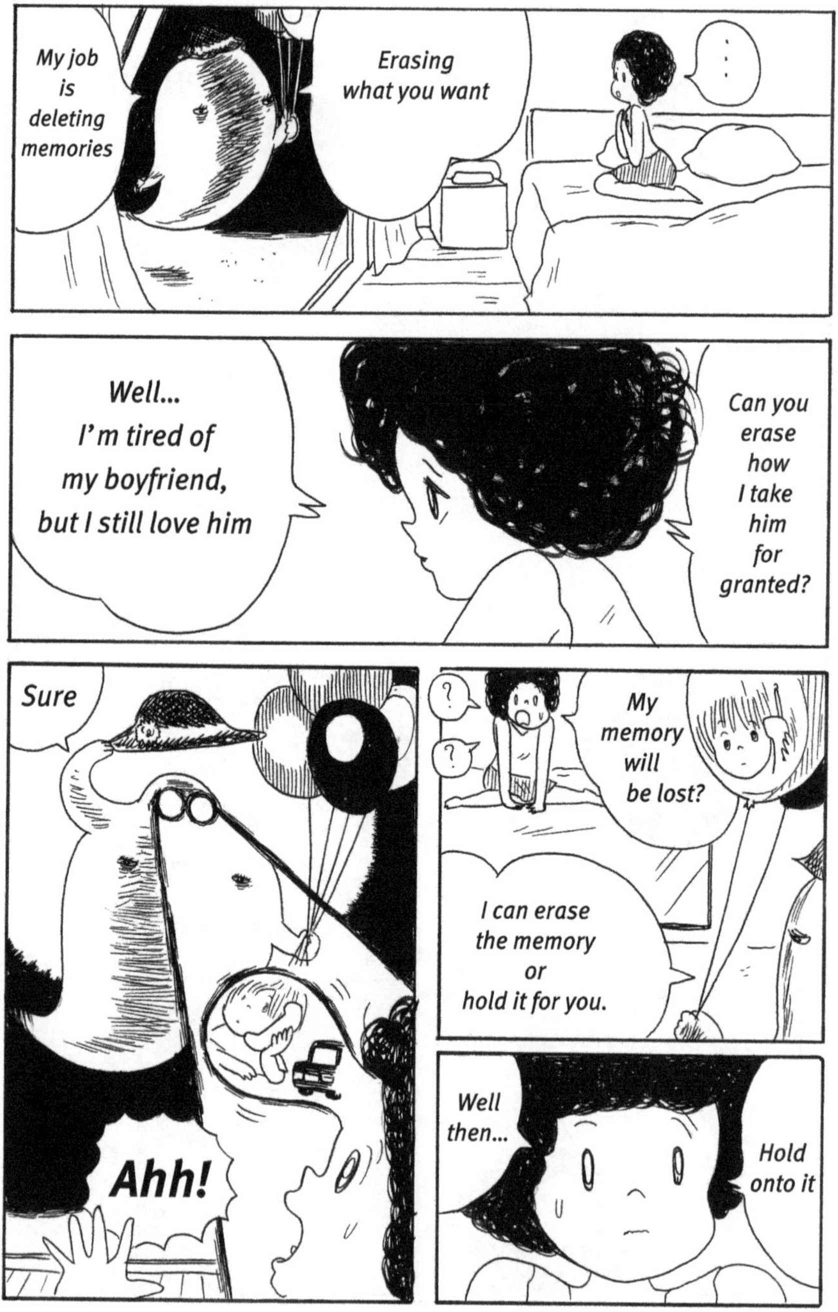
My job is deleting memories
Erasing what you want
. . .
Well... I'm tired of my boyfriend, but I still love him
Can you erase how I take him for granted?
Sure
Ahh!
?
?
My memory will be lost?
I can erase the memory or hold it for you.
Well then...
Hold onto it

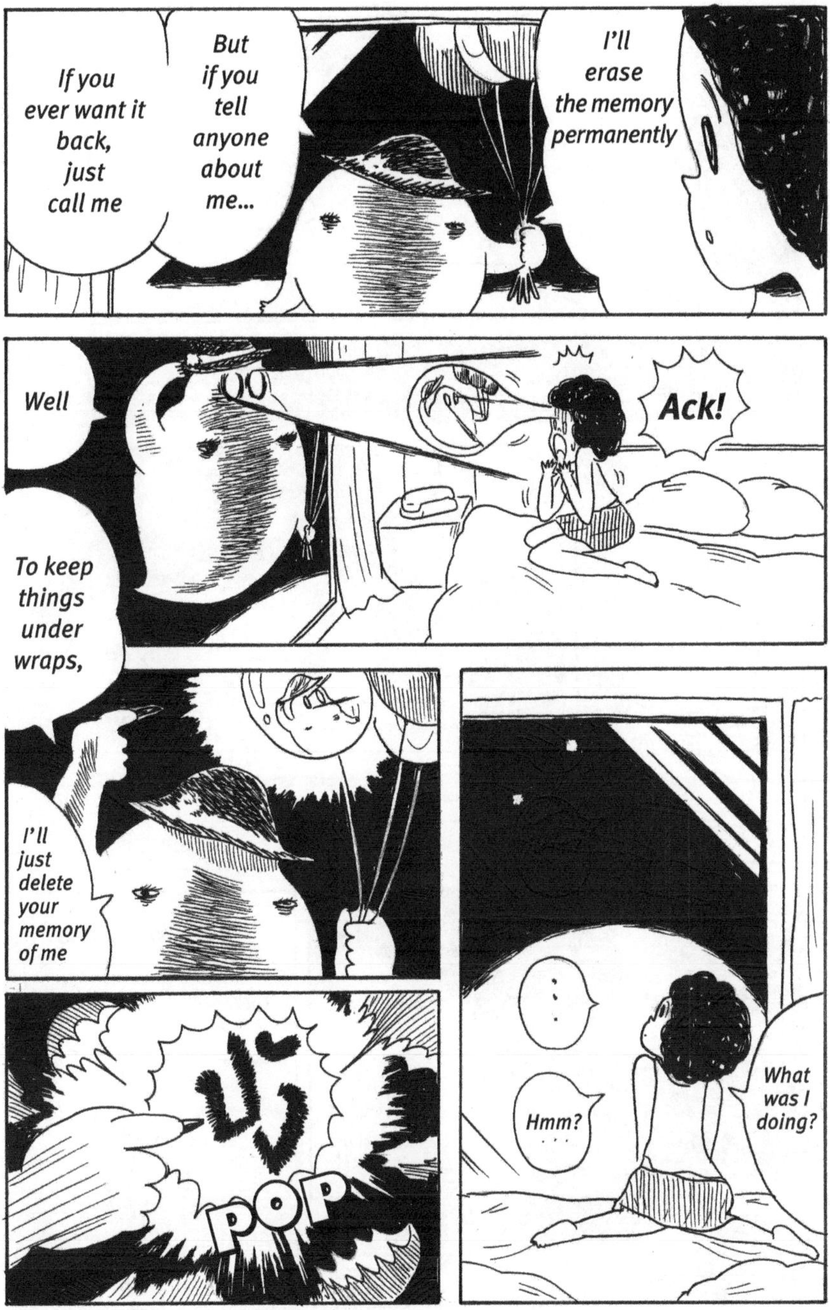
If you ever want it back, just call me
But if you tell anyone about me...
I'll erase the memory permanently
Well
To keep things under wraps,
Ack!
I'll just delete your memory of me
POP
...
Hmm?
What was I doing?

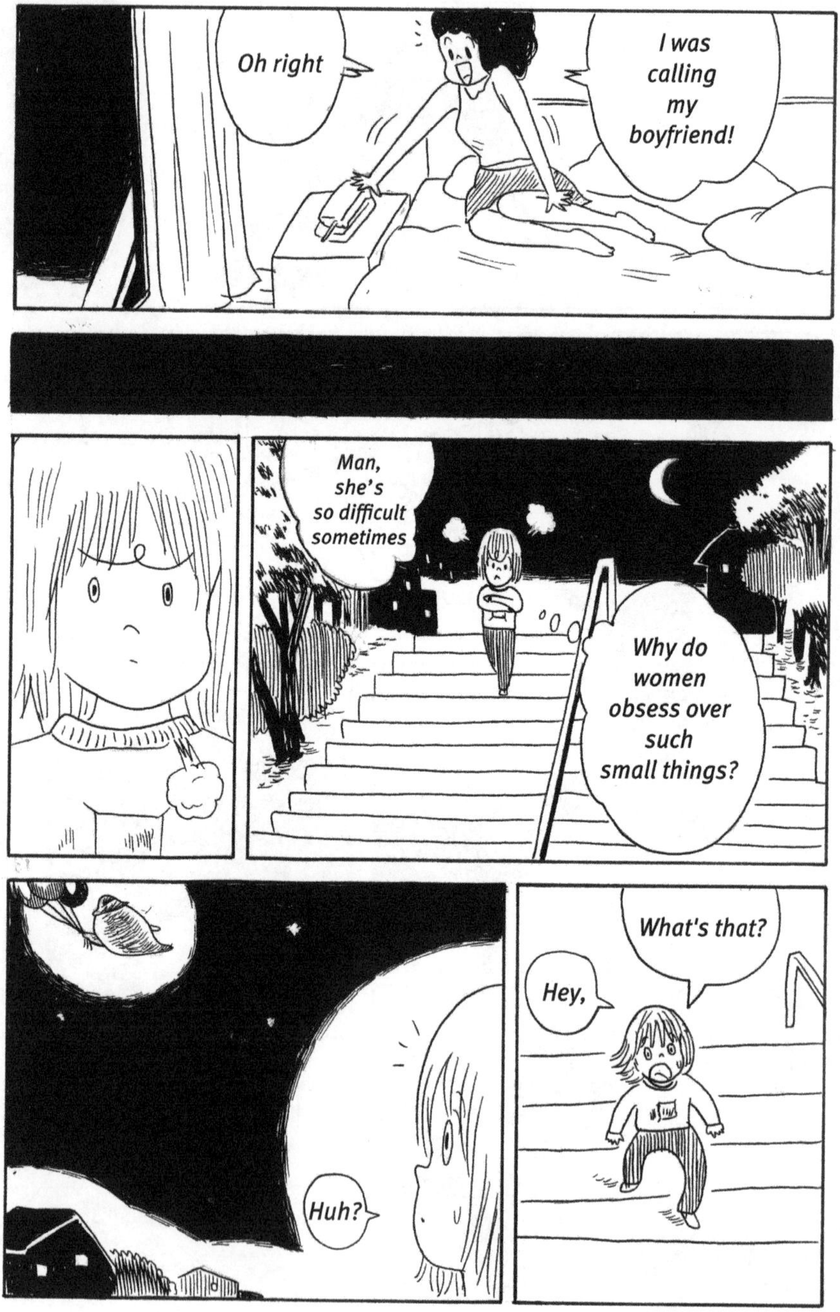
Oh right
I was calling my boyfriend!
Man, she's so difficult sometimes
Why do women obsess over such small things?
Huh?
Hey,
What's that?

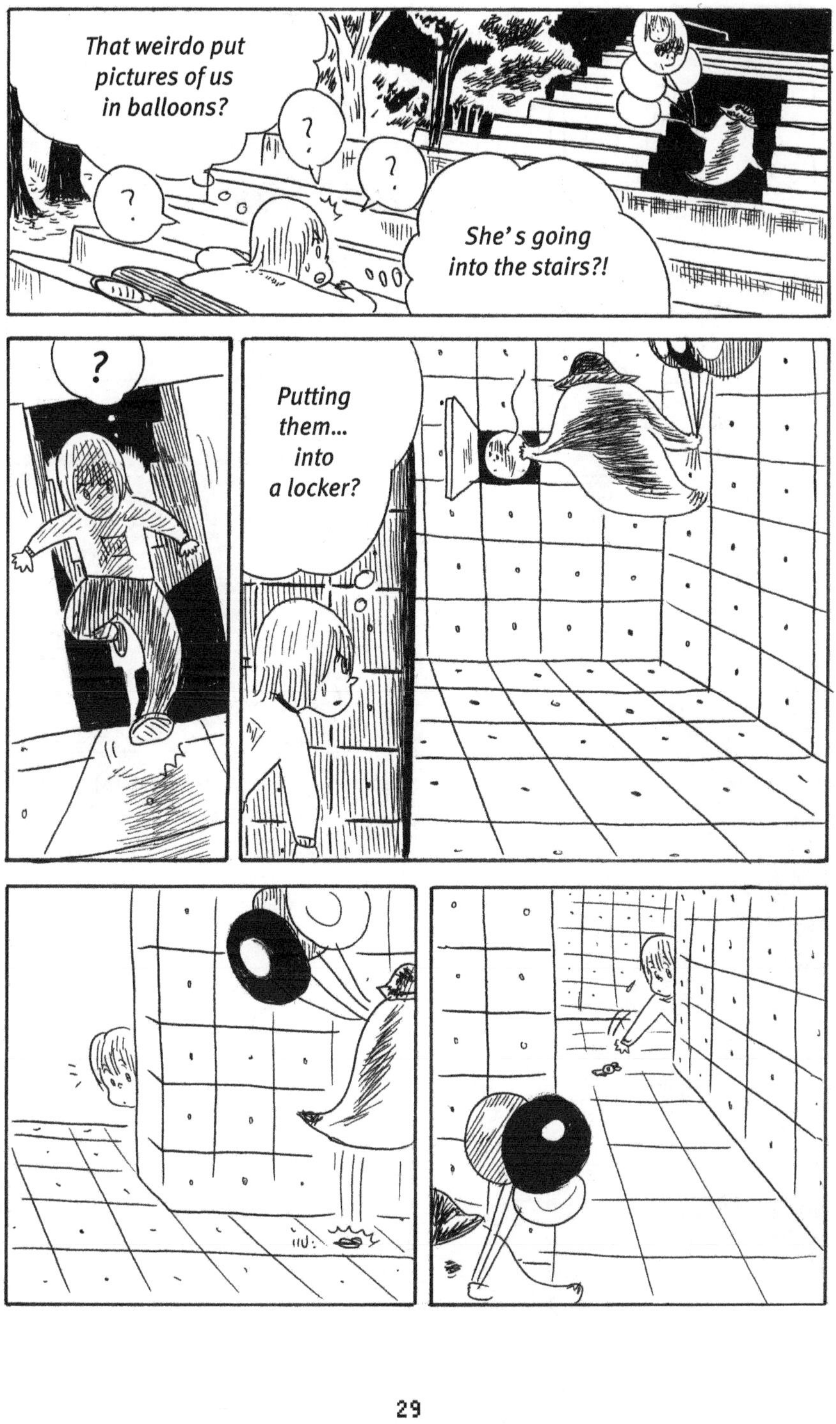
That weirdo put pictures of us in balloons?
?
?
?
She's going into the stairs?!
?
Putting them... into a locker?

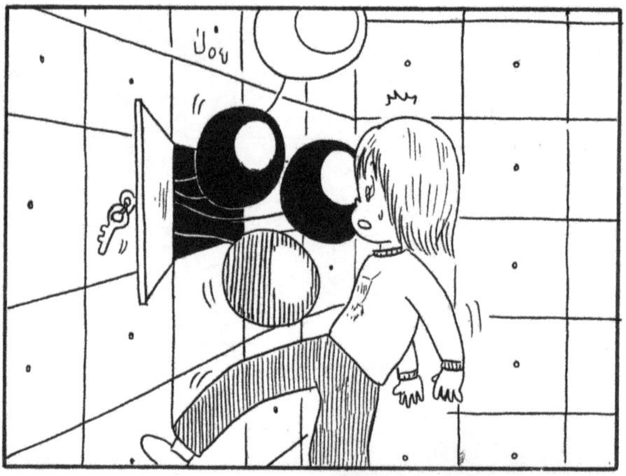

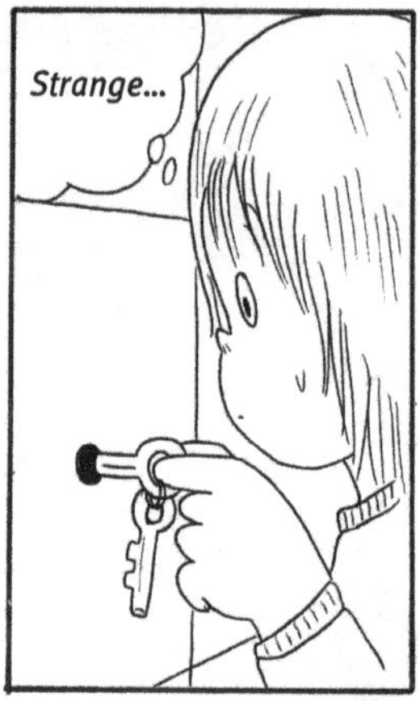
Strange...

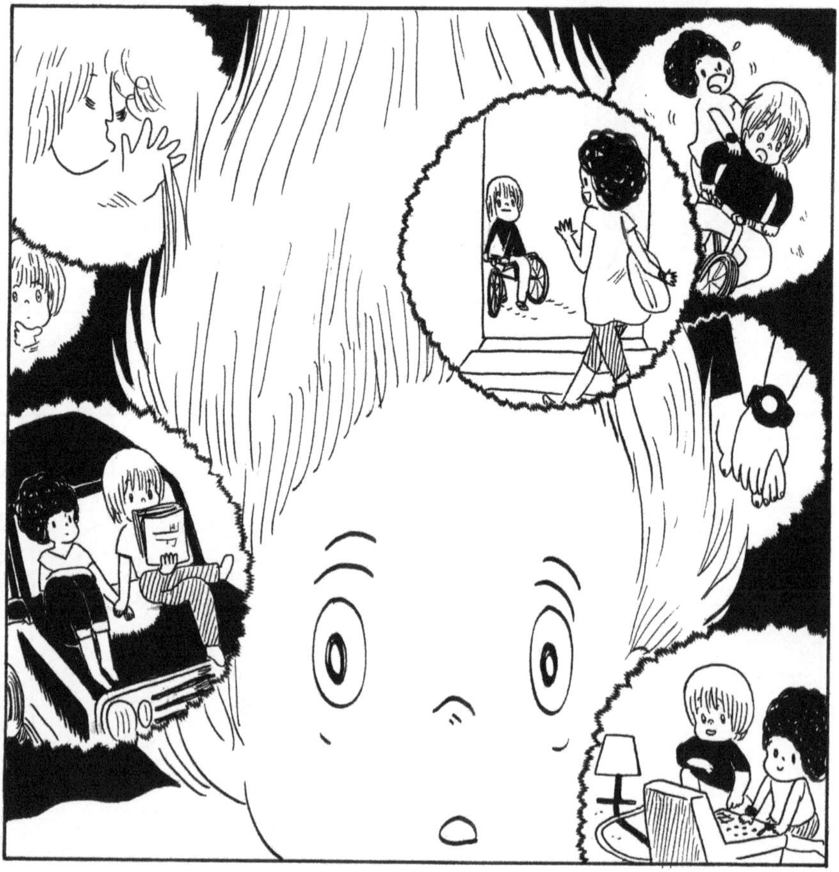

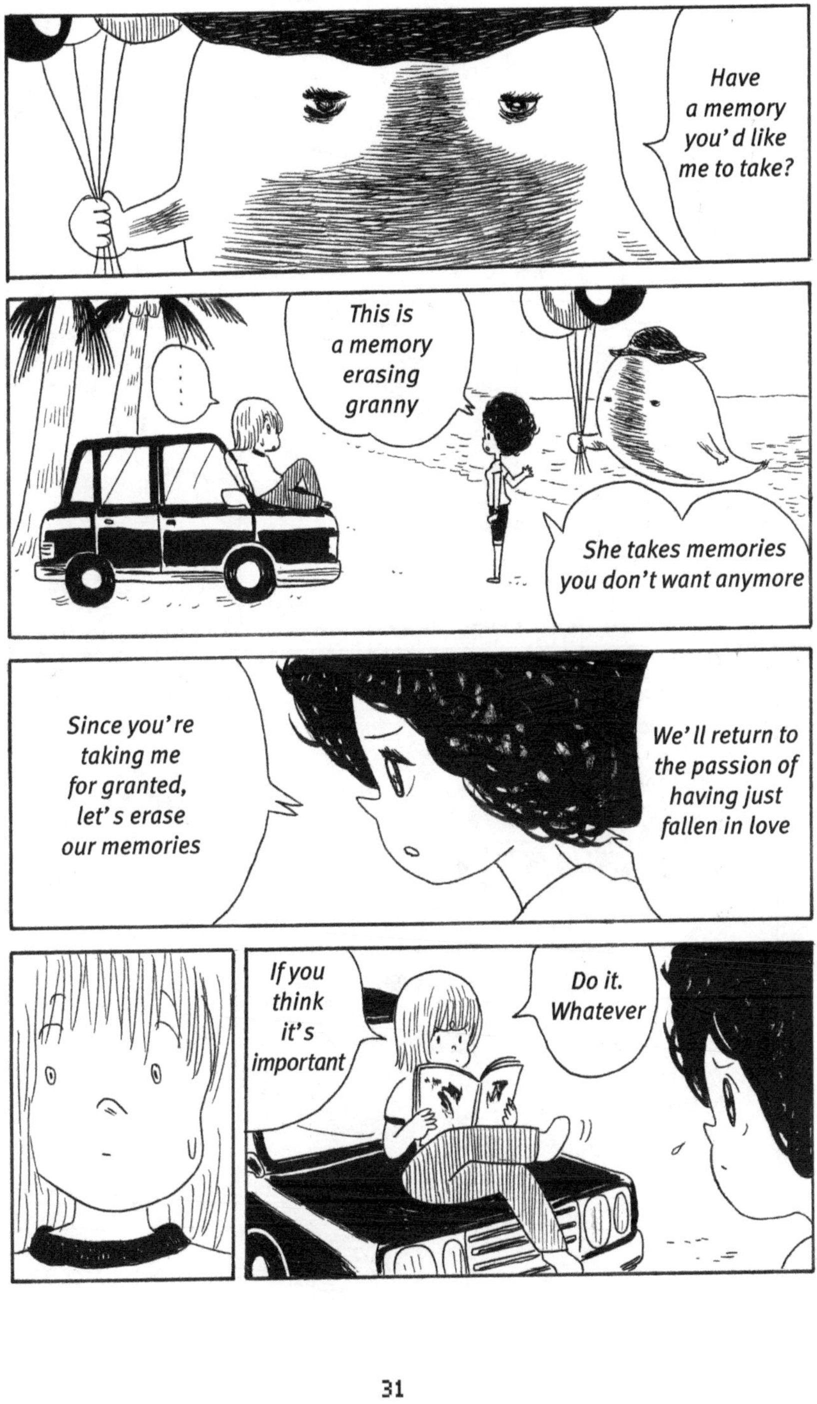
Have a memory you'd like me to take?
This is a memory erasing granny
....
She takes memories you don't want anymore
Since you're taking me for granted, let's erase our memories
We'll return to the passion of having just fallen in love
If you think it's important
Do it. Whatever

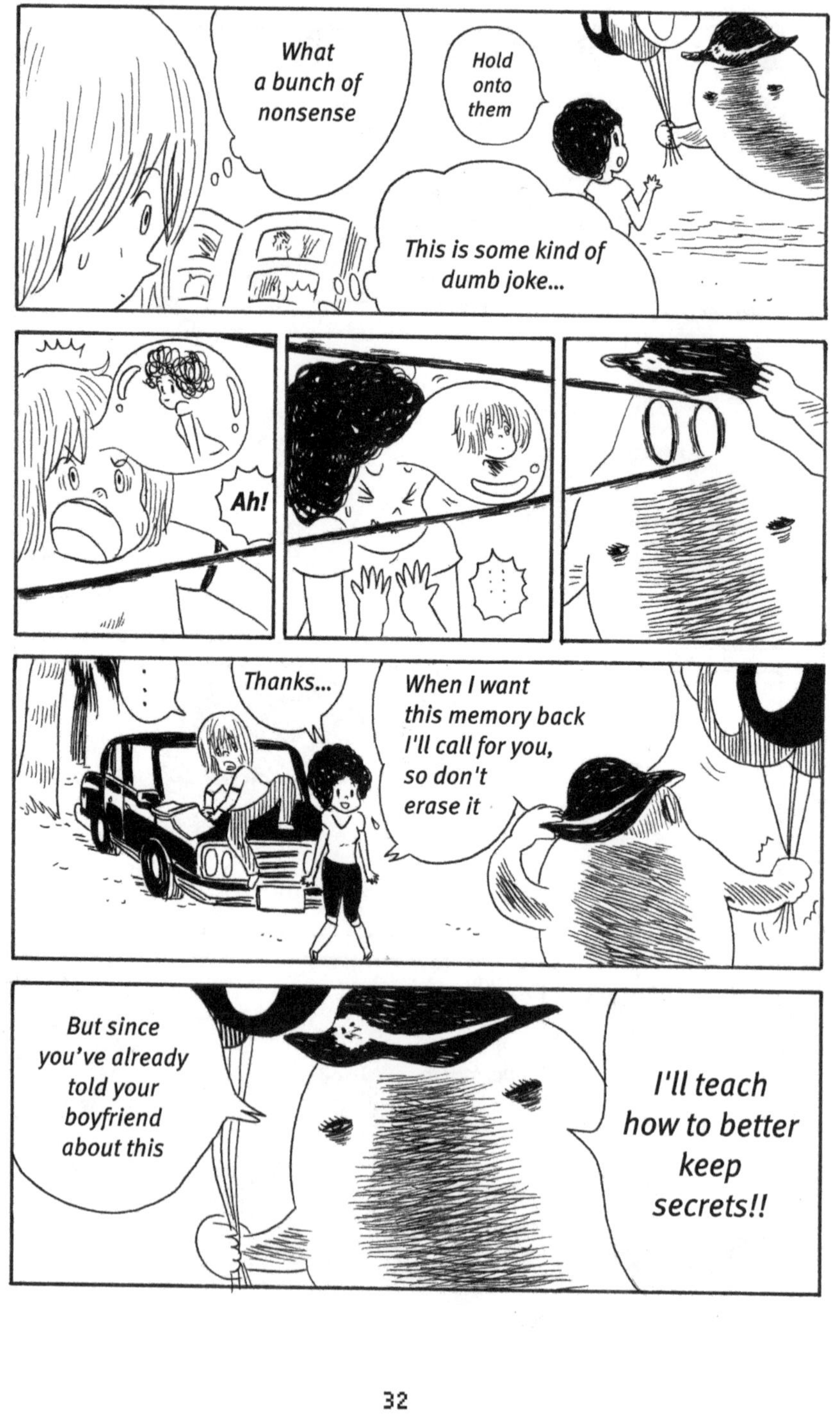
What a bunch of nonsense
Hold onto them
This is some kind of dumb joke...
Ah!
...
Thanks...
When I want this memory back I'll call for you, so don't erase it
But since you've already told your boyfriend about this
I'll teach how to better keep secrets!!

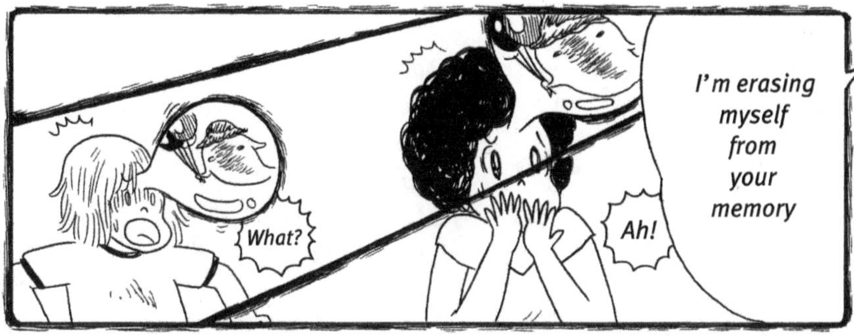
I'm erasing myself from your memory
Ah!
What?

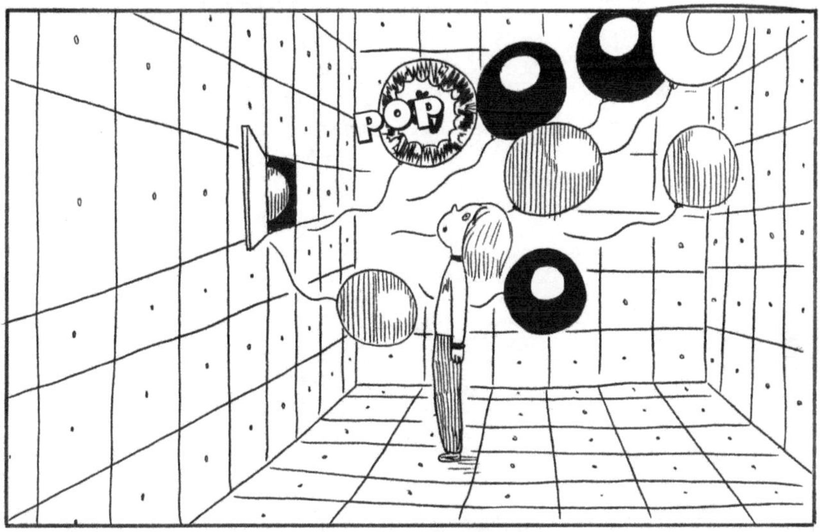
POP!

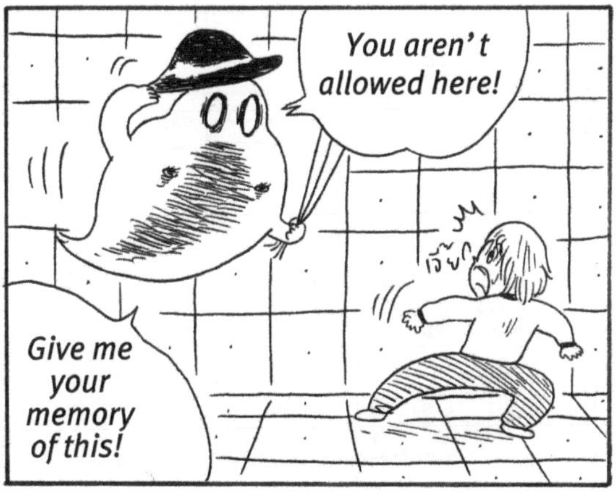
You aren't allowed here!
Give me your memory of this!

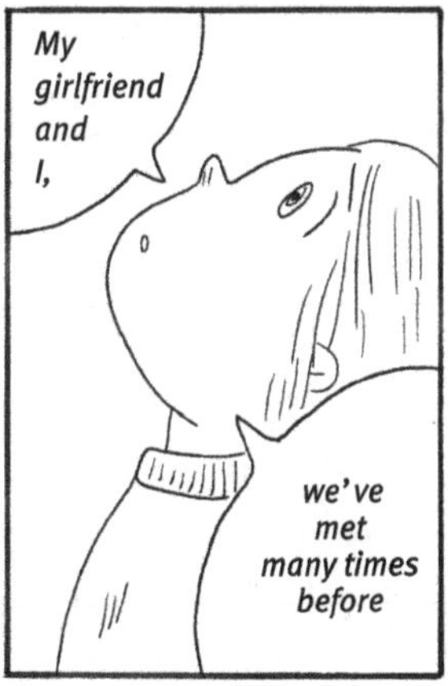
My girlfriend and I,
we've met many times before

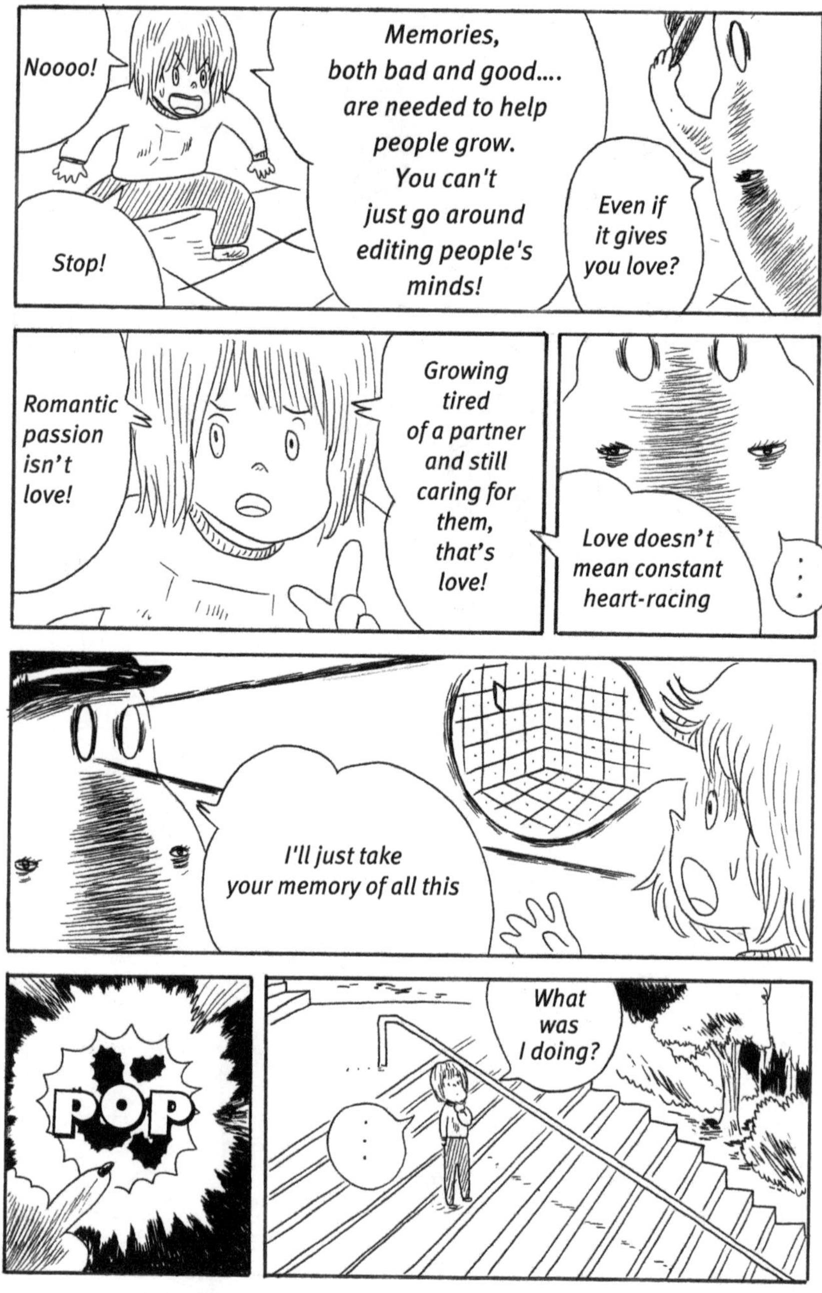
Noooo!
Stop!
Memories, both bad and good.... are needed to help people grow. You can't just go around editing people's minds!
Even if it gives you love?
Romantic passion isn't love!
Growing tired of a partner and still caring for them, that's love!
Love doesn't mean constant heart-racing
. . .
I'll just take your memory of all this
POP
What was I doing?
. . .

RING
RING
Hello?
Yeah, I'm taking a walk
What are you up to?
I'm sorry but I had to do it. It's my job, after all....
I hope someday your girlfriend understands what you told me...
You two are a good couple!
But, you're cute!
I like you

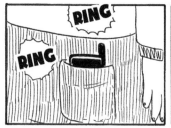

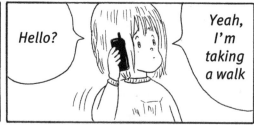

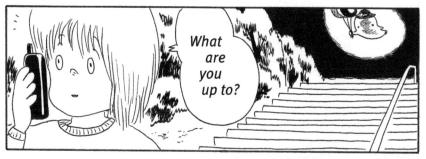

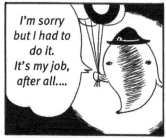

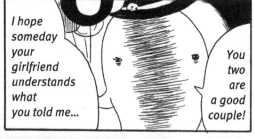

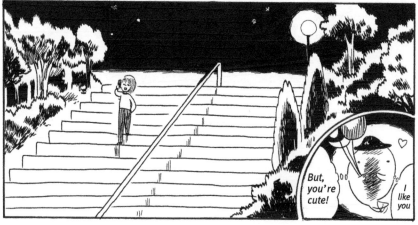

LOVE ELEVATOR

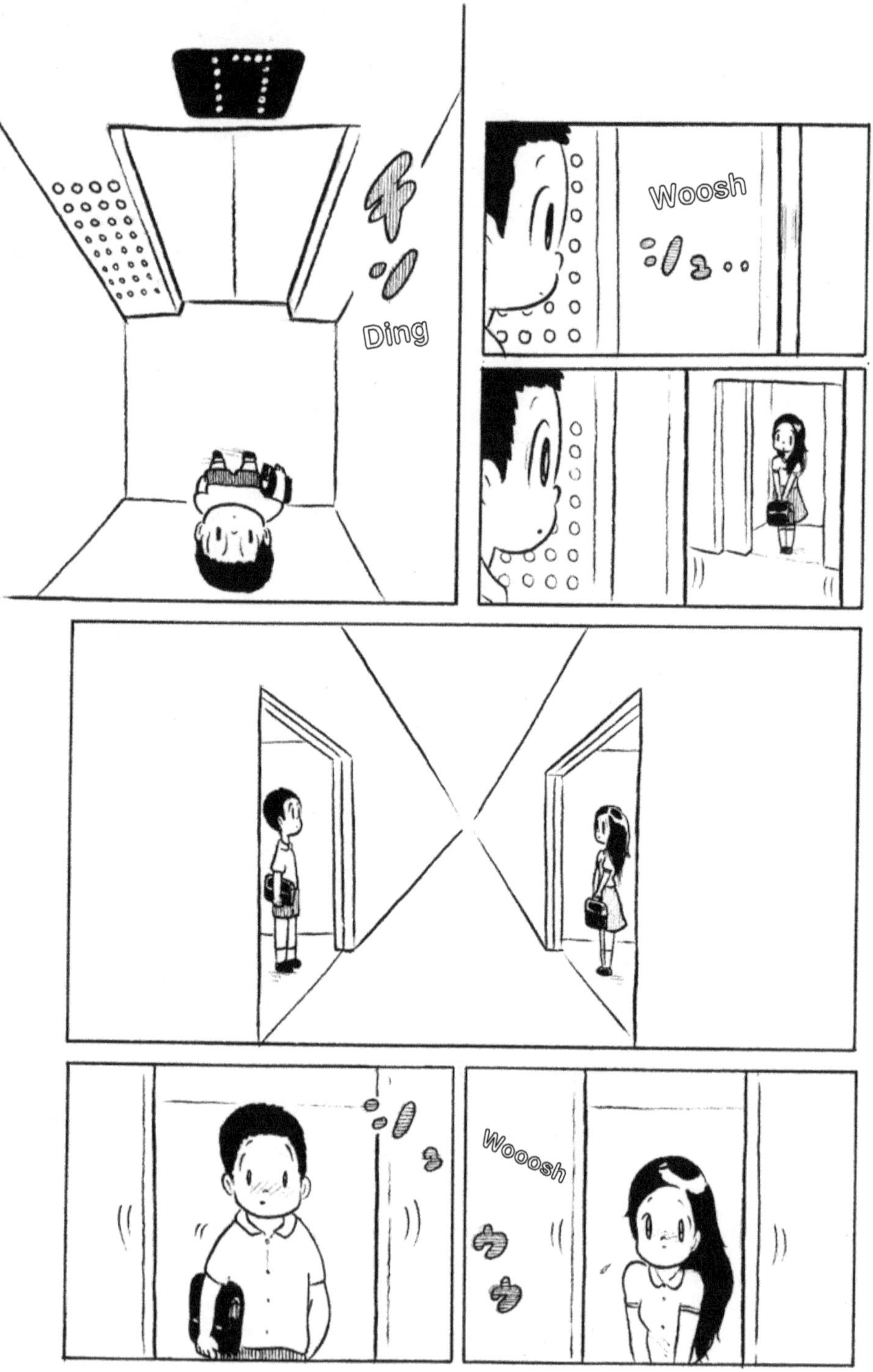
Ding
Woosh
Wooosh

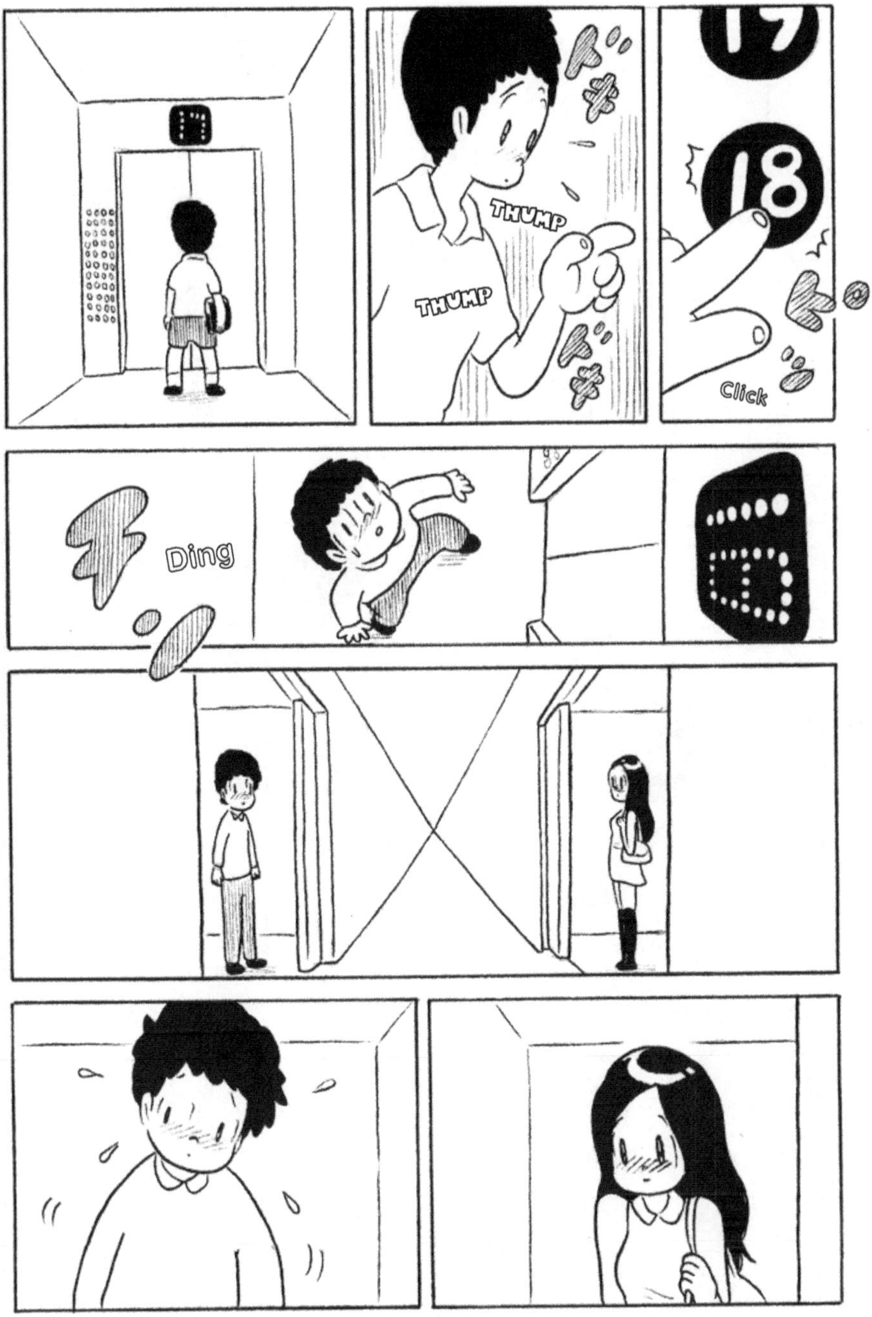
THUMP
THUMP
Click
Ding

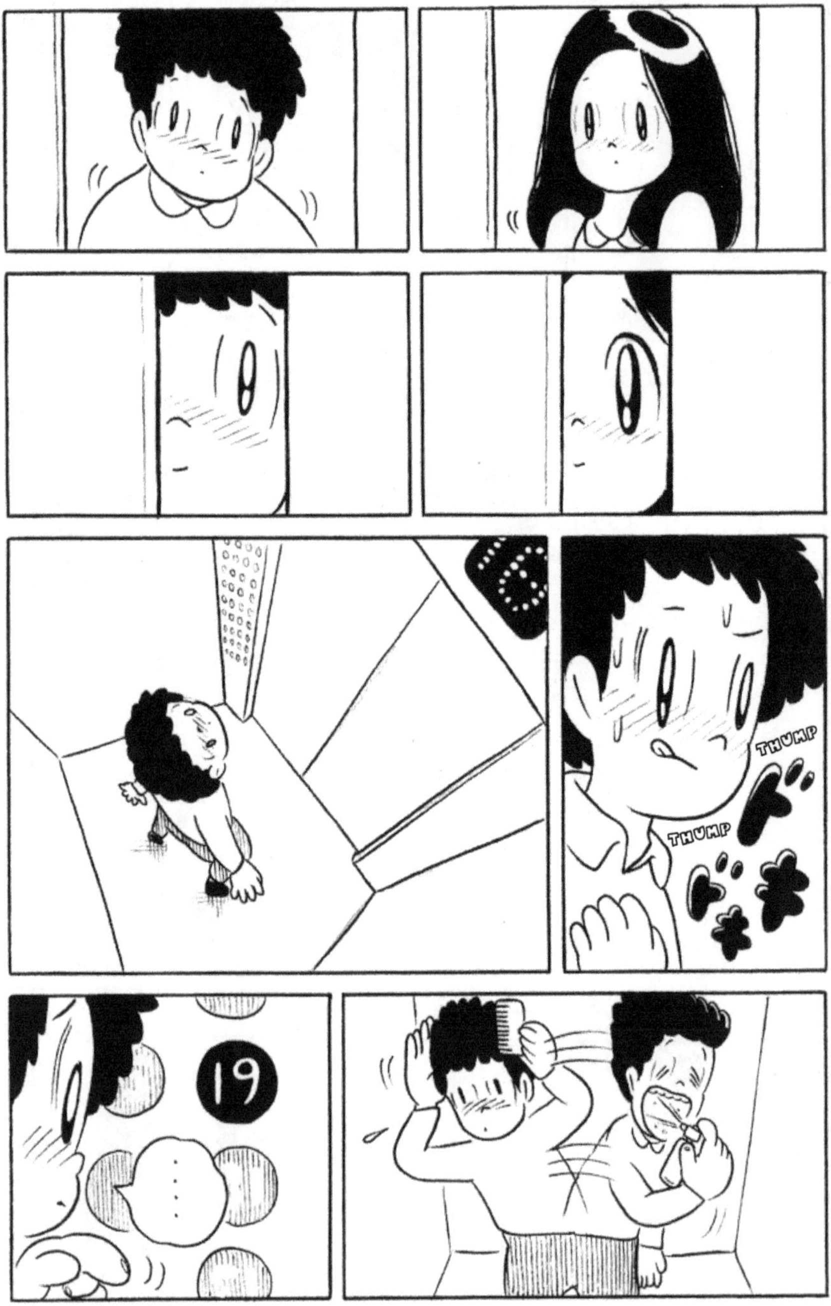
THUMP
THUMP
19
.....

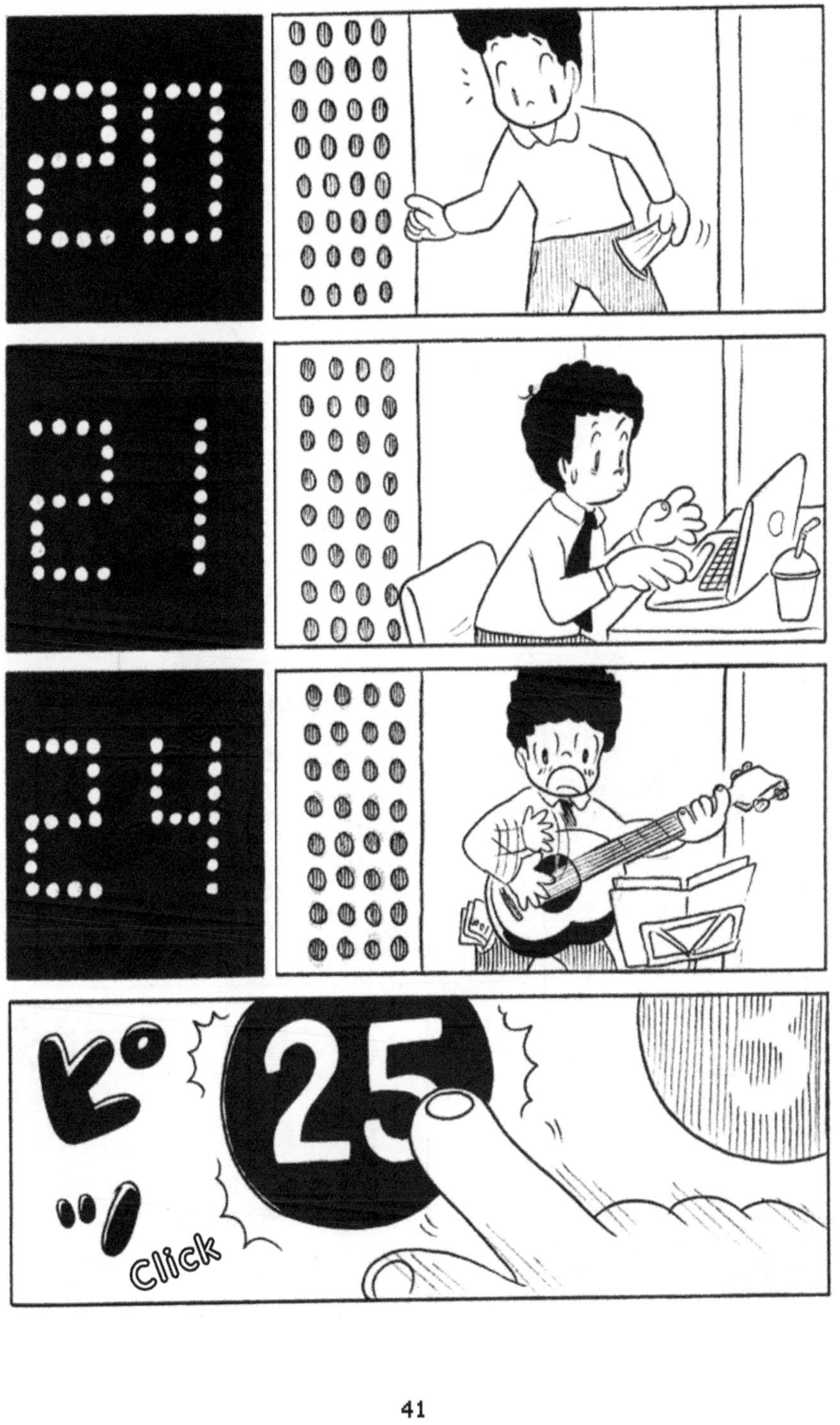
20
21
24
25
ピッ
Click

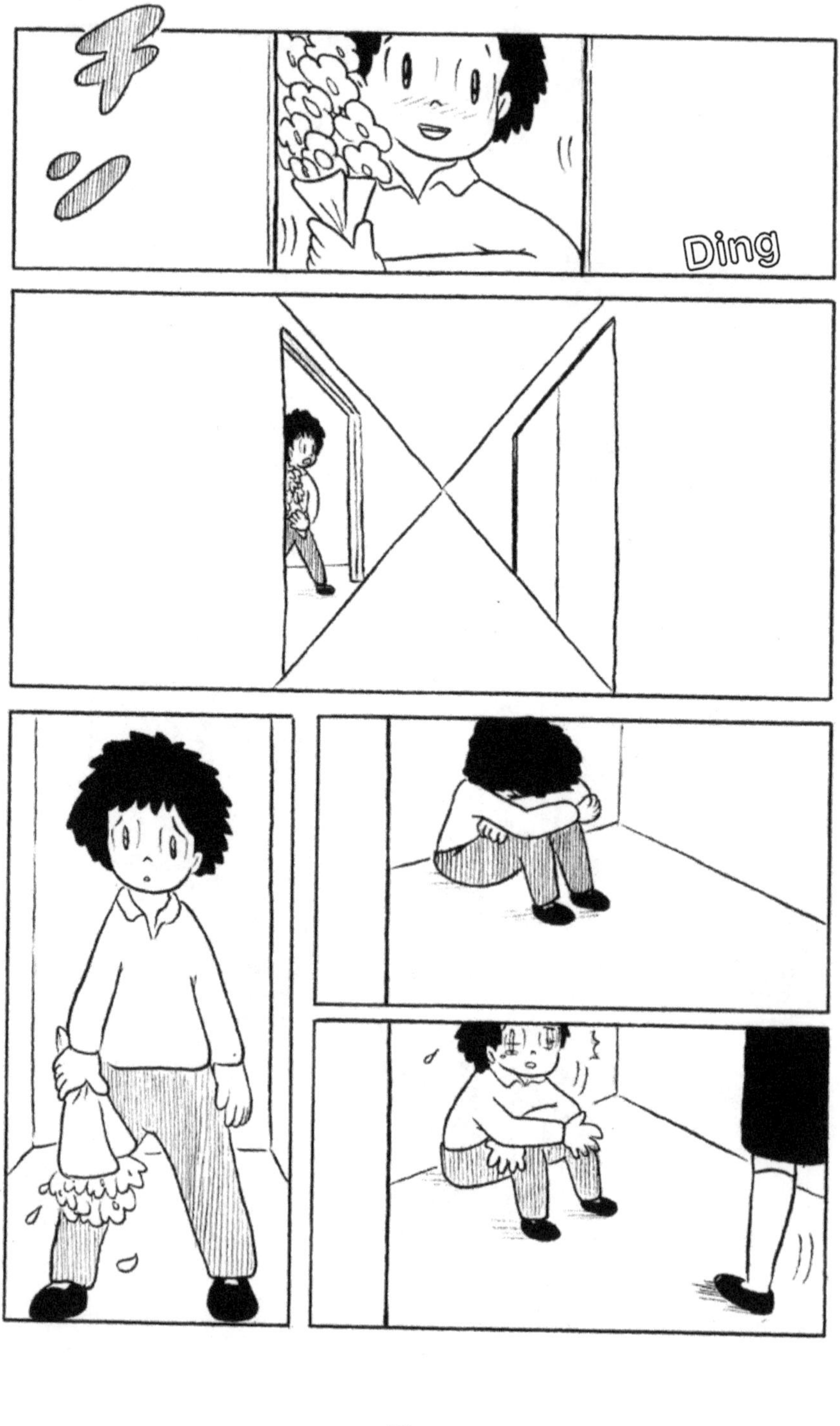
Ding

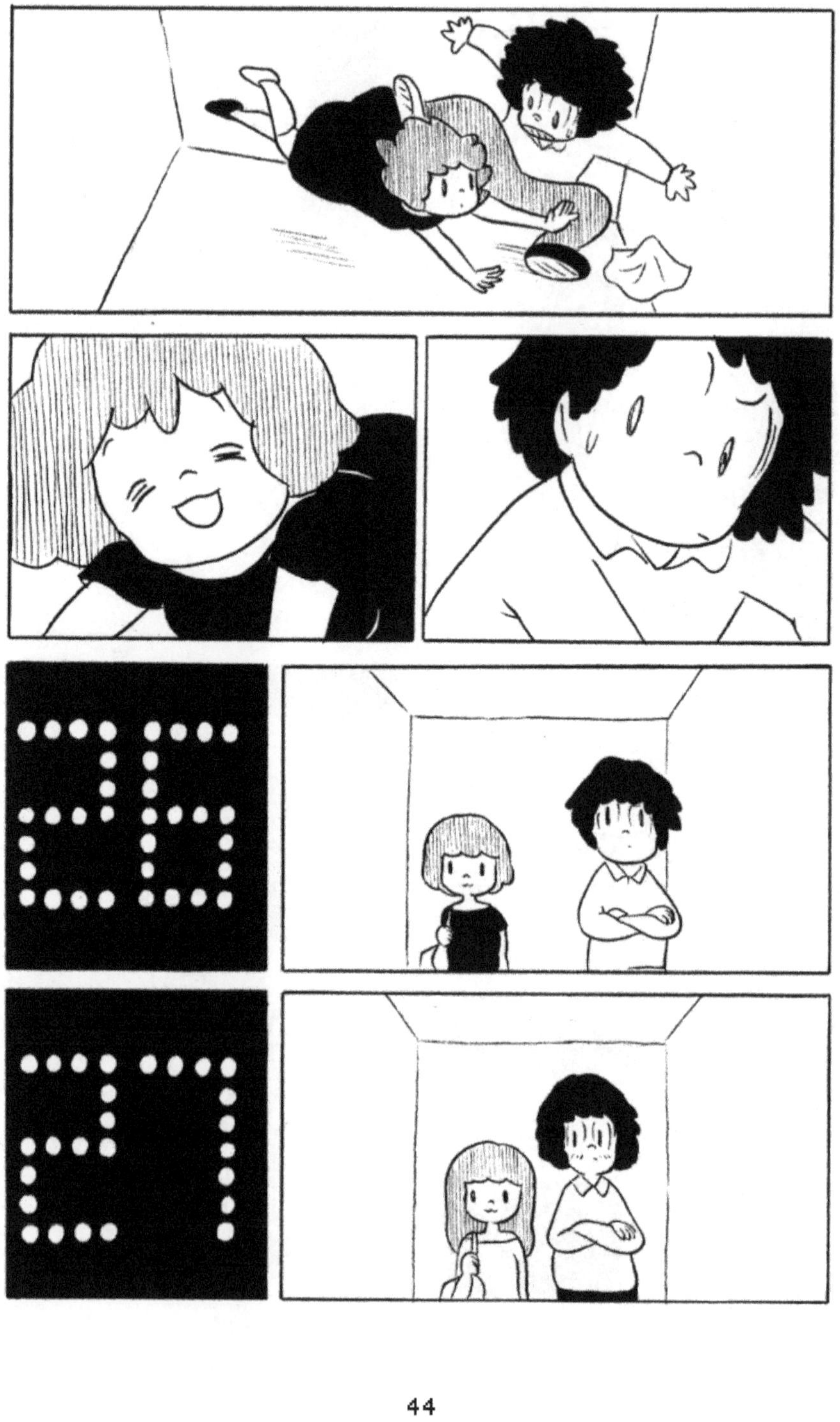
26
27

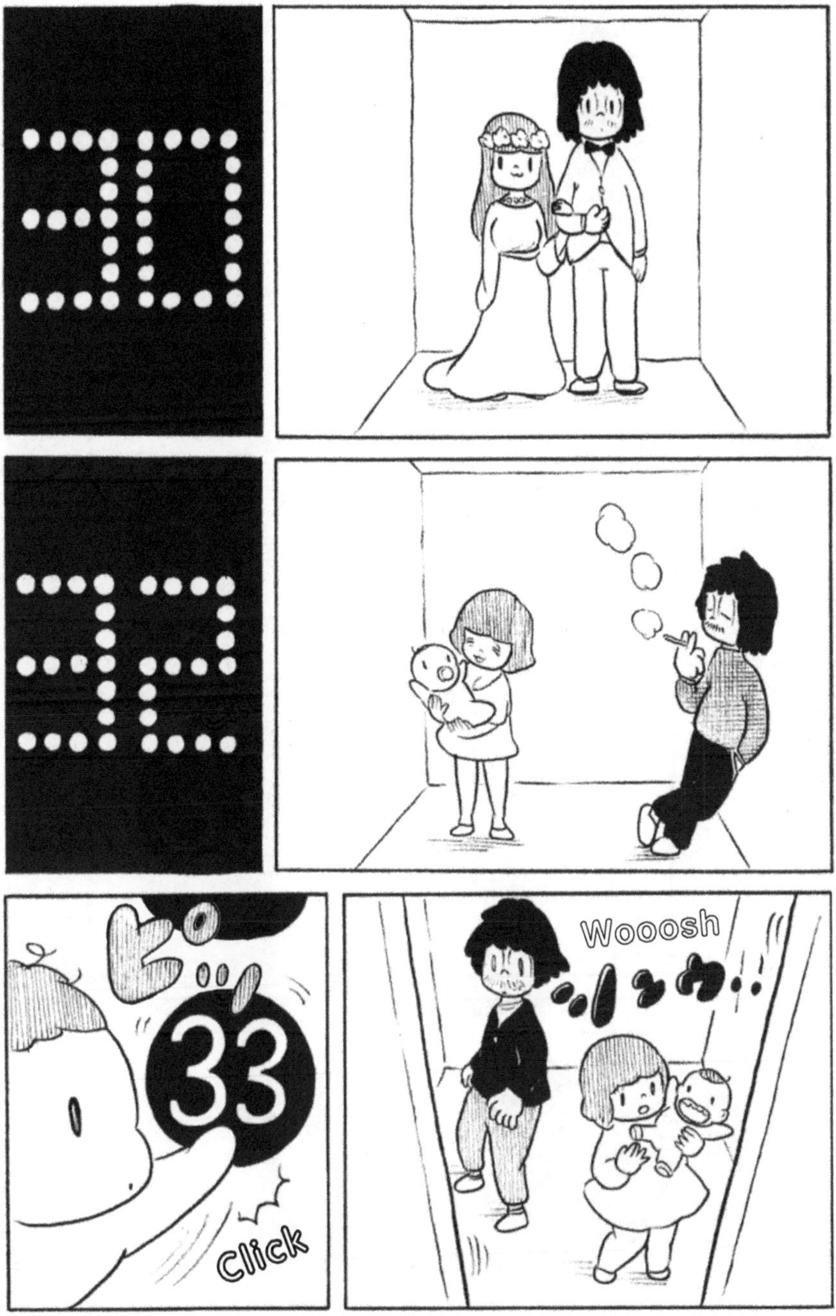
Wooosh
33
Click

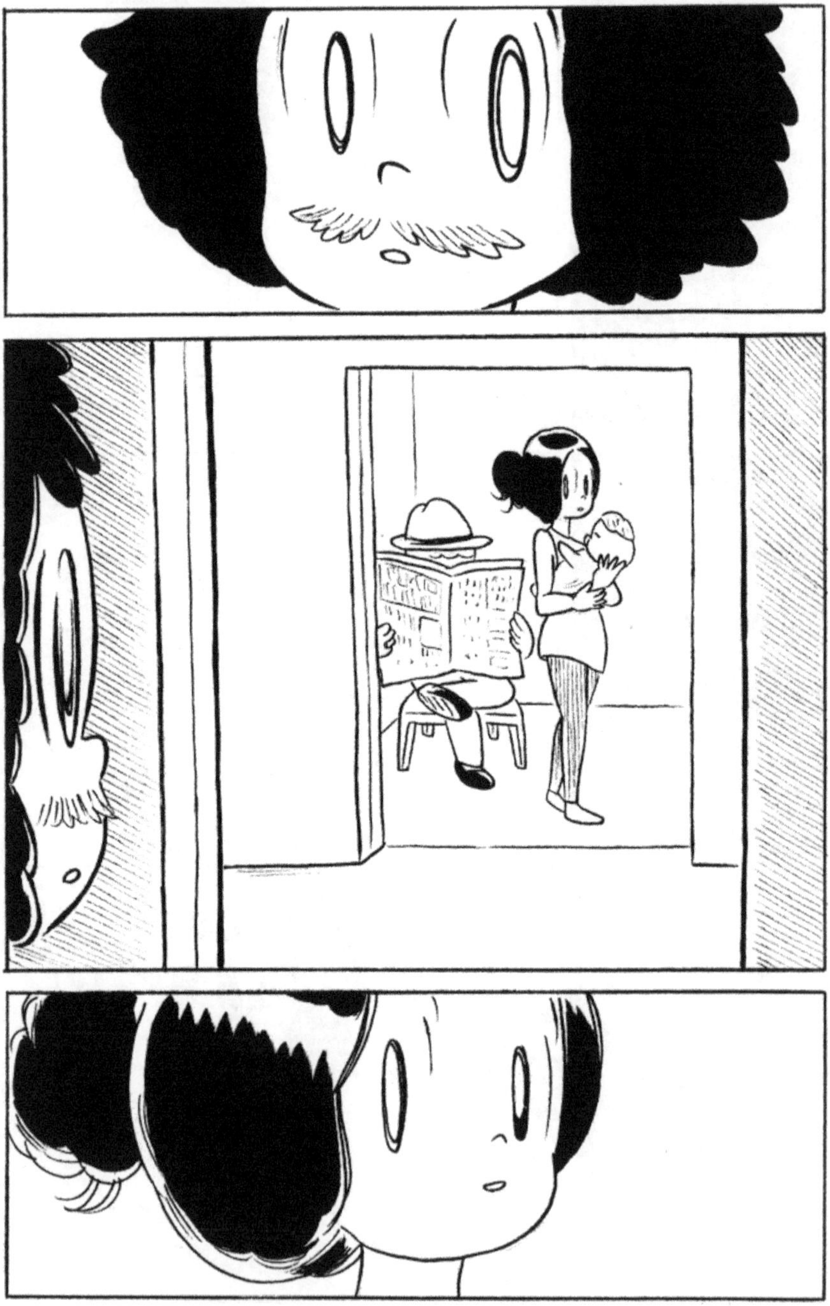

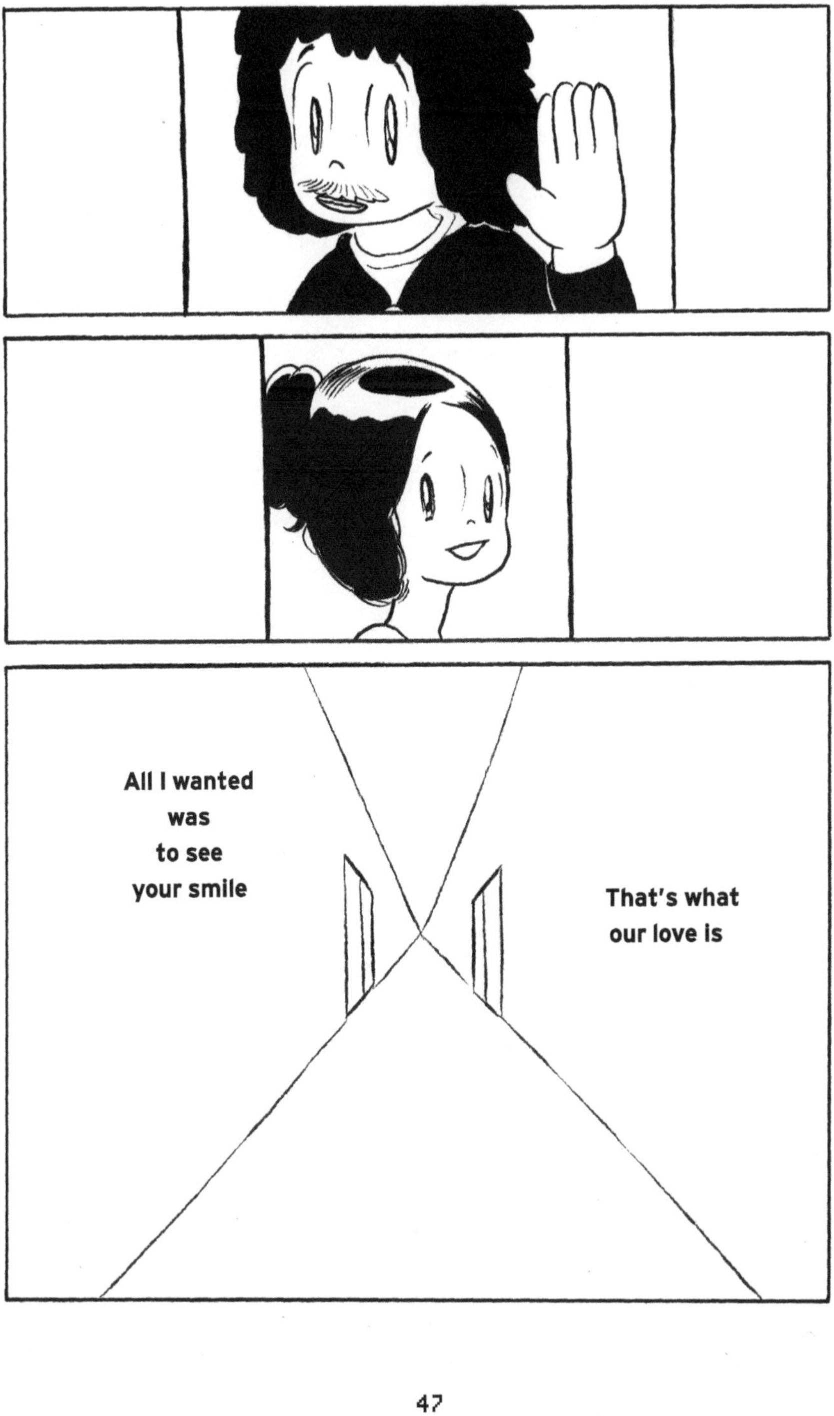
All I wanted was to see your smile
That's what our love is

Bird

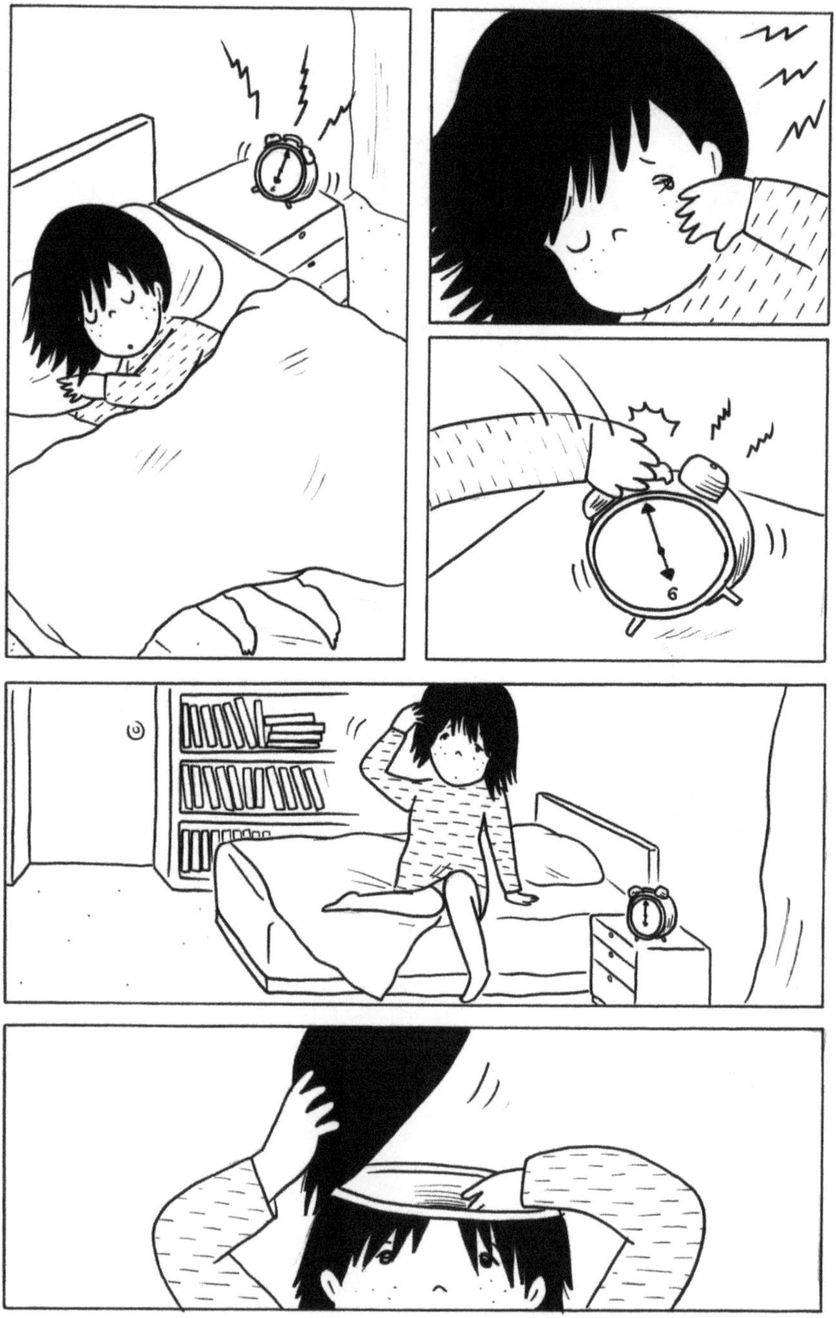

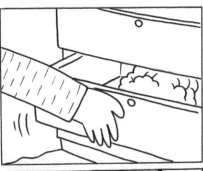

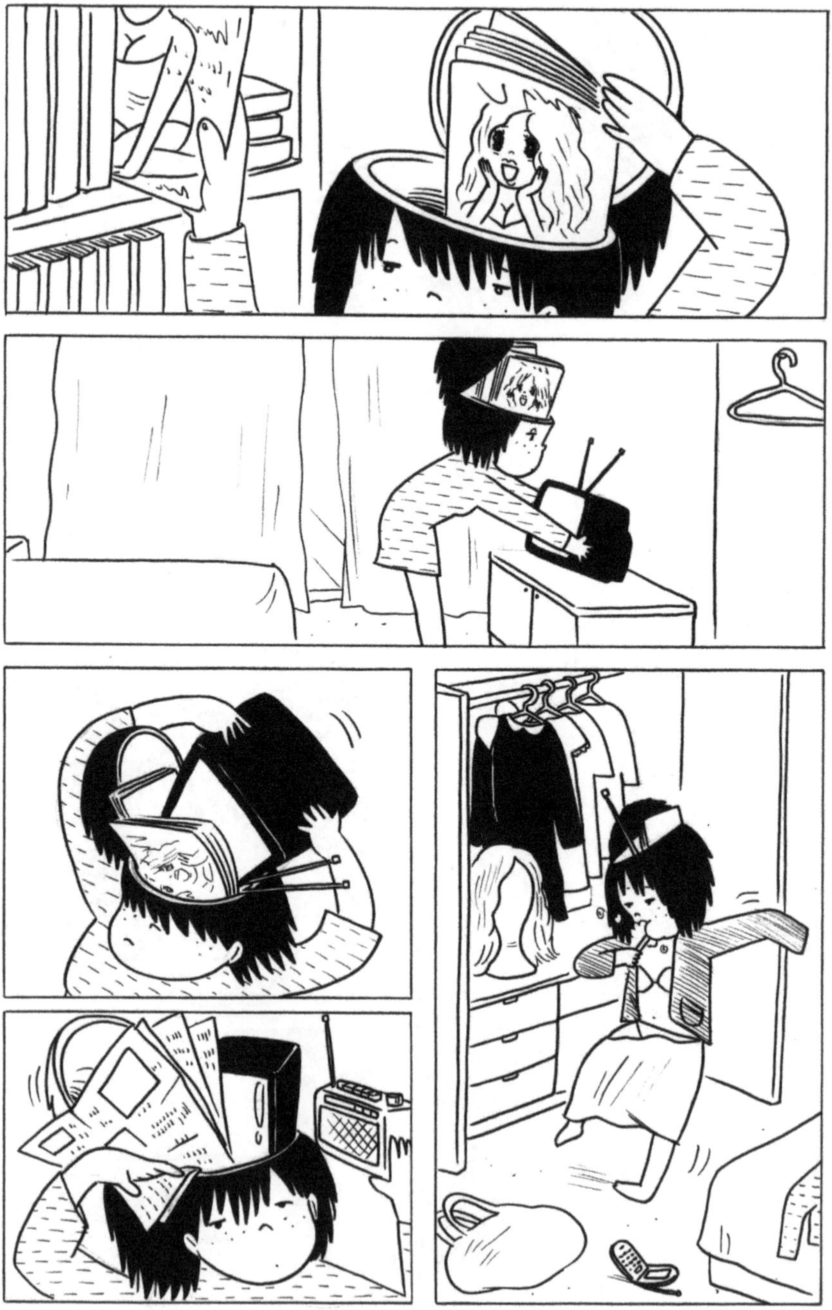

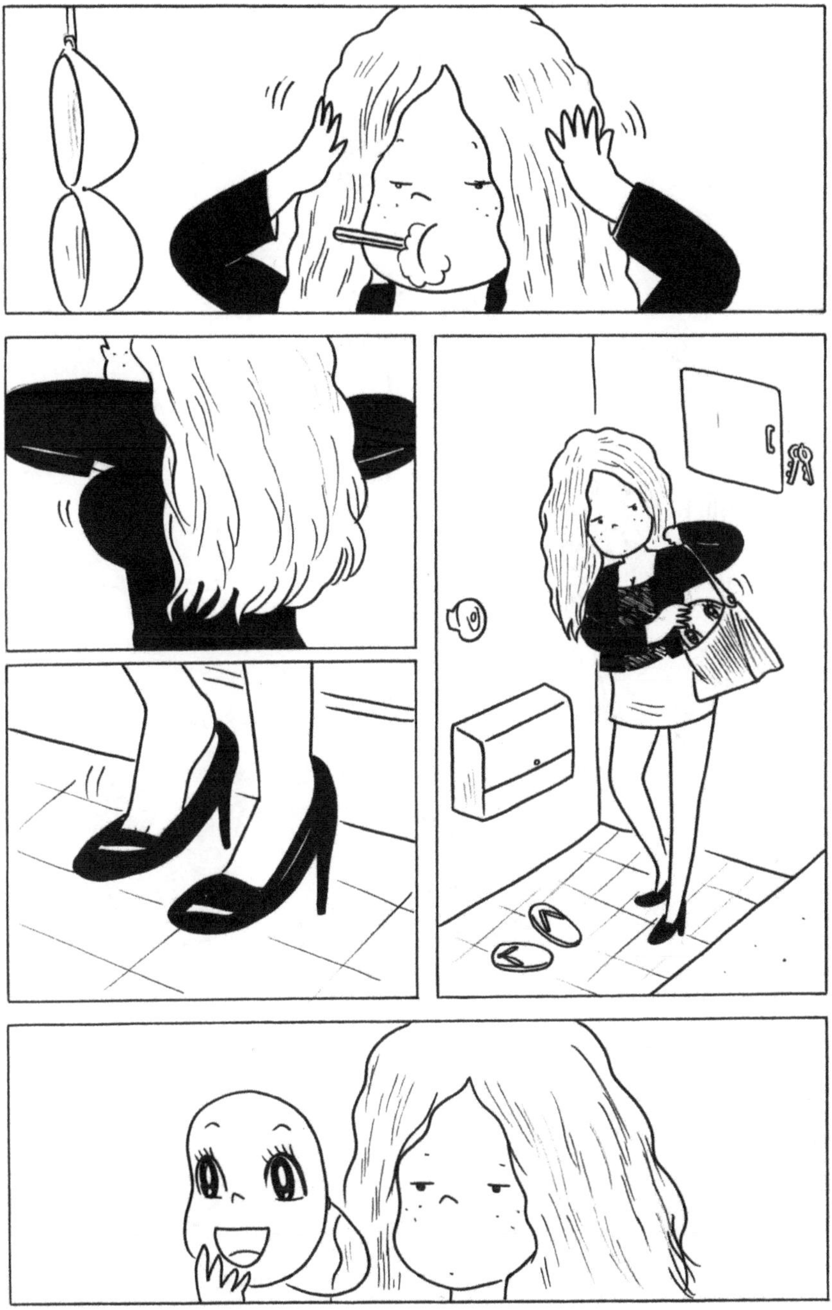

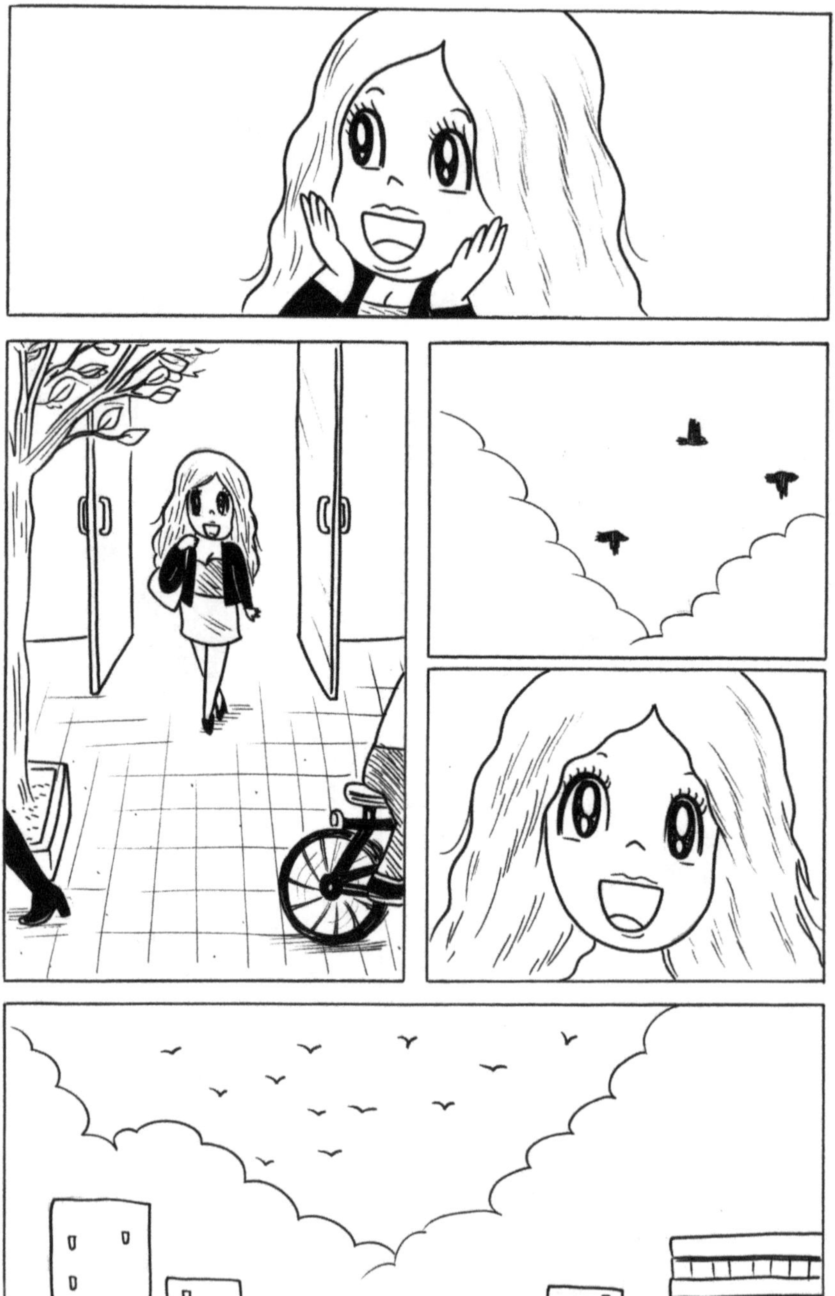

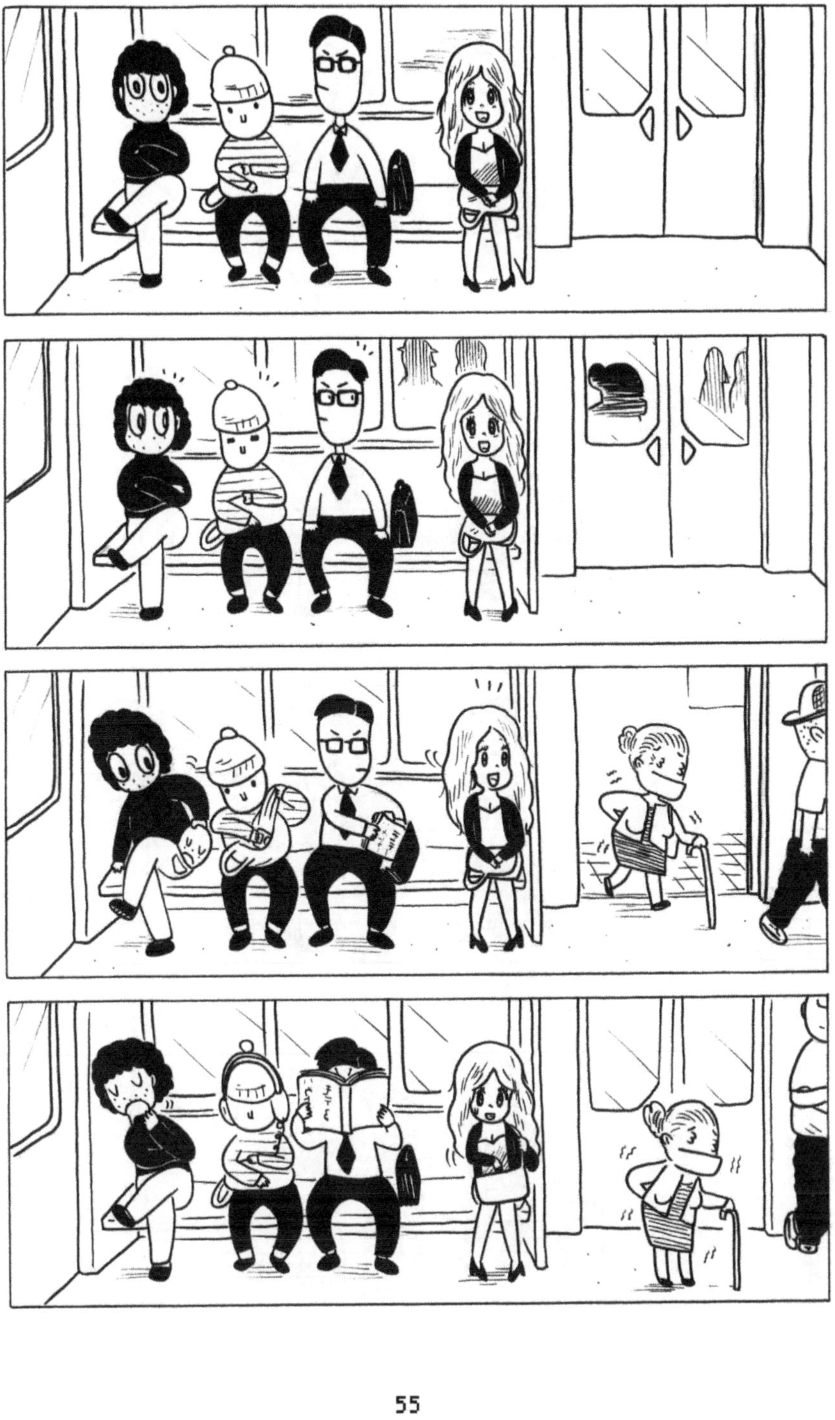

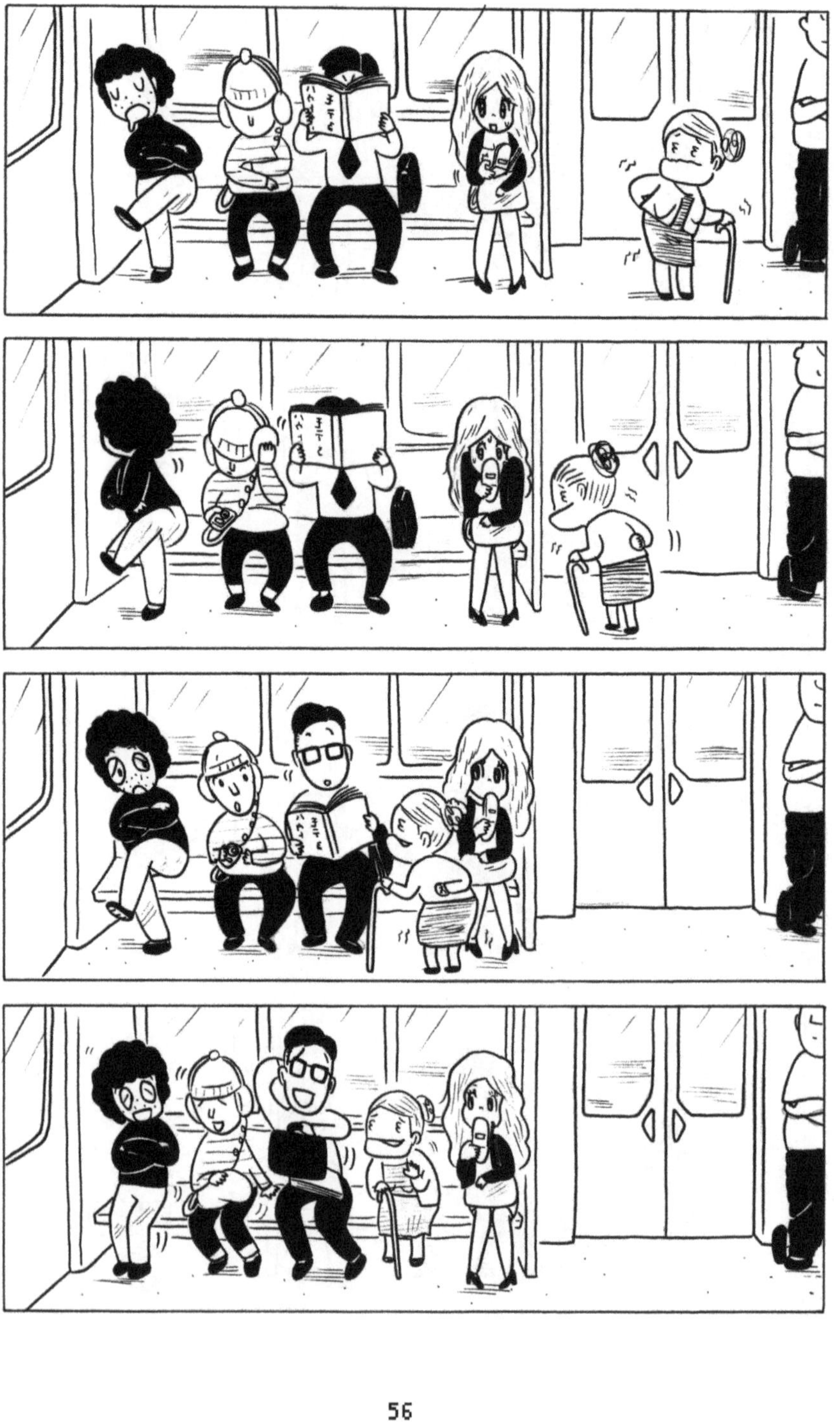

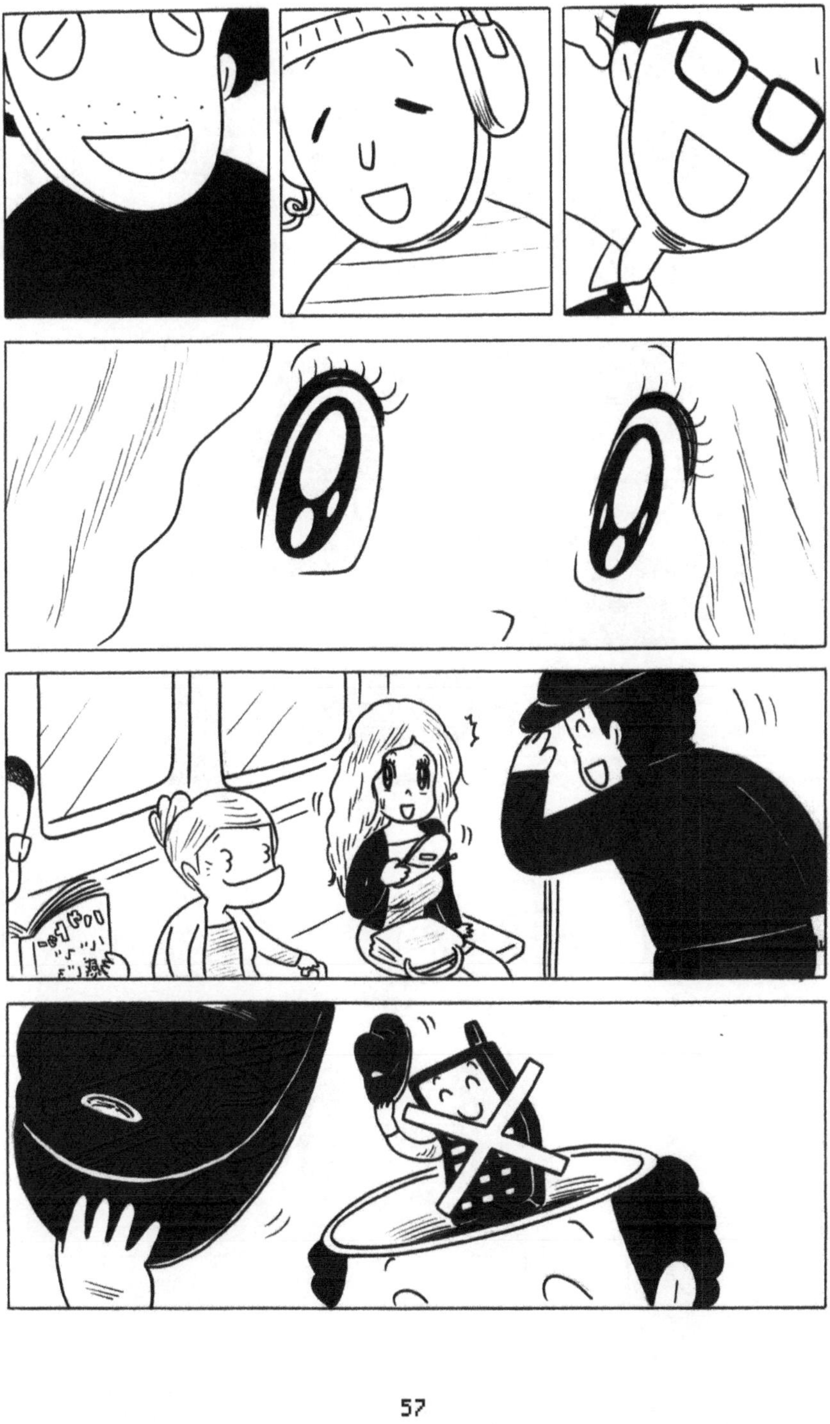

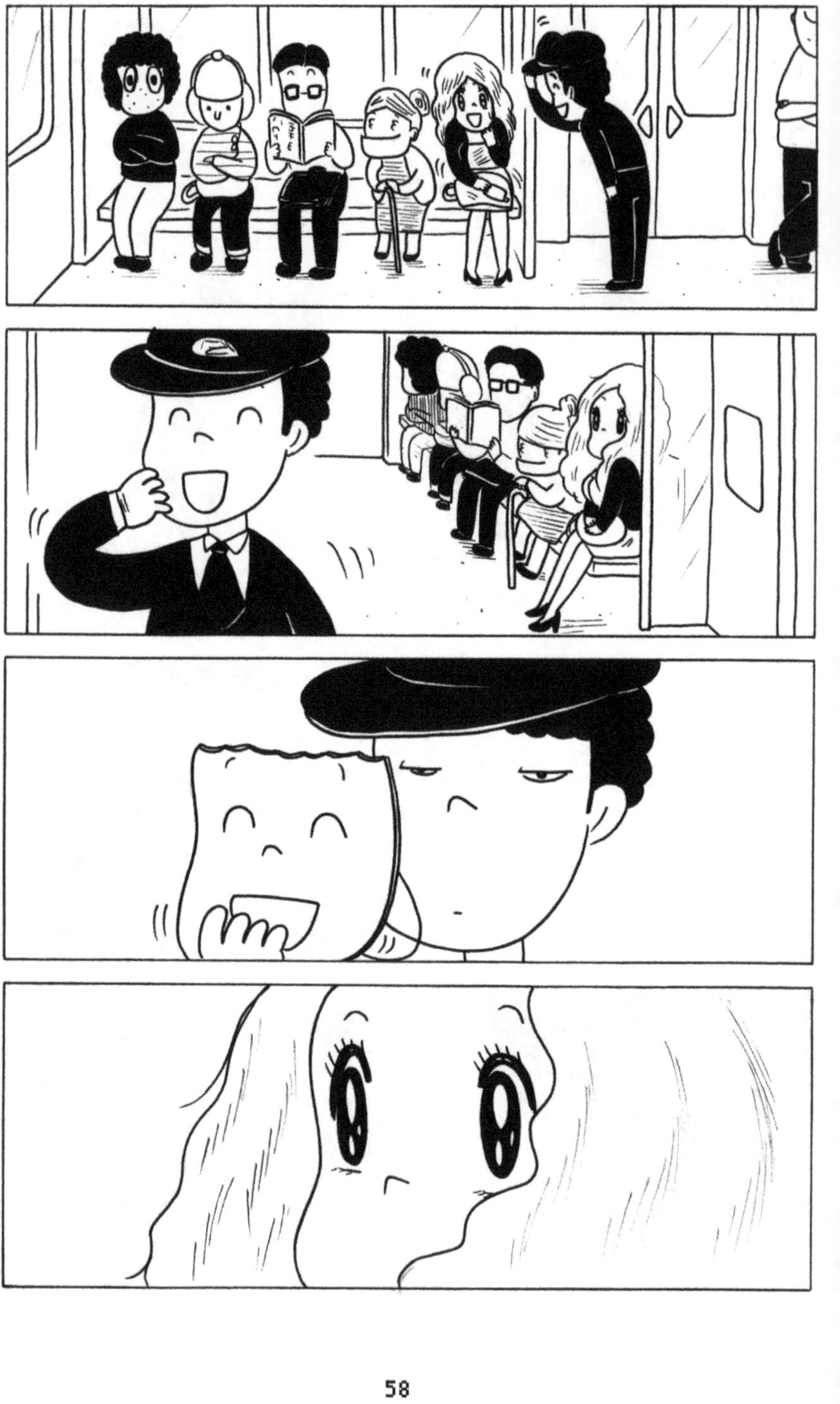

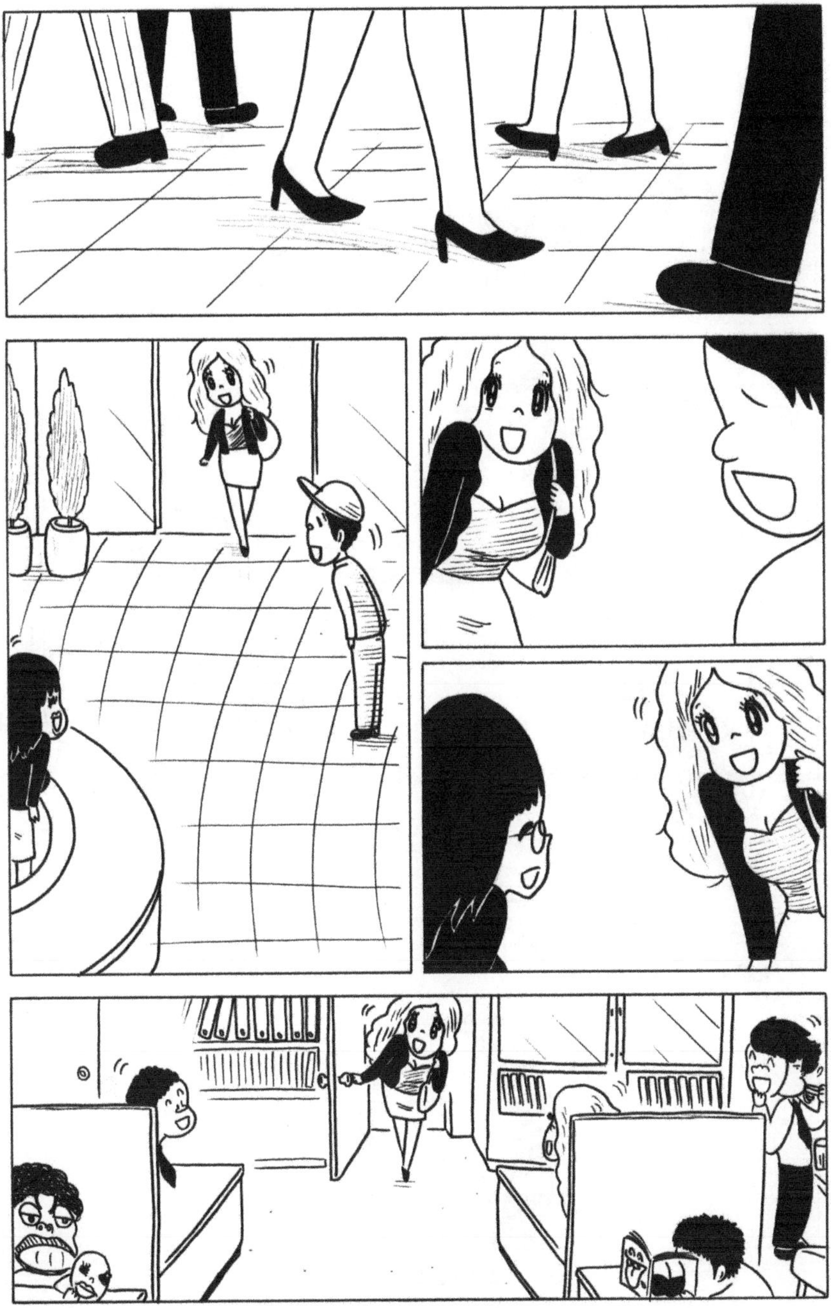

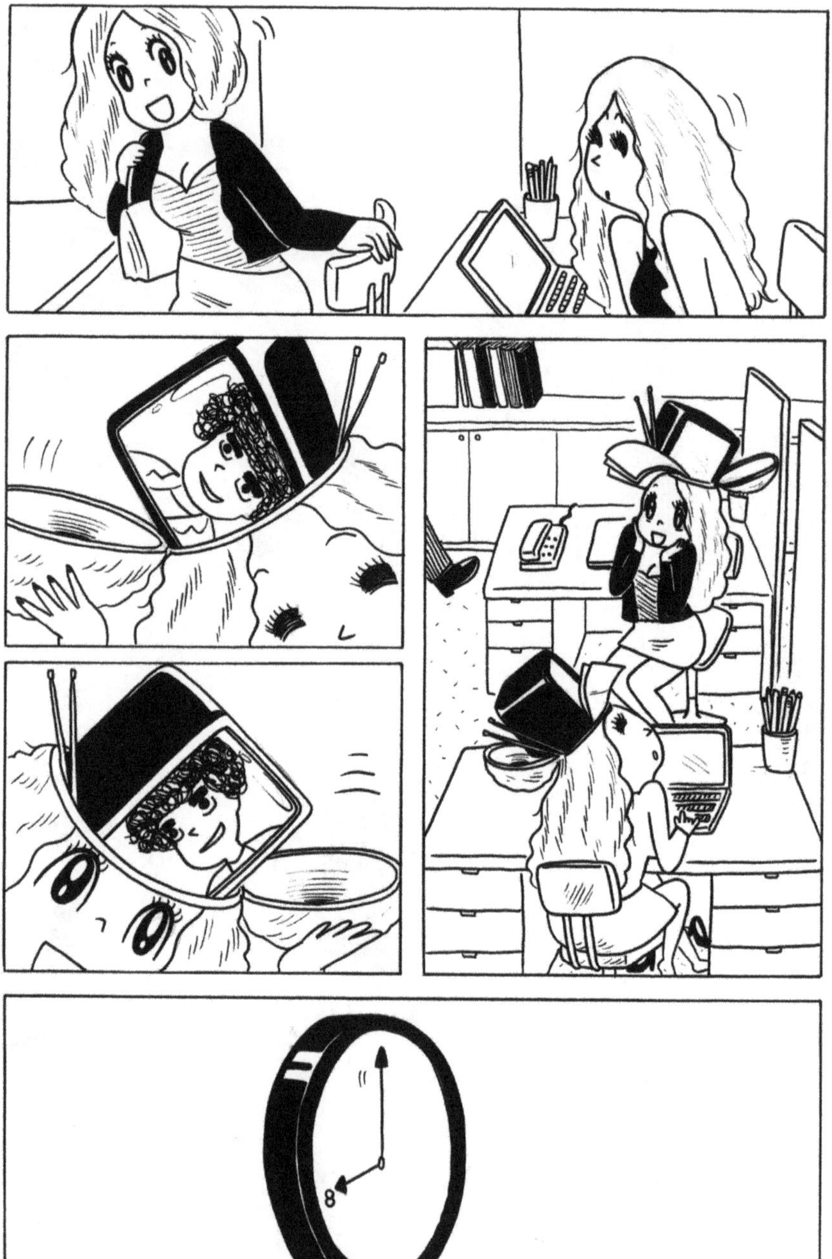

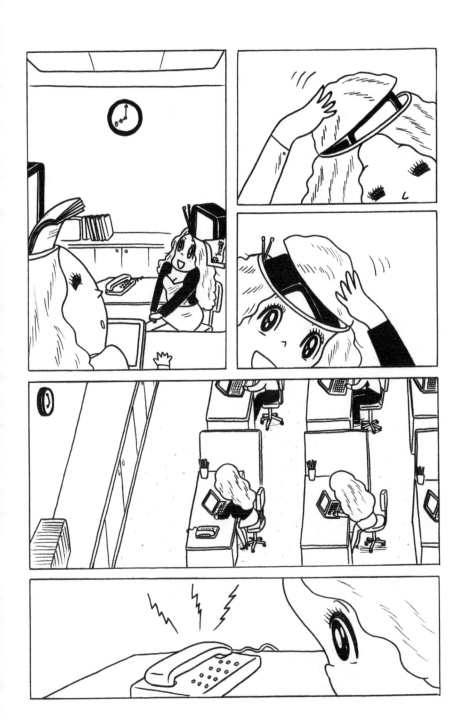

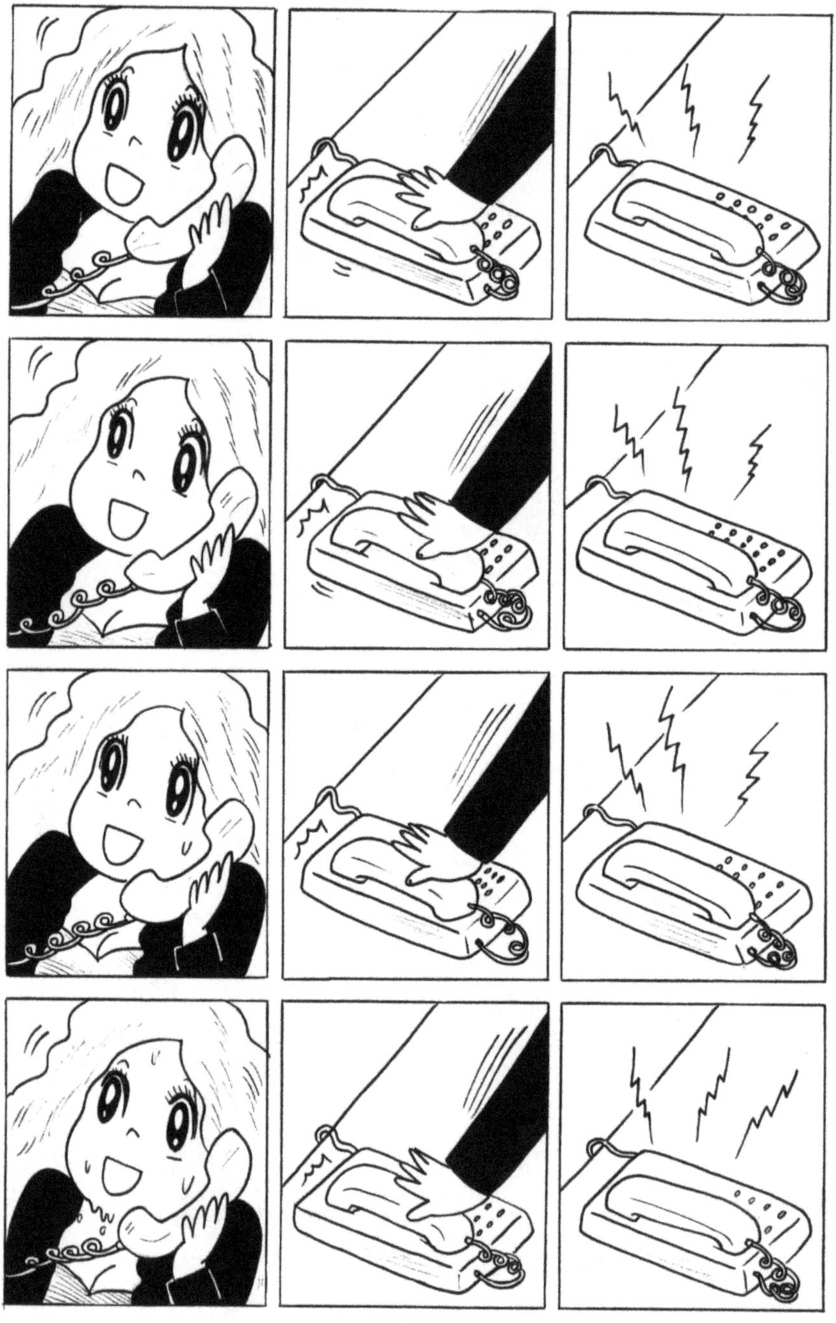

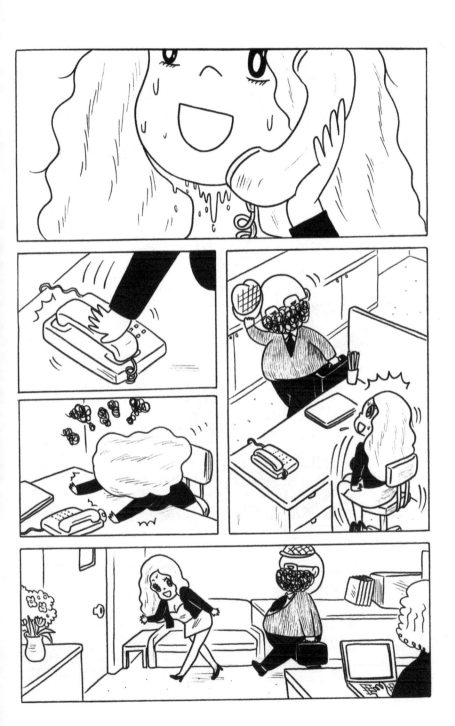

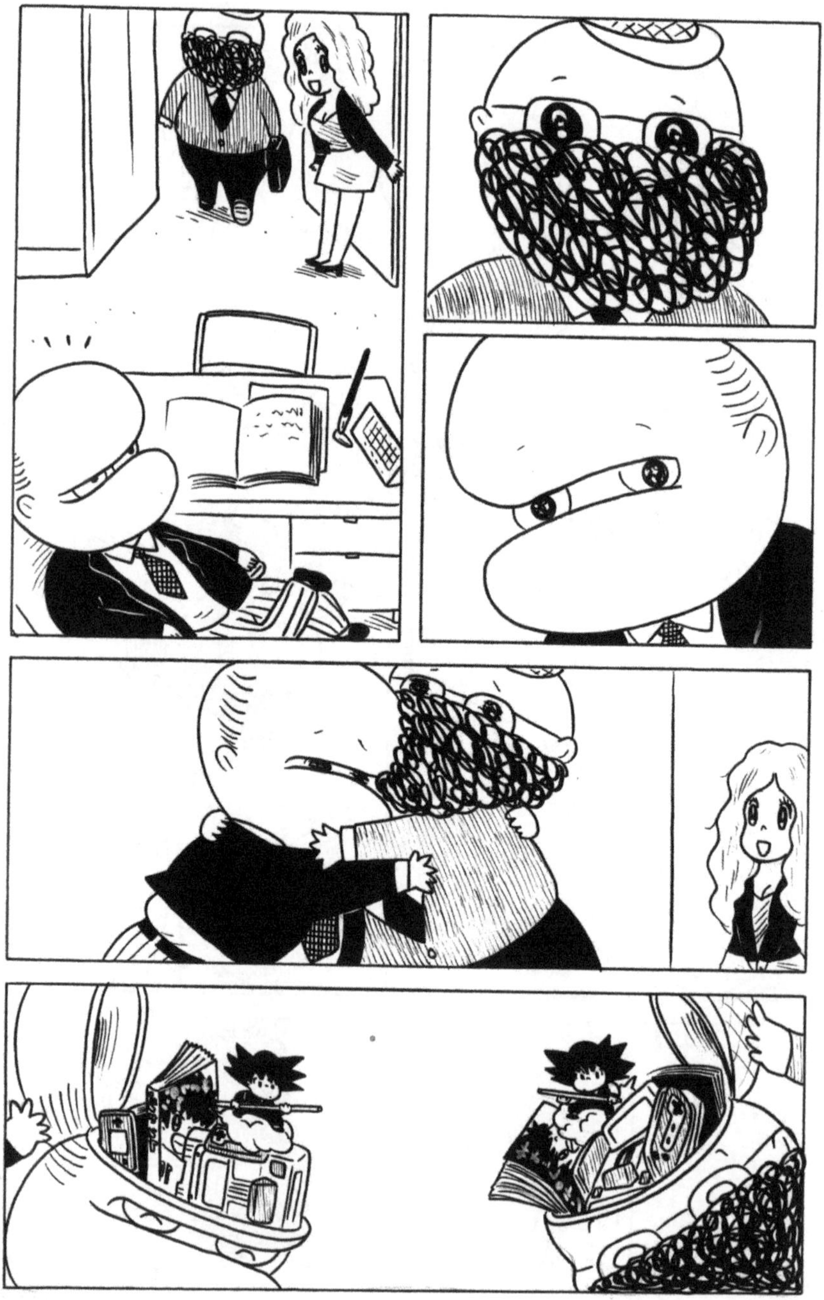

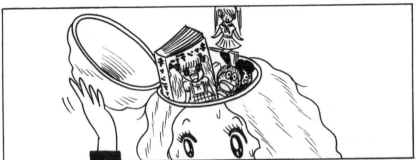

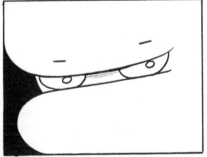

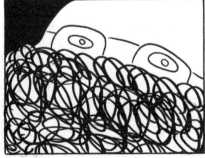

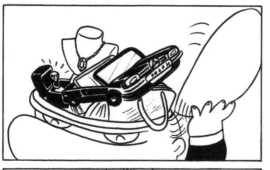

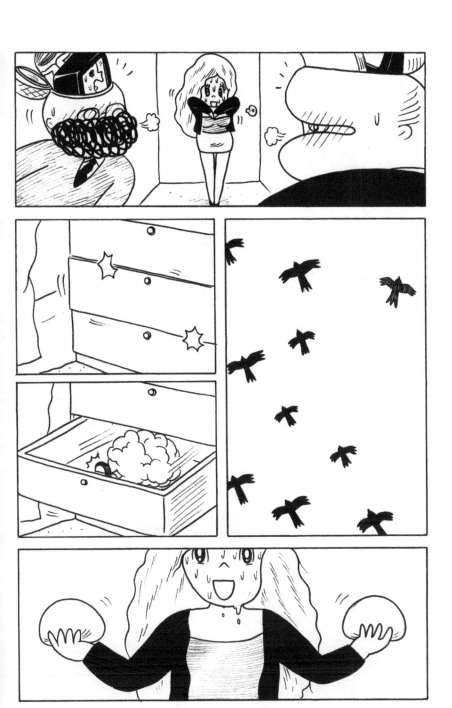

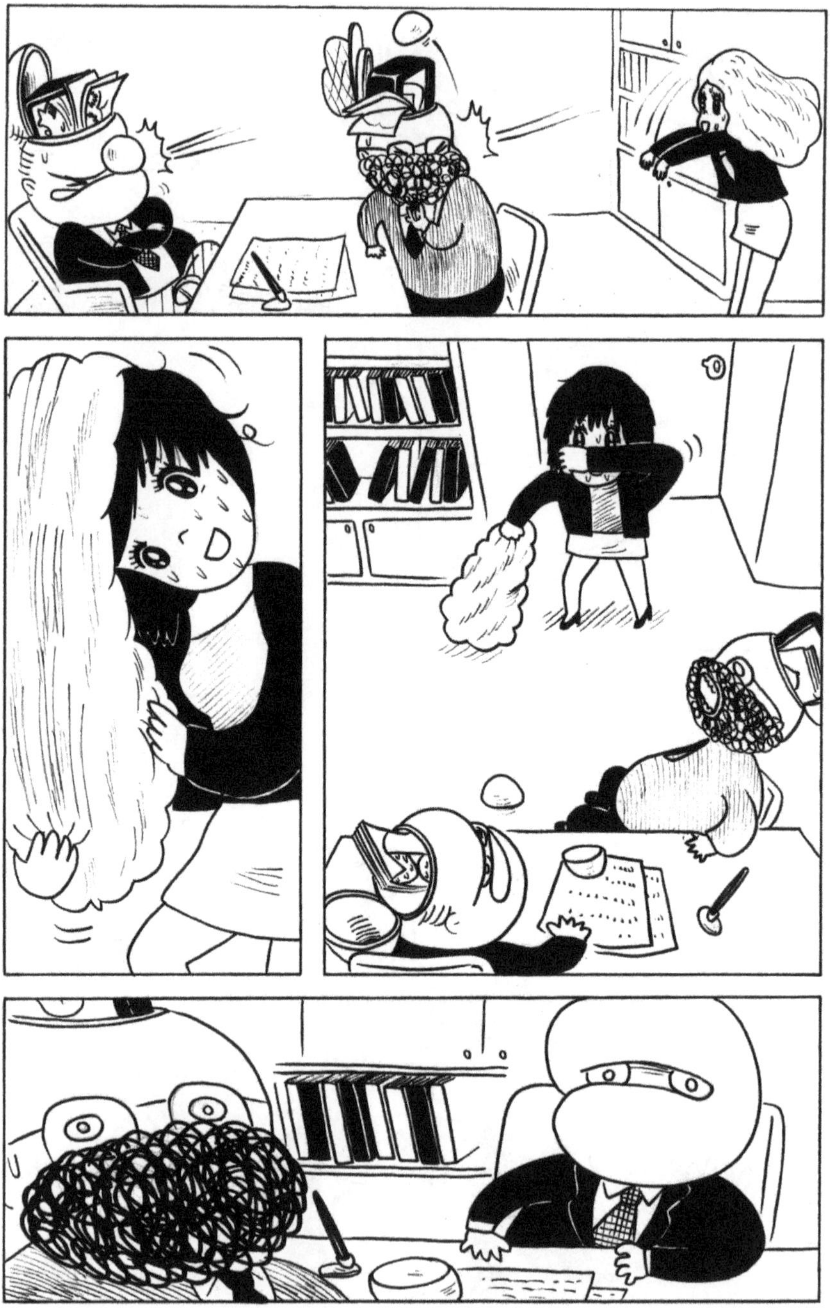

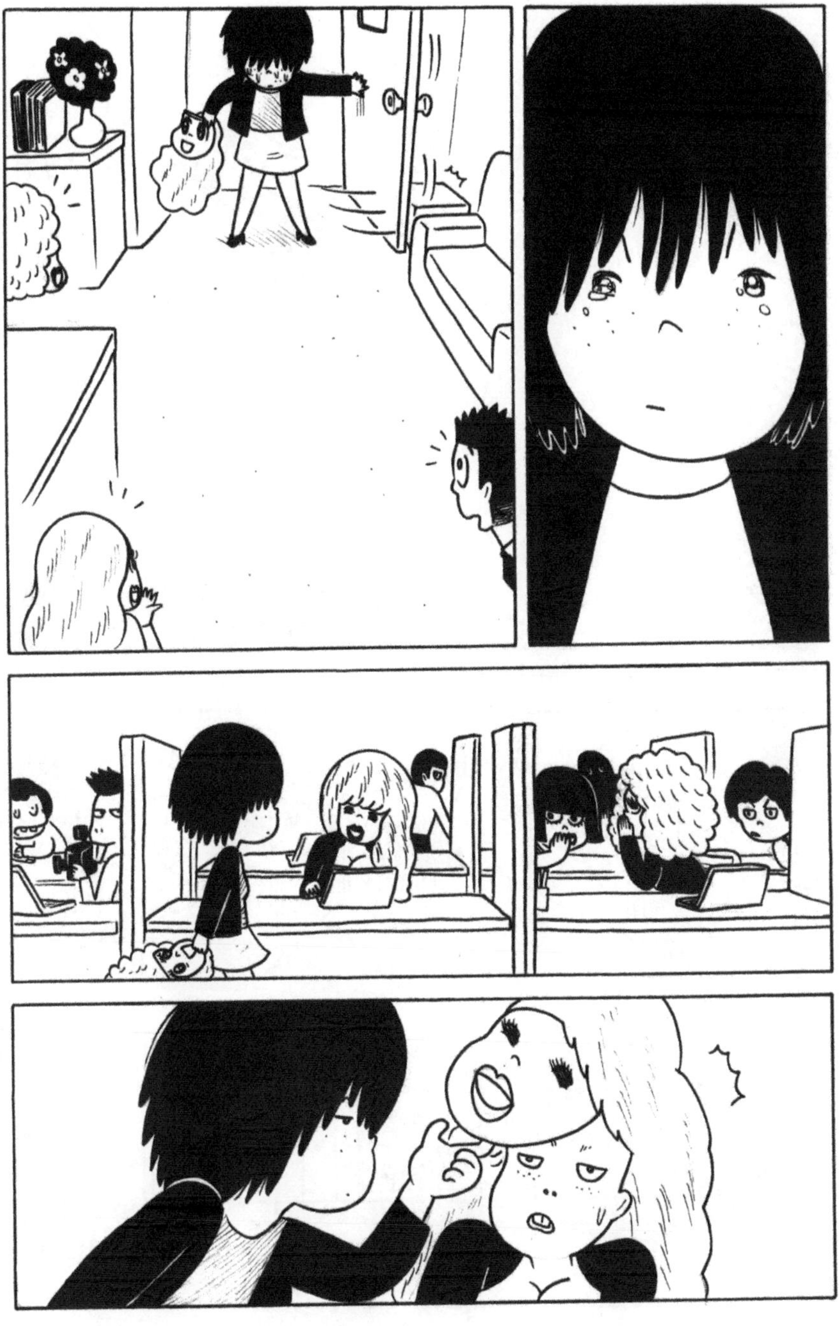

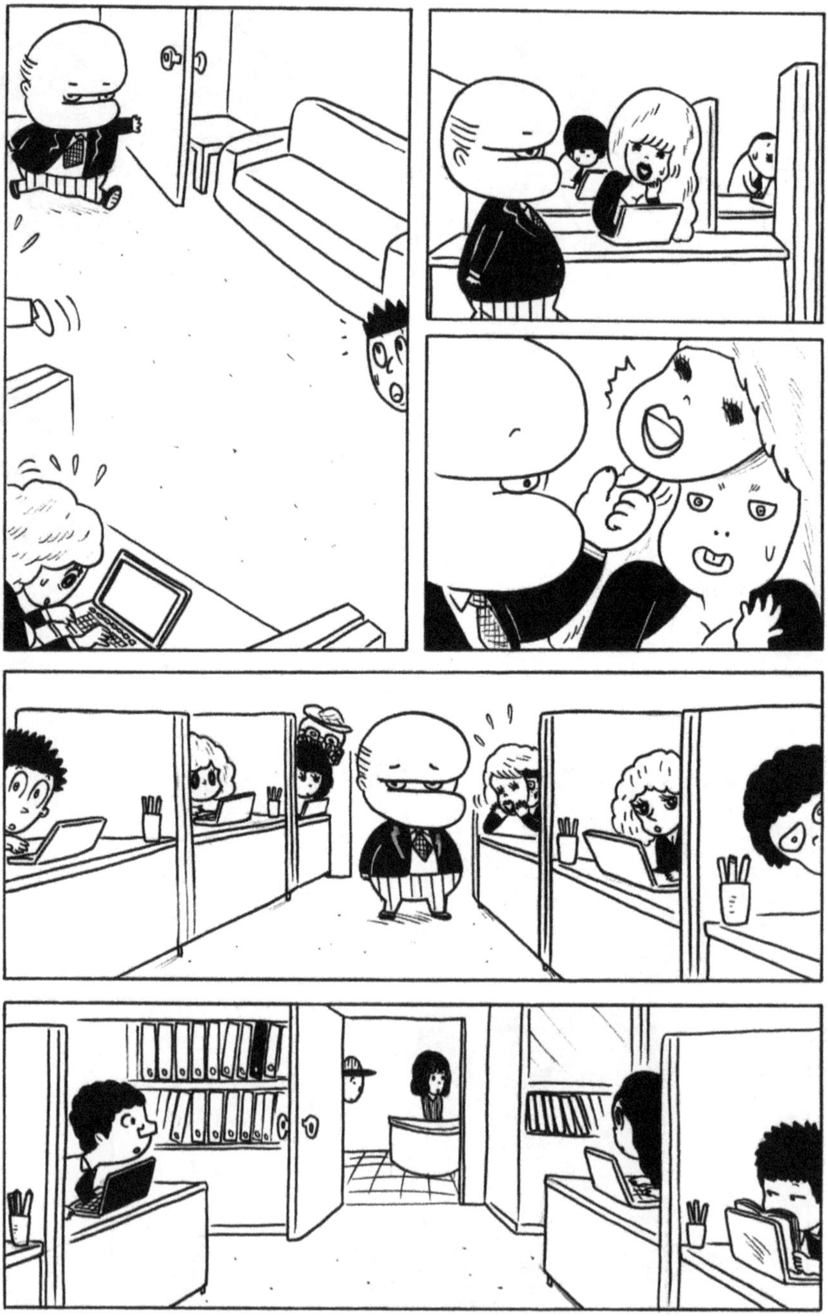

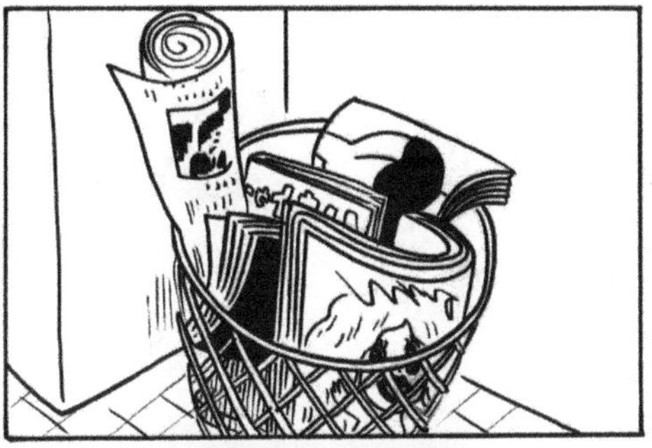

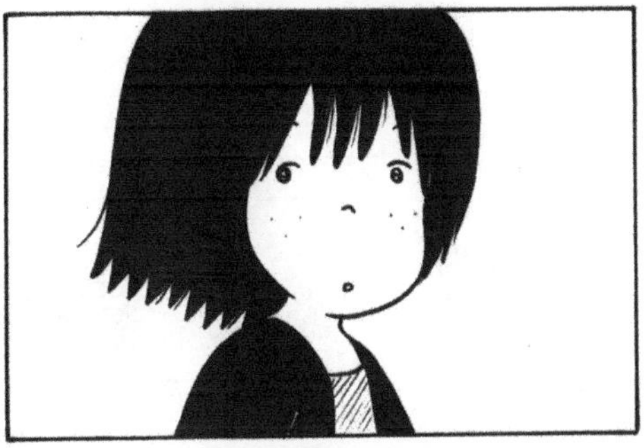

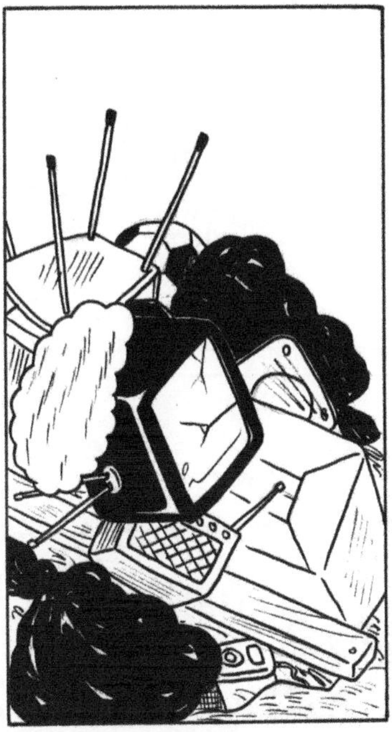

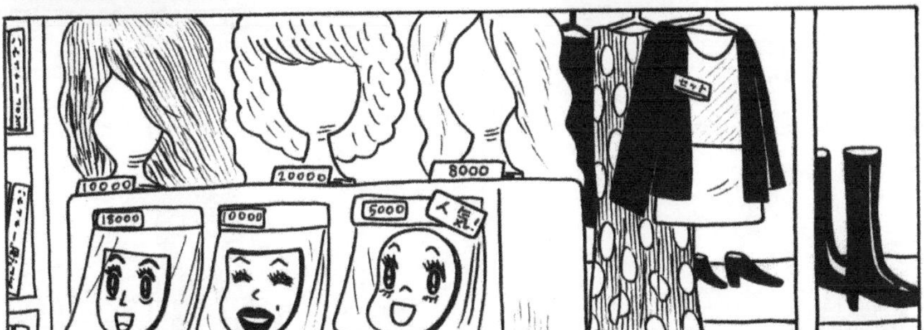
セット
8000
人気!
5000
20000
10000
10000
18000

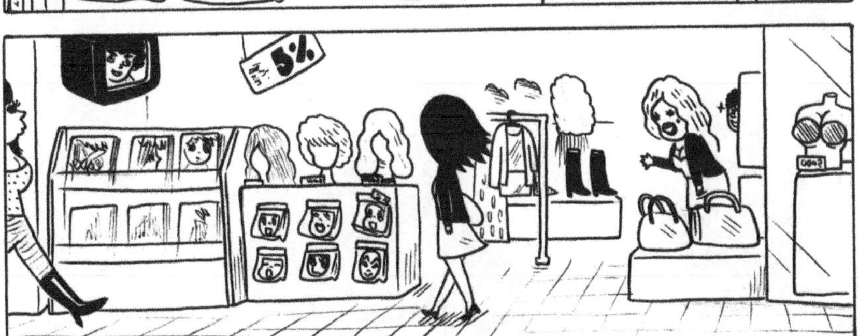
5%

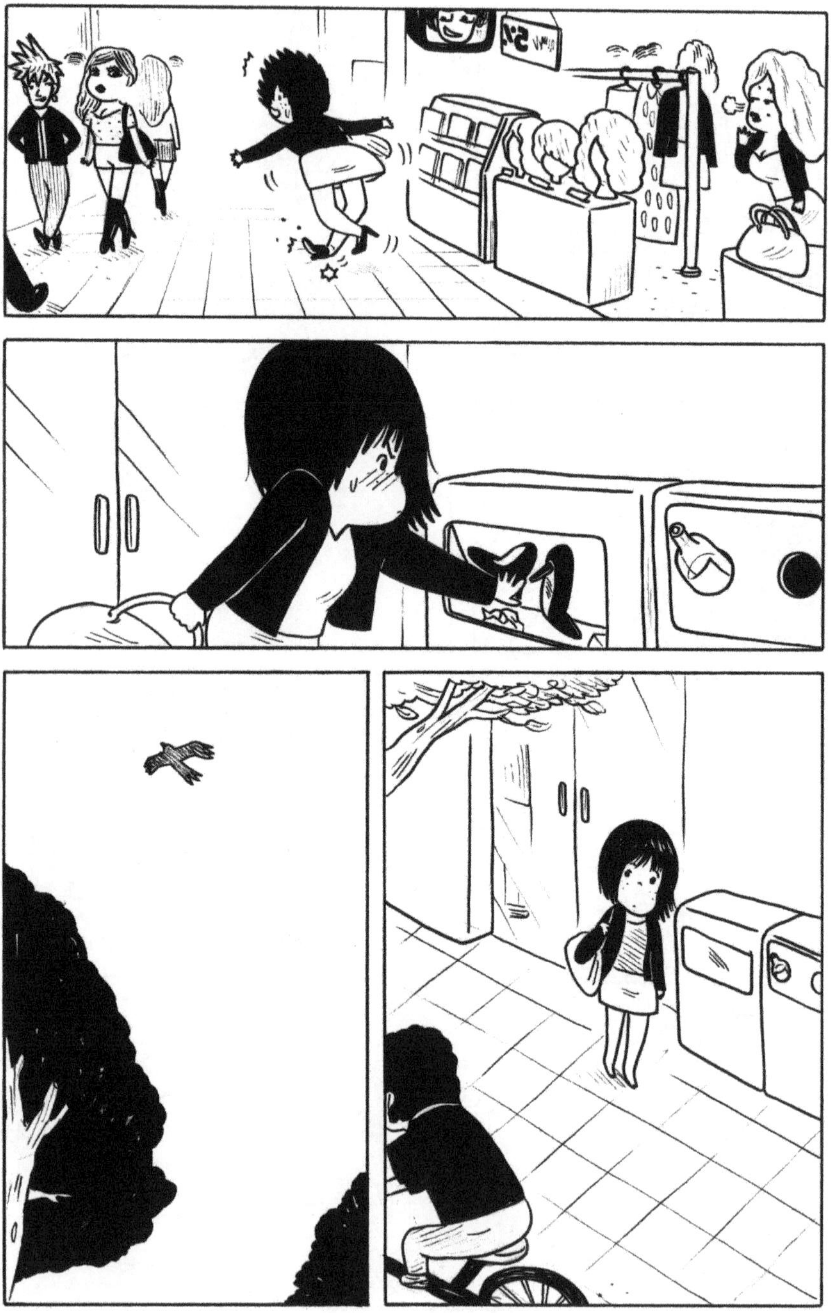

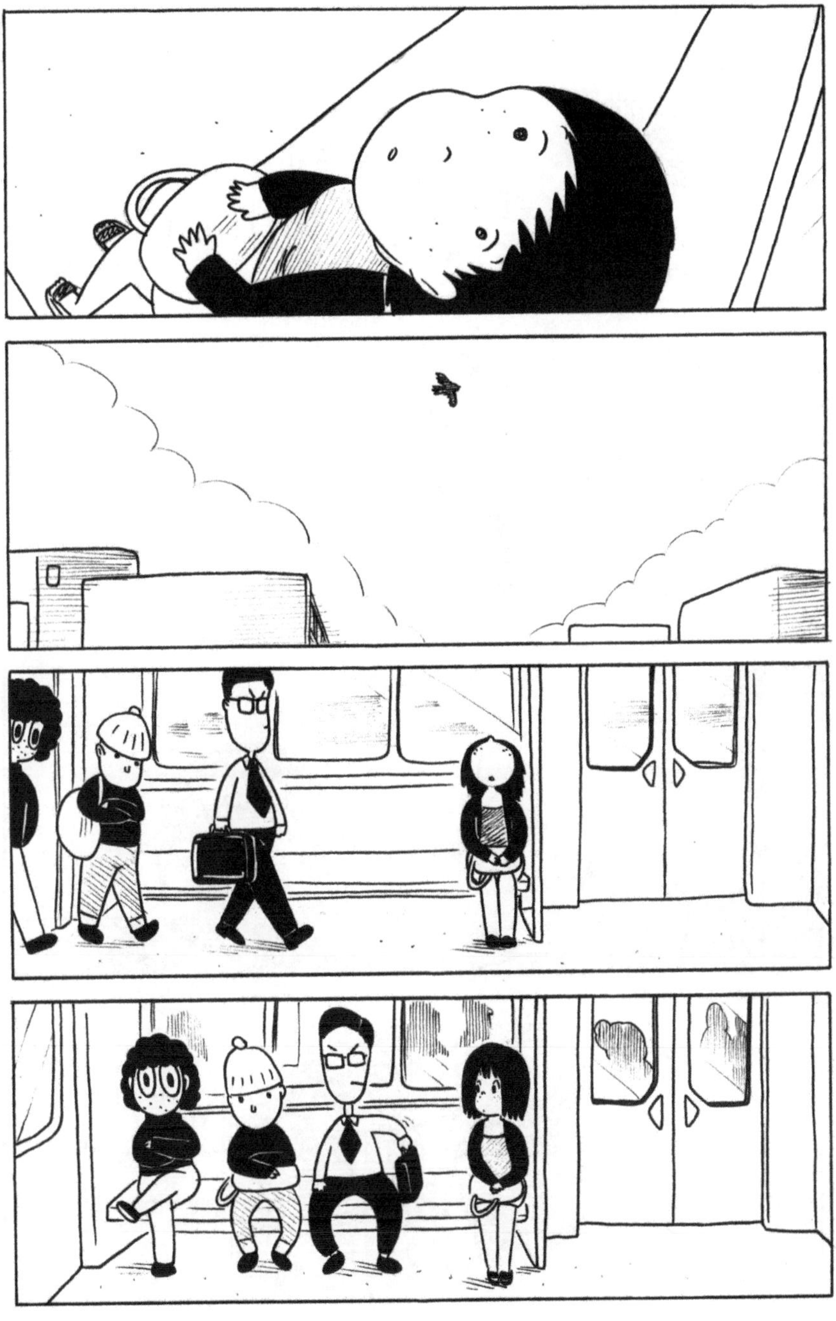

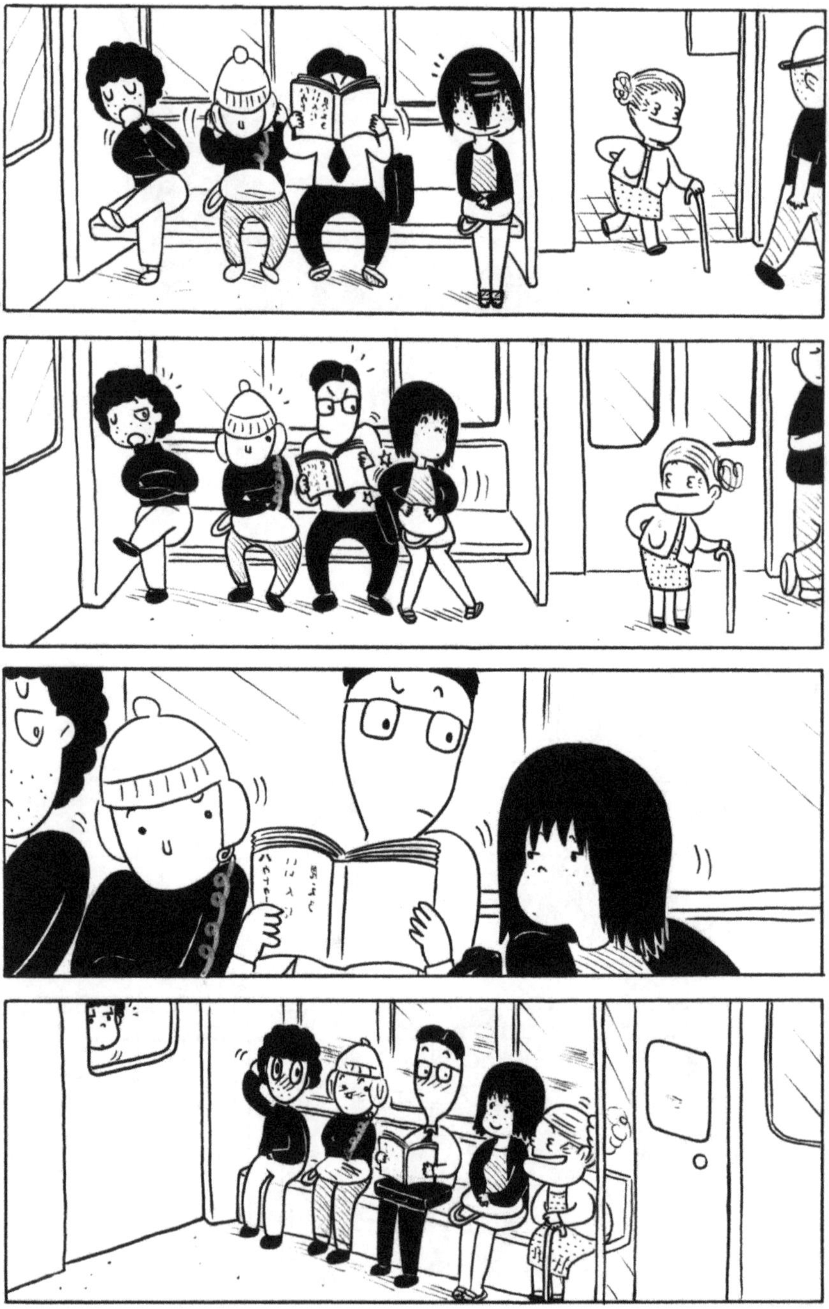

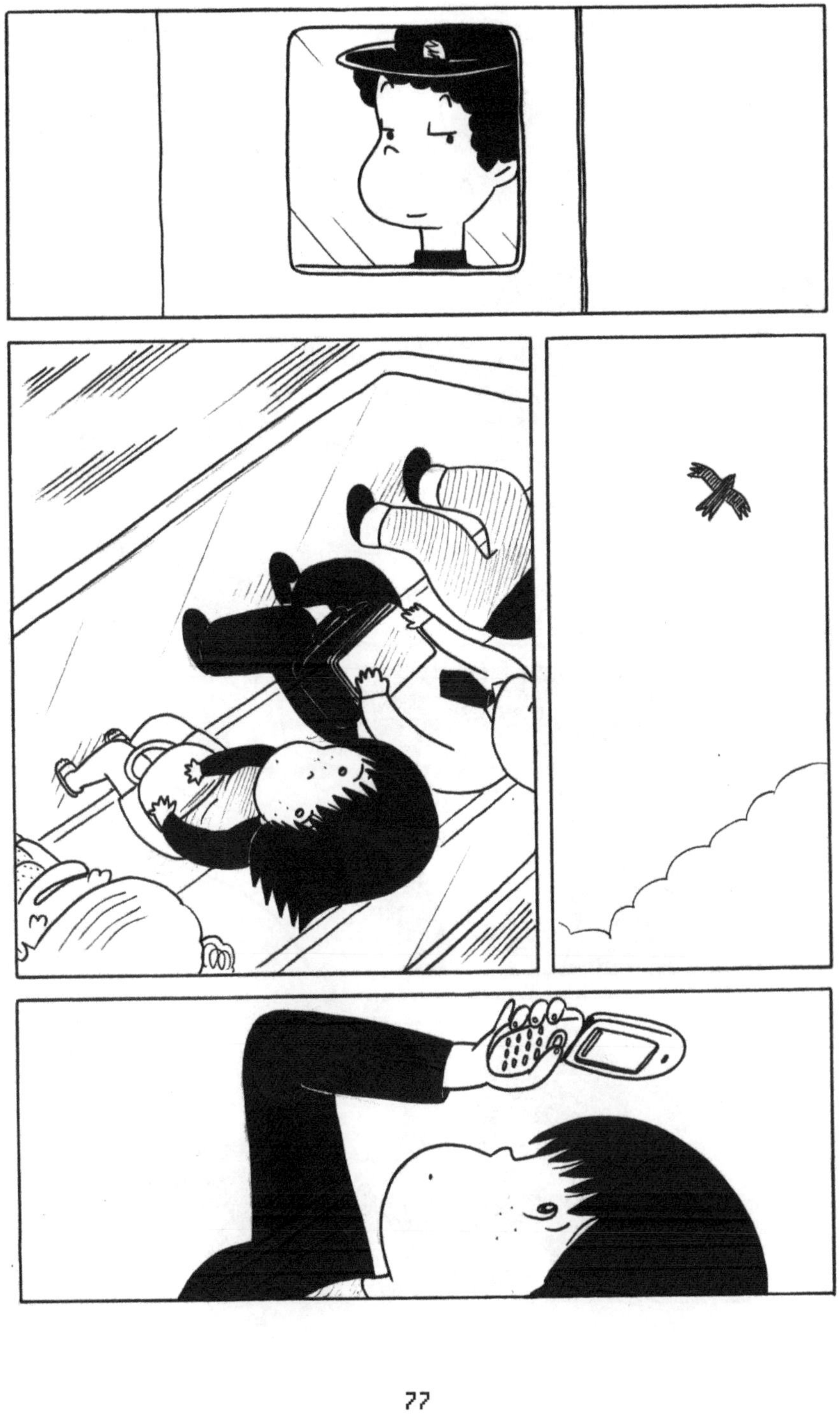

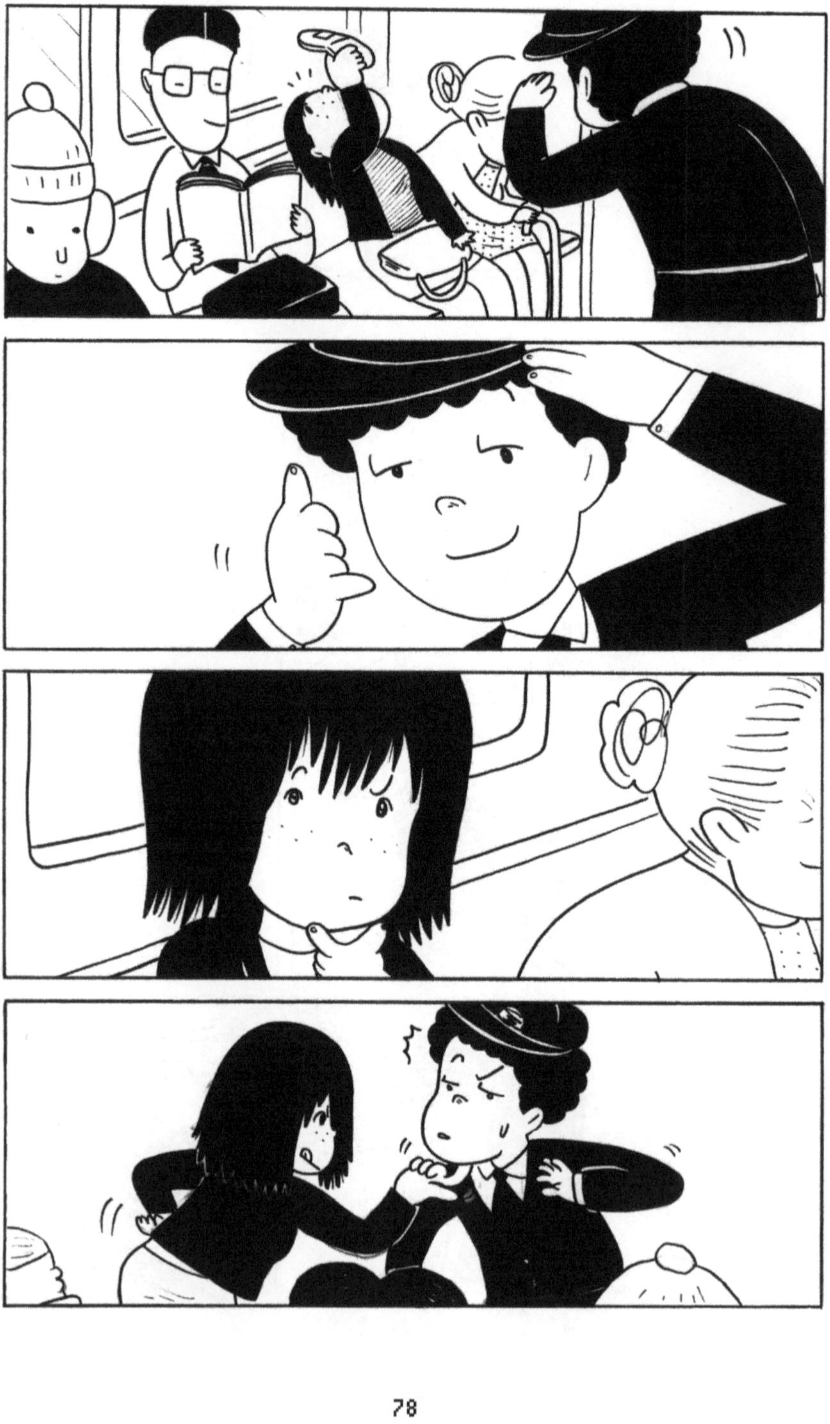

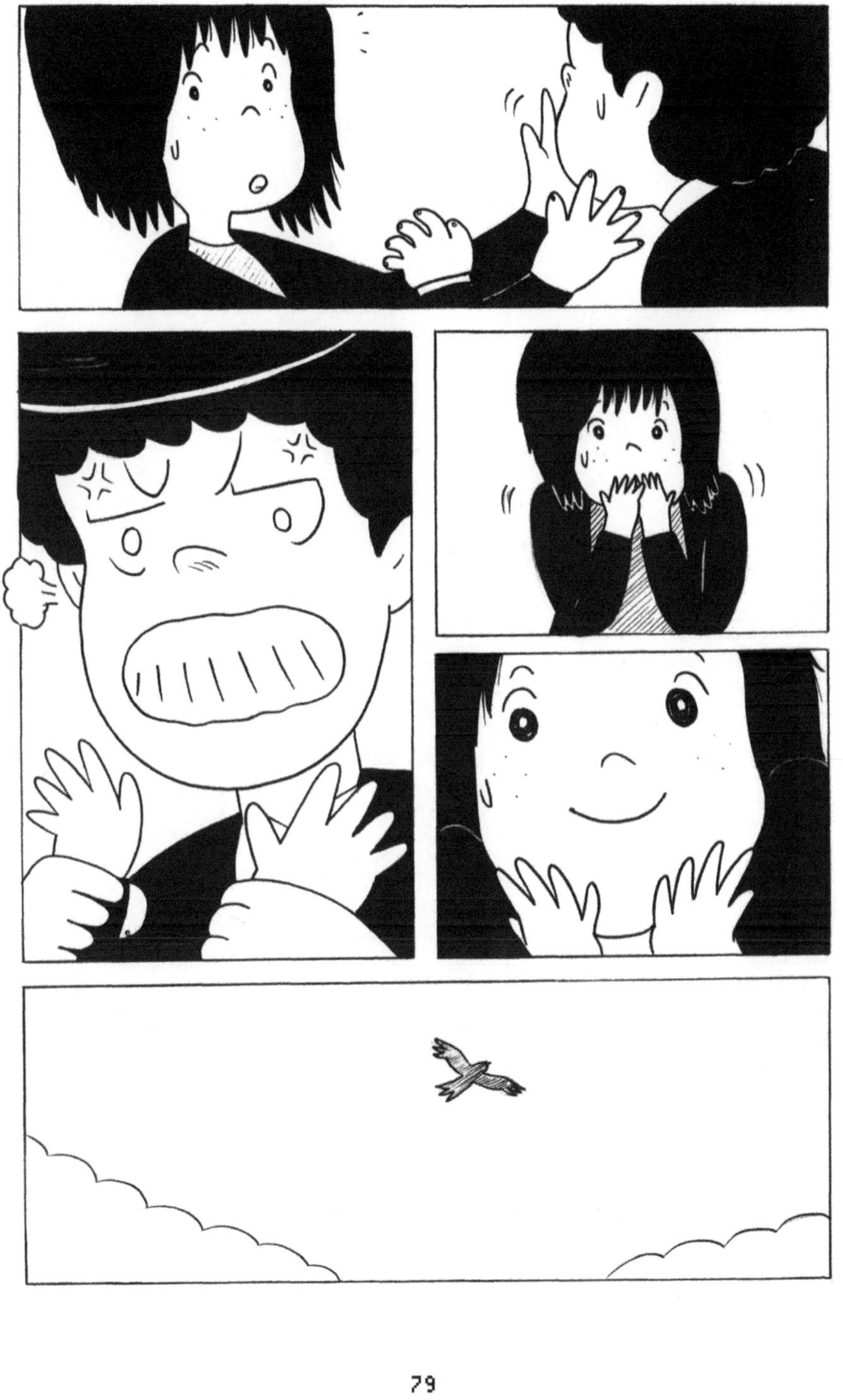

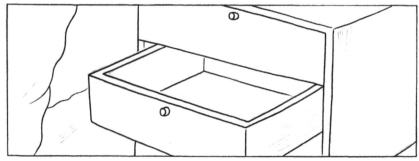

floating

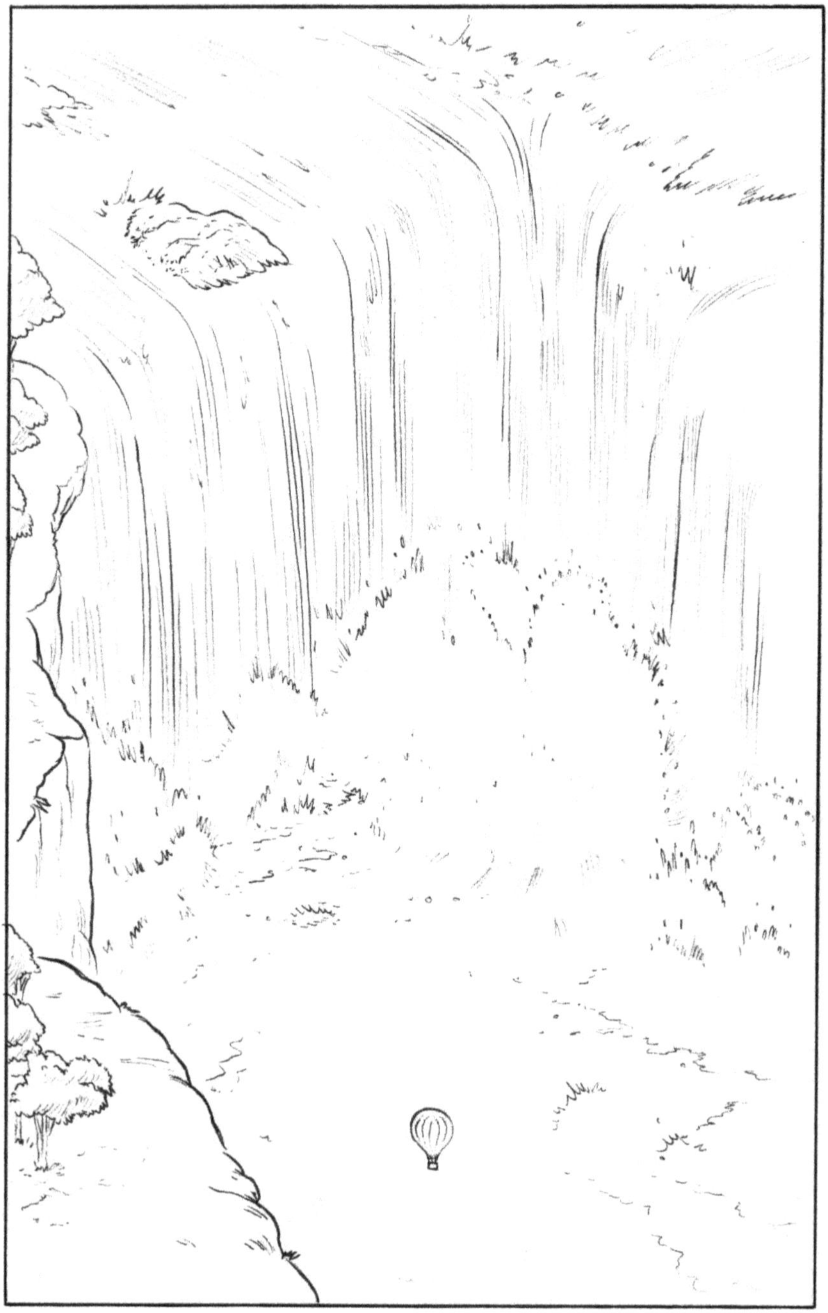

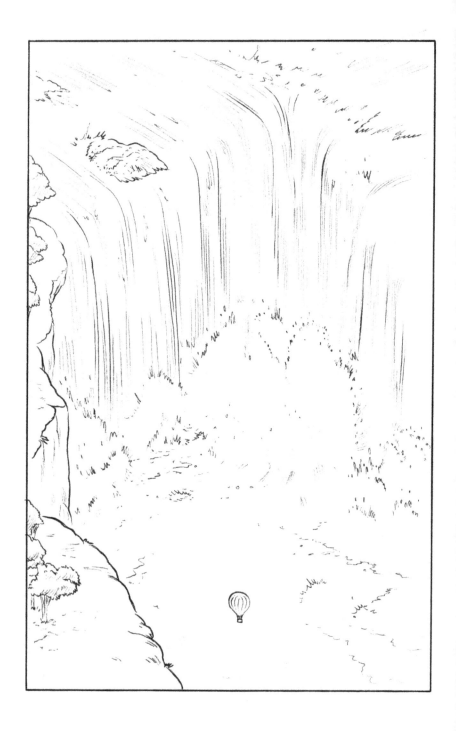

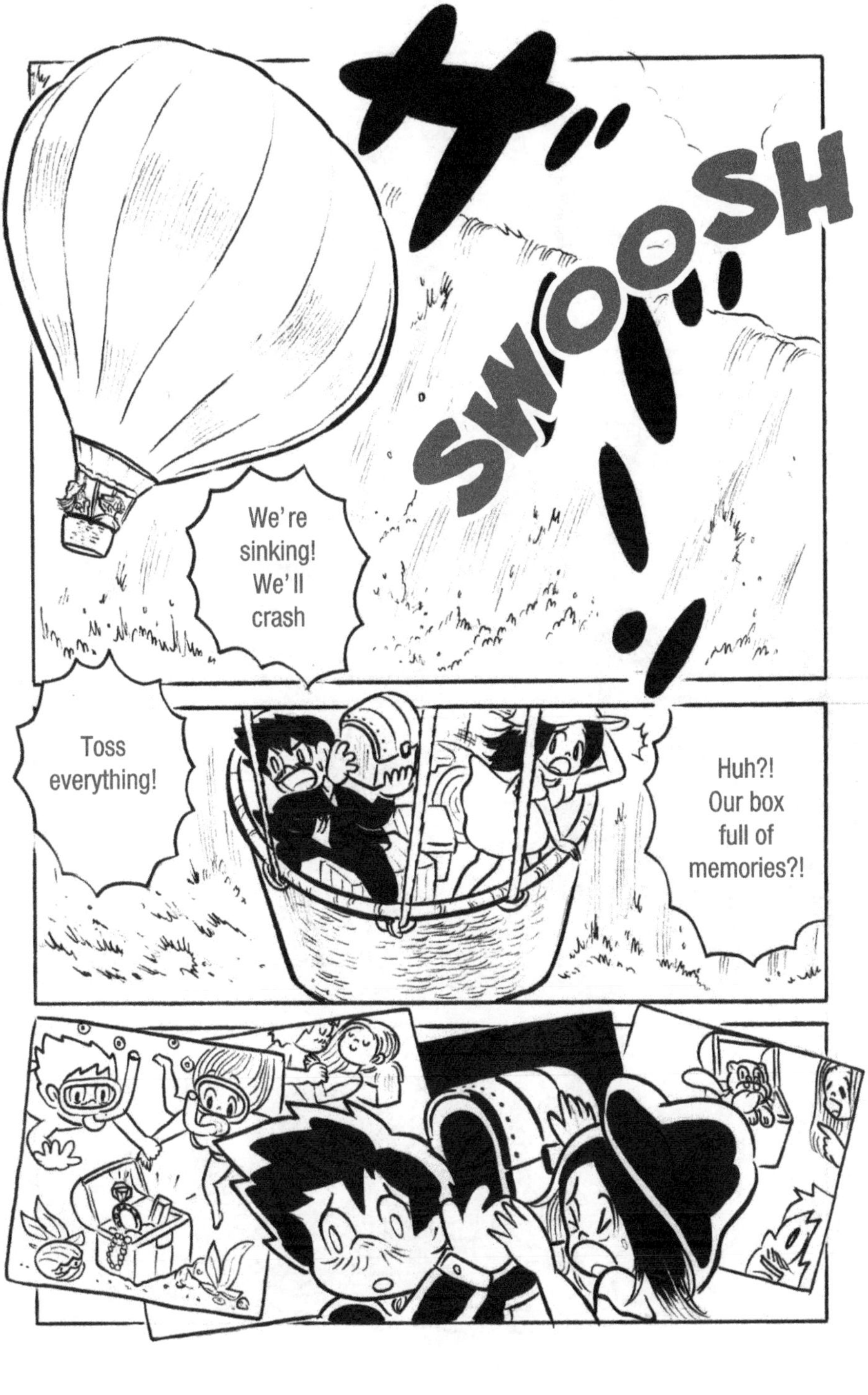
SWOOSH
We're sinking! We'll crash
Huh?! Our box full of memories?!
Toss everything!

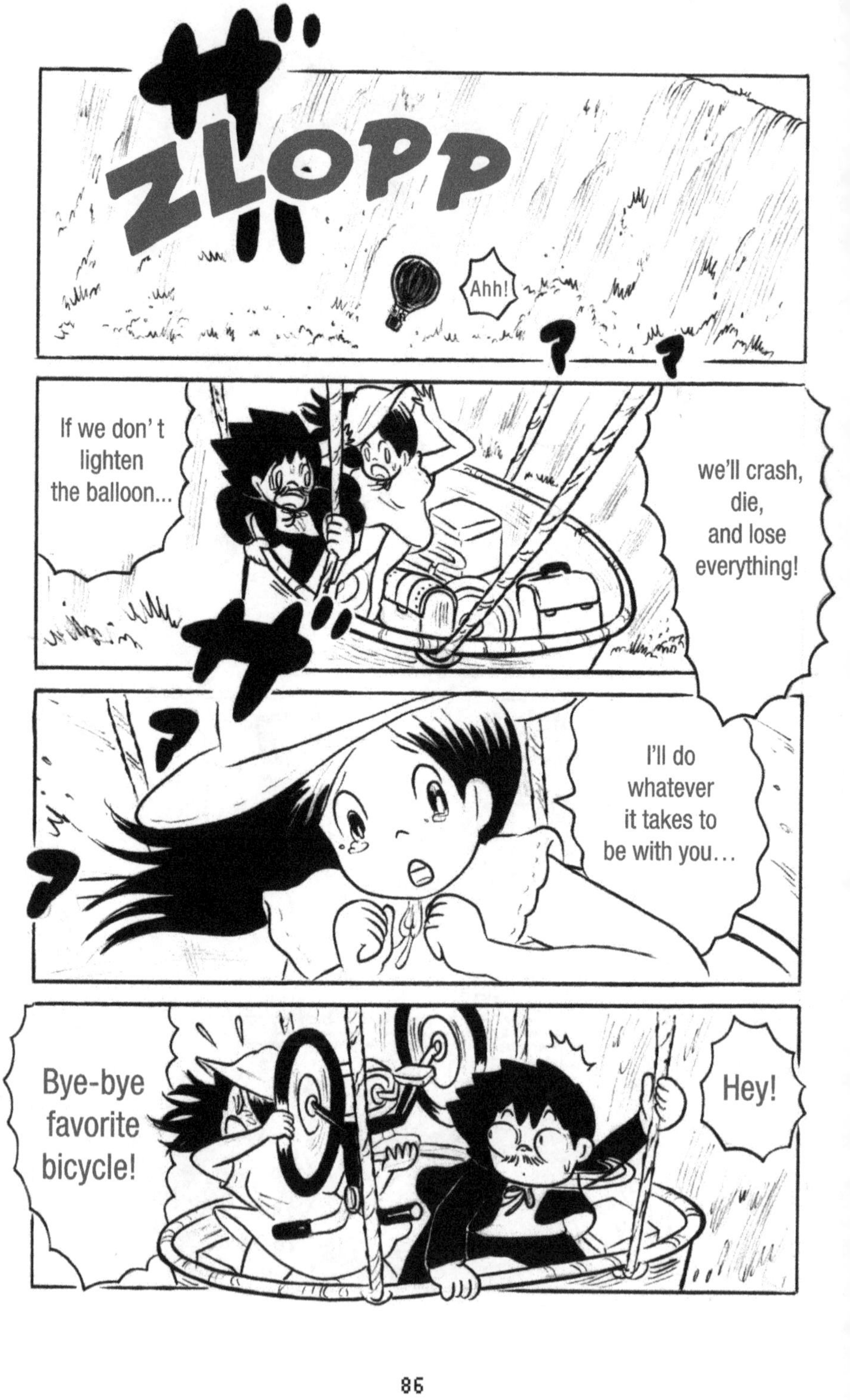
ZLOPP
Ahh!
If we don't t lighten the balloon...
we'll crash, die, and lose everything!
I'll do whatever it takes to be with you…
Bye-bye favorite bicycle!
Hey!

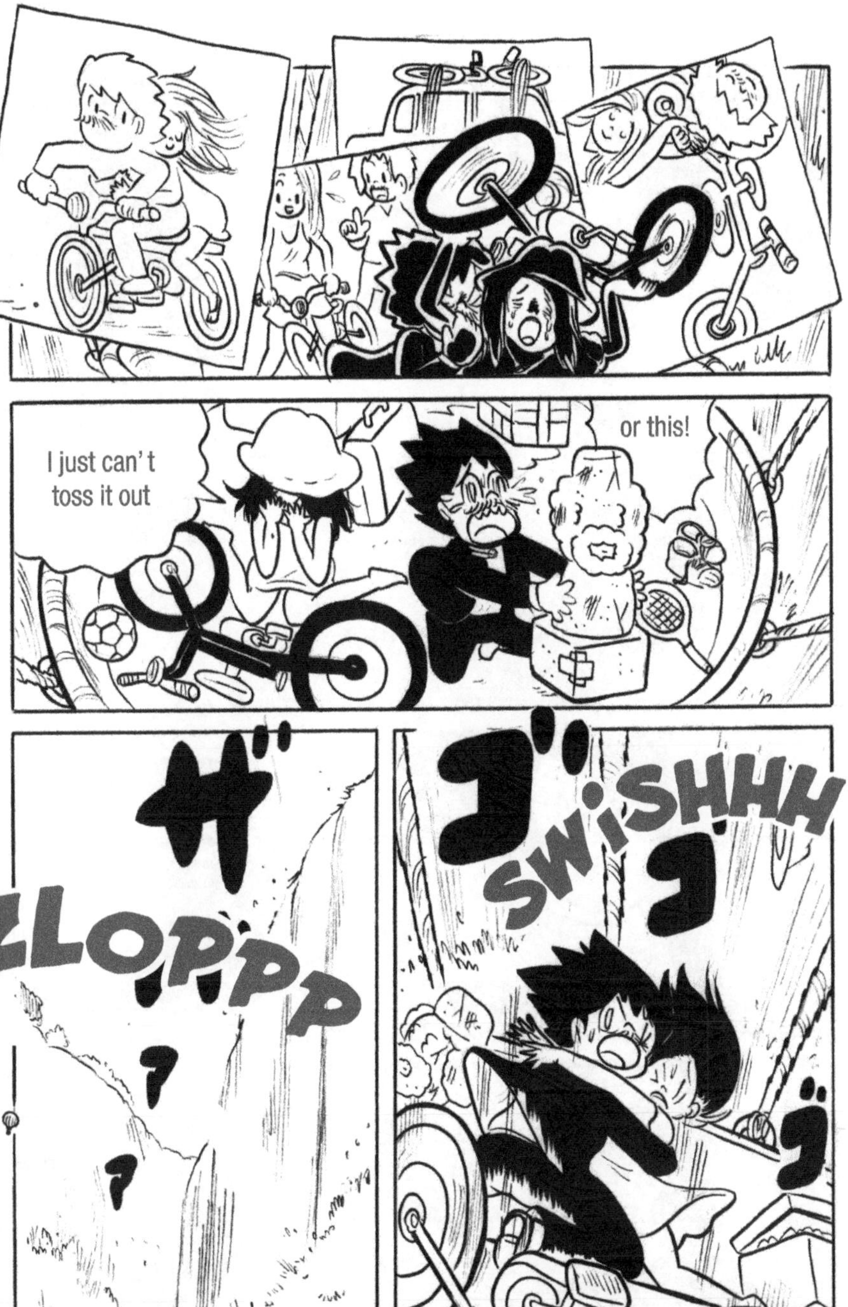

I just can’t toss it out
or this!
ZLOPPP
SWISHHH

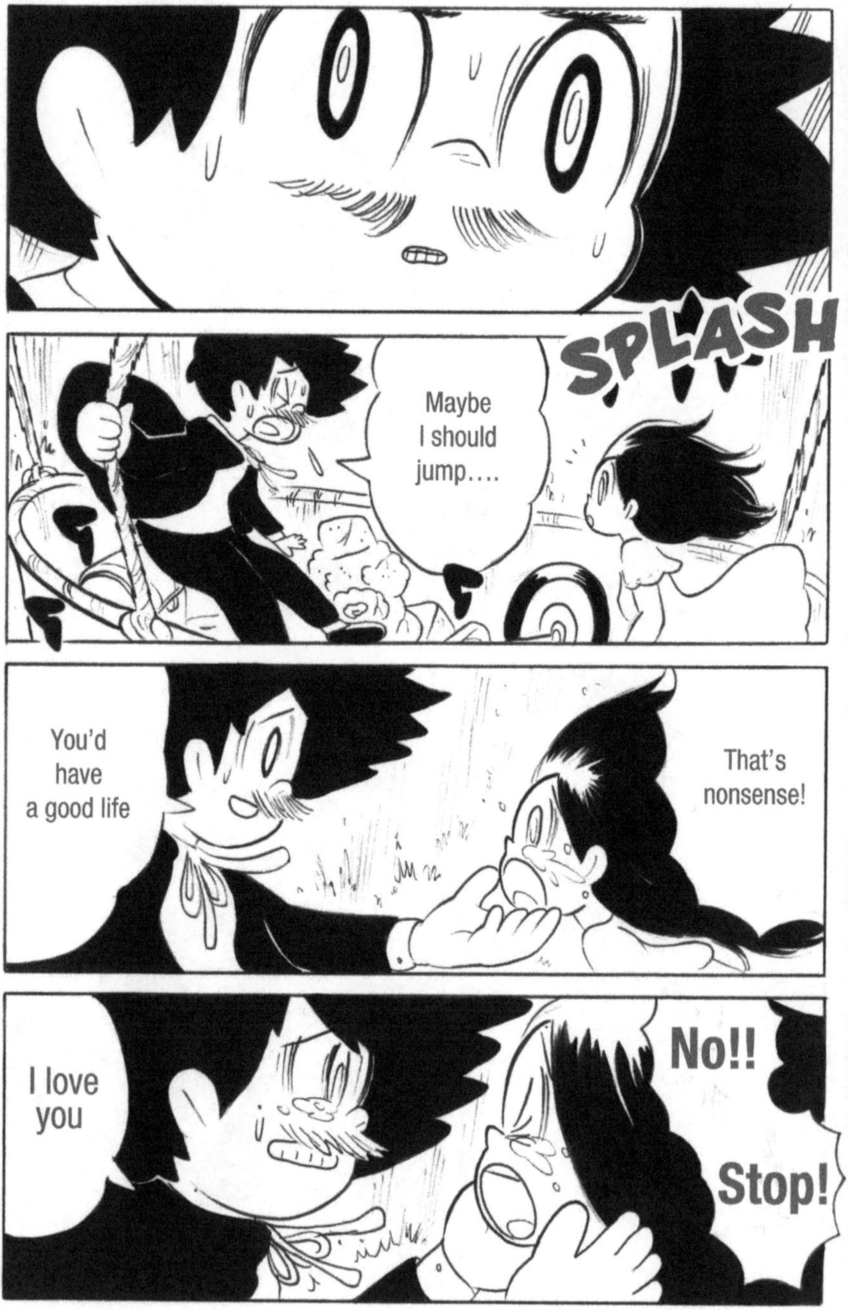
Maybe I should jump….
SPLASH
You'd have a good life
That's nonsense!
I love you
No!!
Stop!

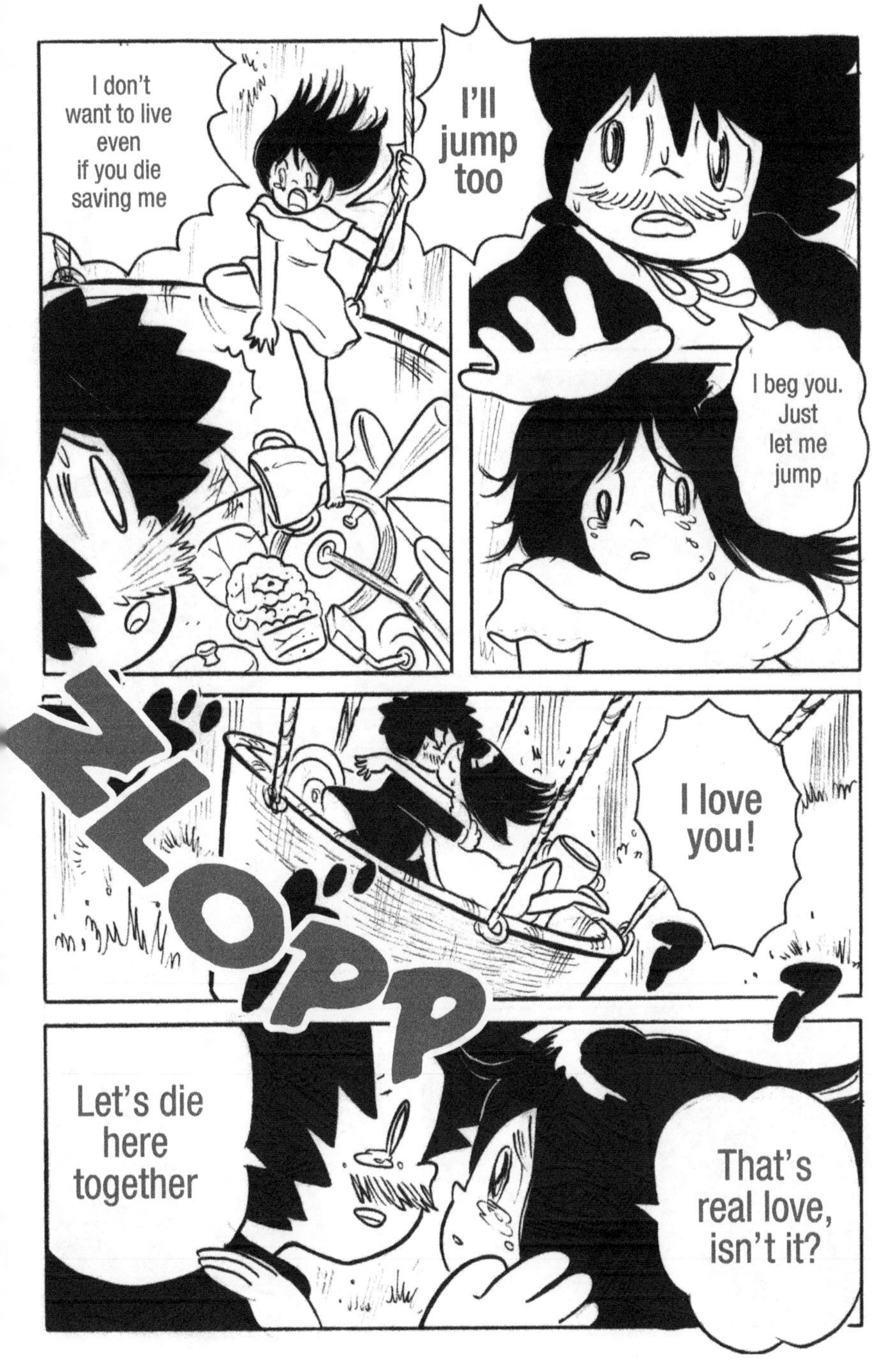
I'll jump too
I beg you. Just let me jump
I don't want to live even if you die saving me
I love you!
FLOPP
Let's die here together
That's real love, isn't it?

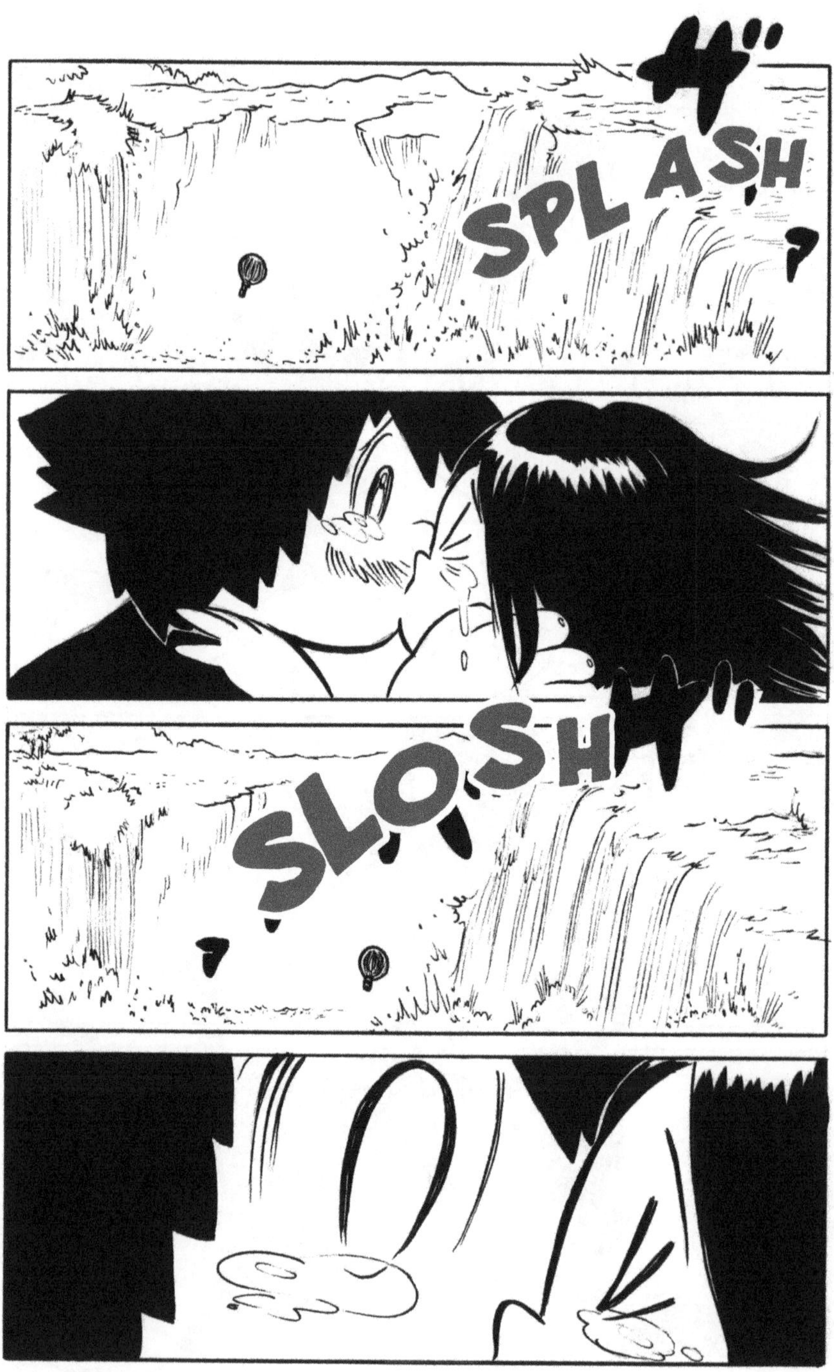
SPLASH
SLOSH

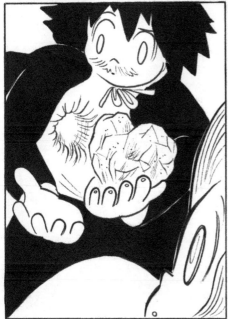

This is
not
love…

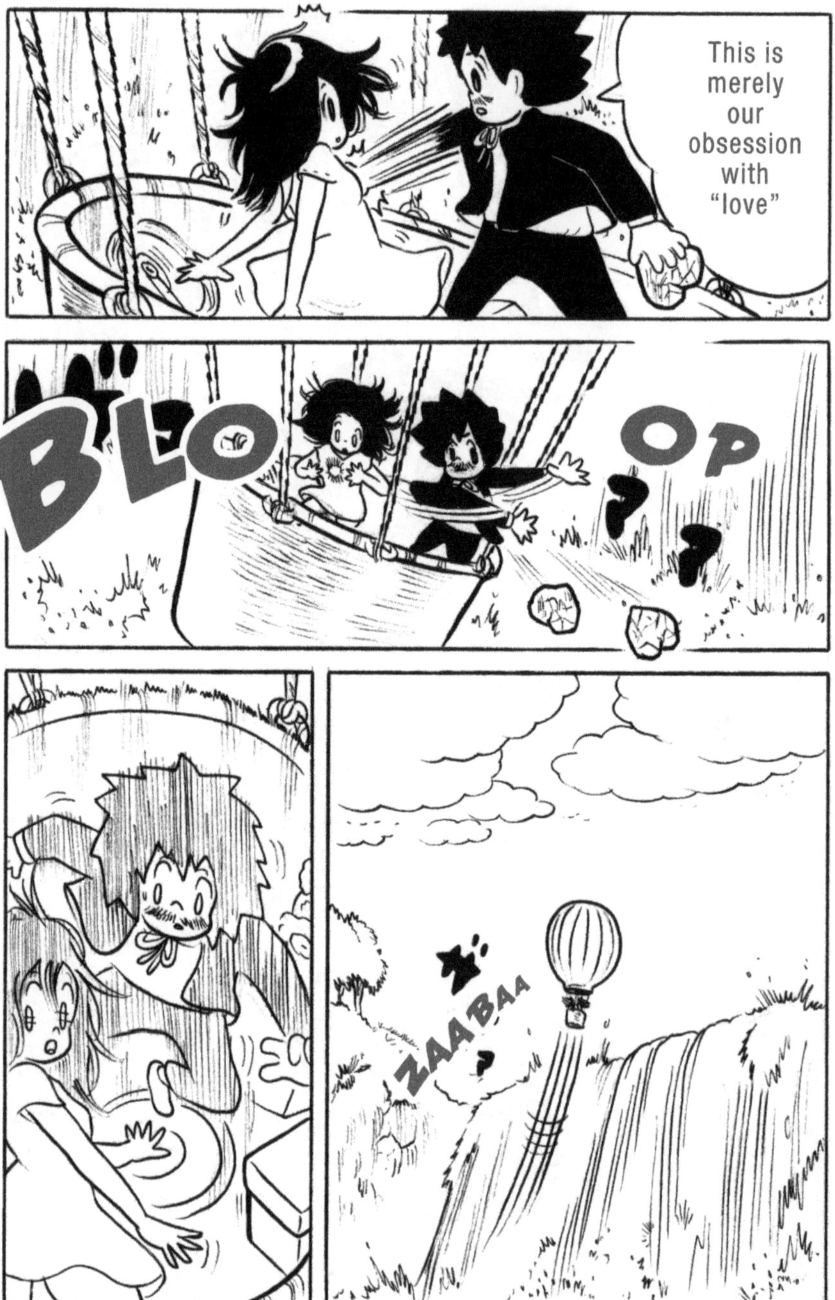
This is merely our obsession with “love”
BLO OP
ZAABAA

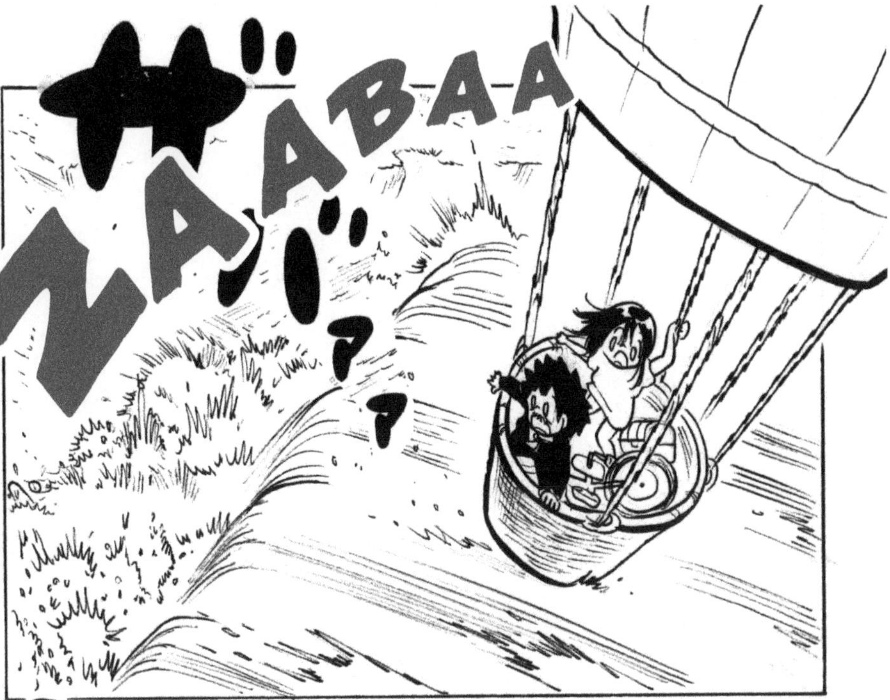
ZAABAA
ザバァァ

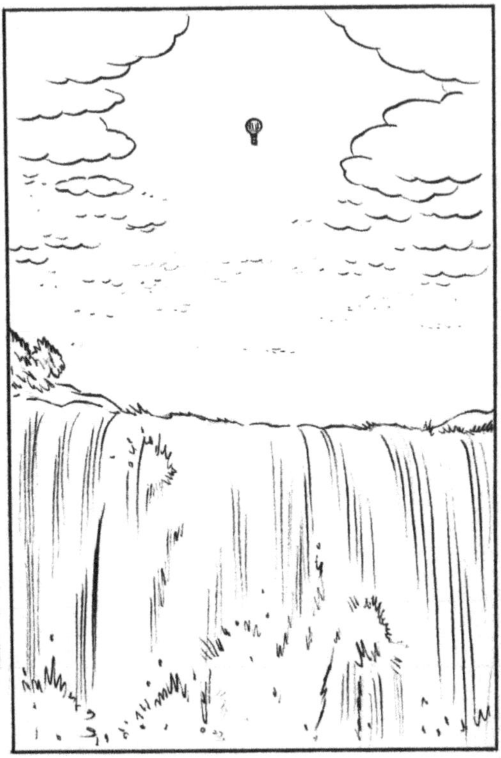

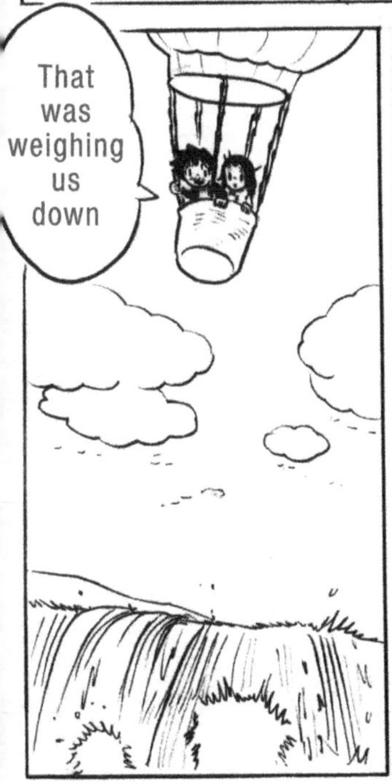
That was weighing us down

HoldingHands

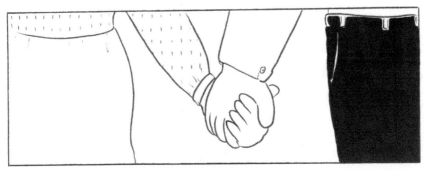

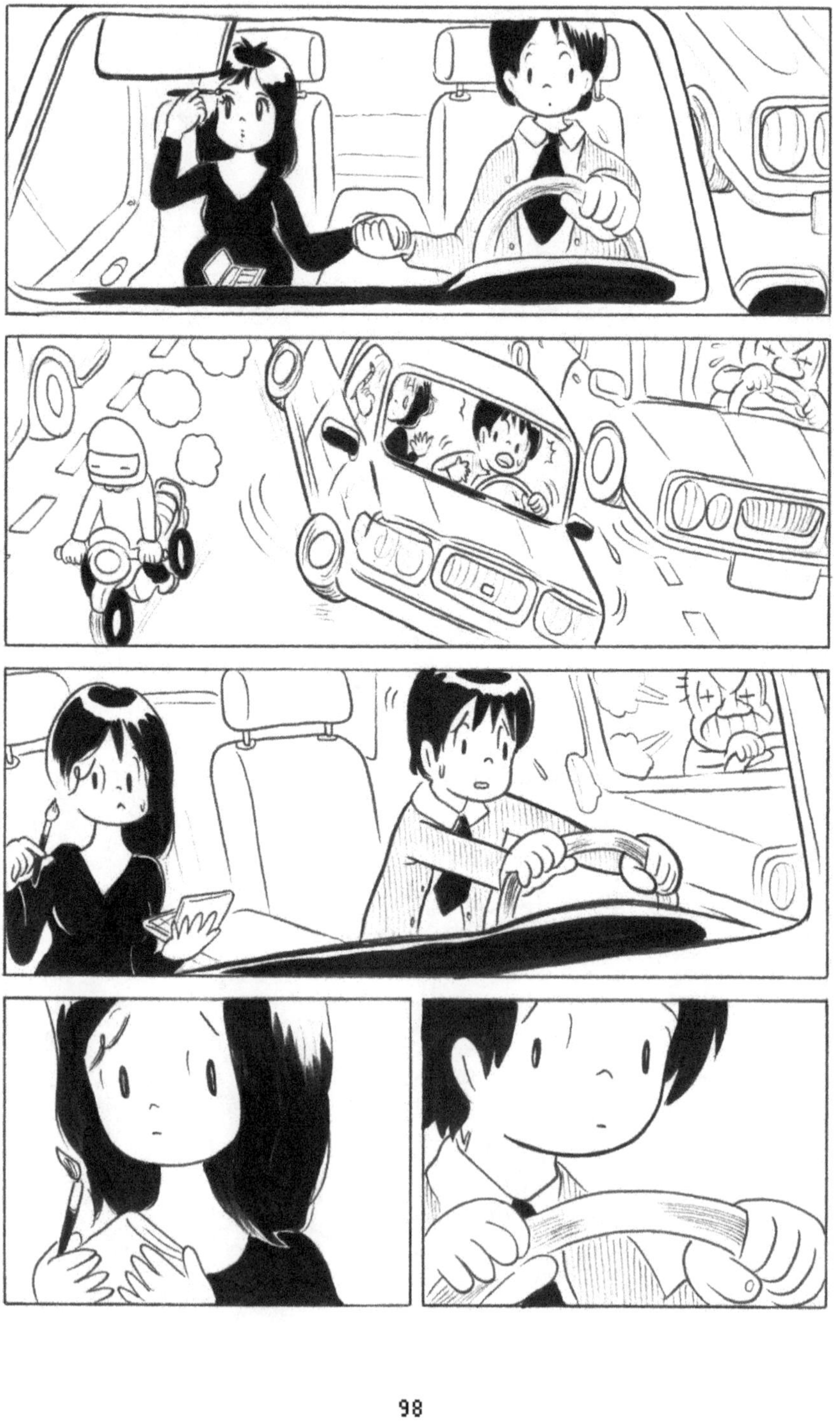

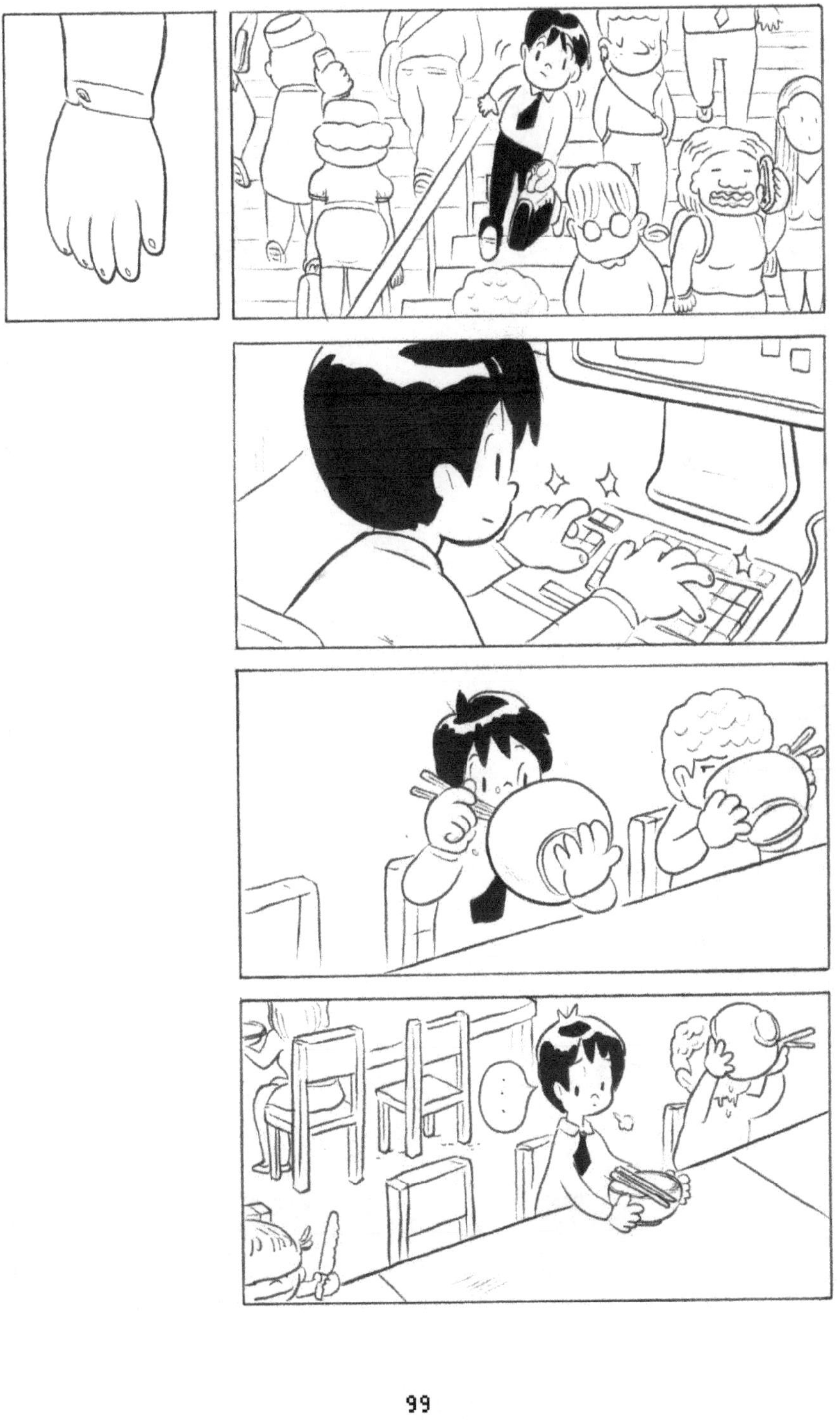
...

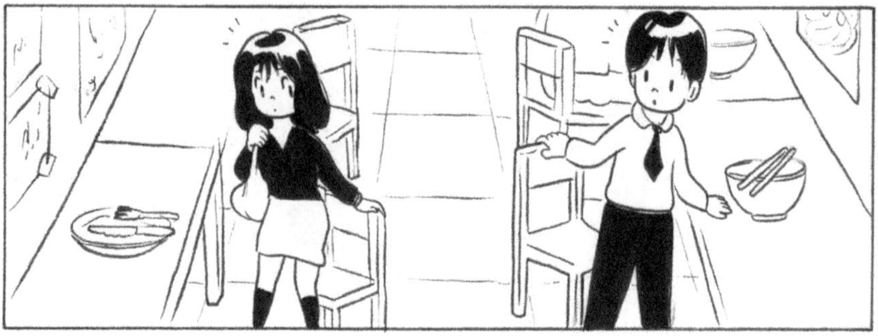
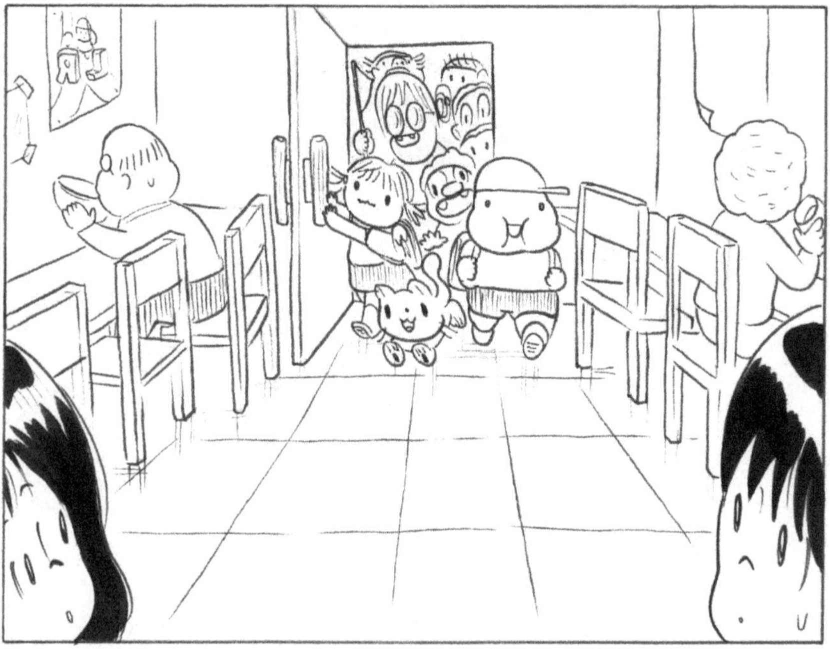
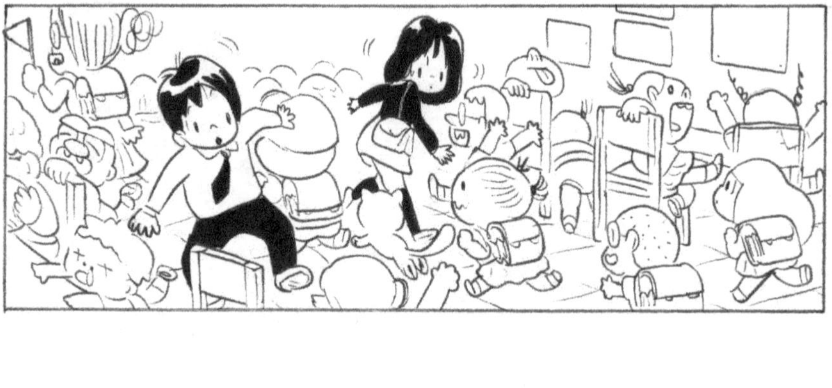

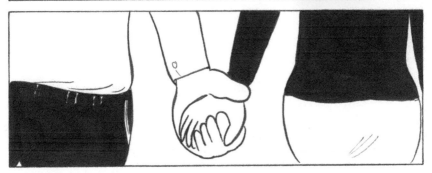

Dinner

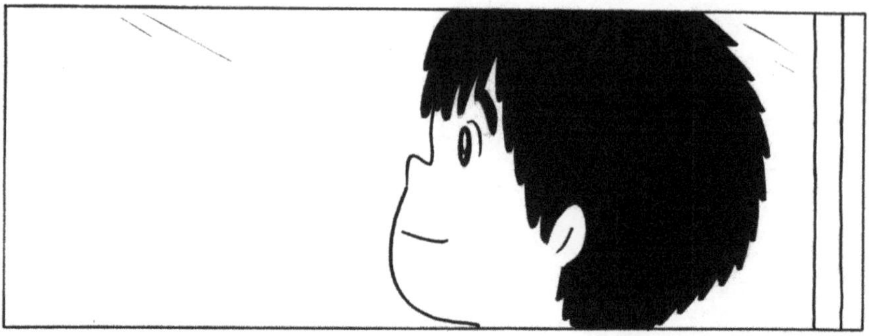
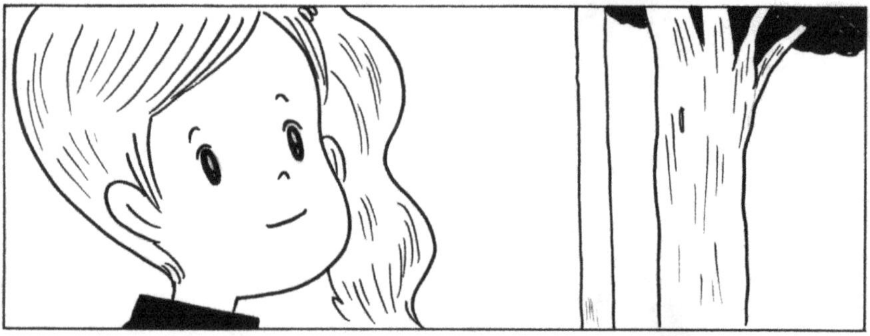
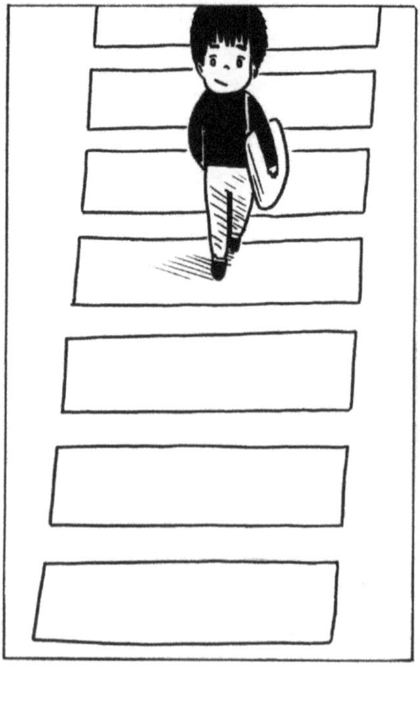
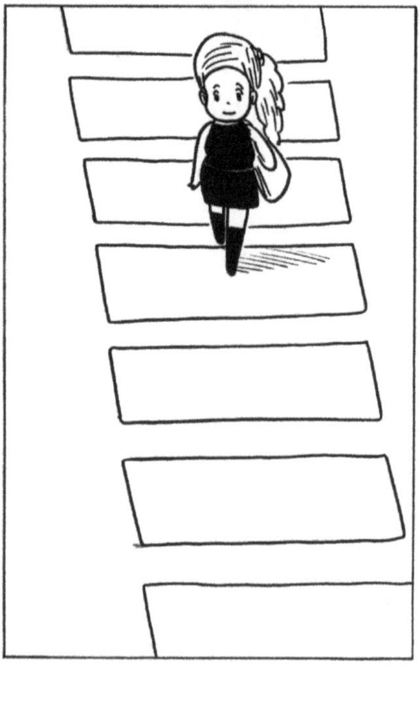

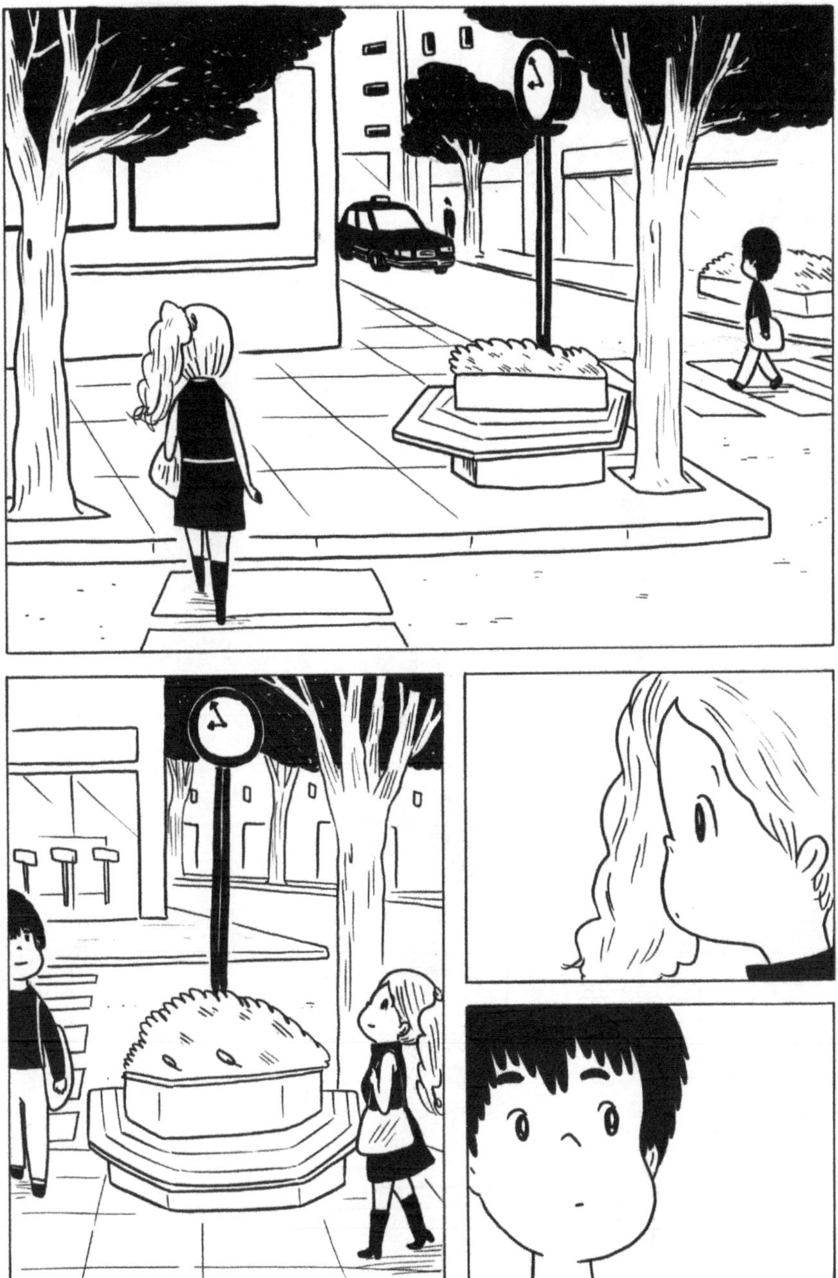

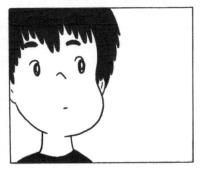

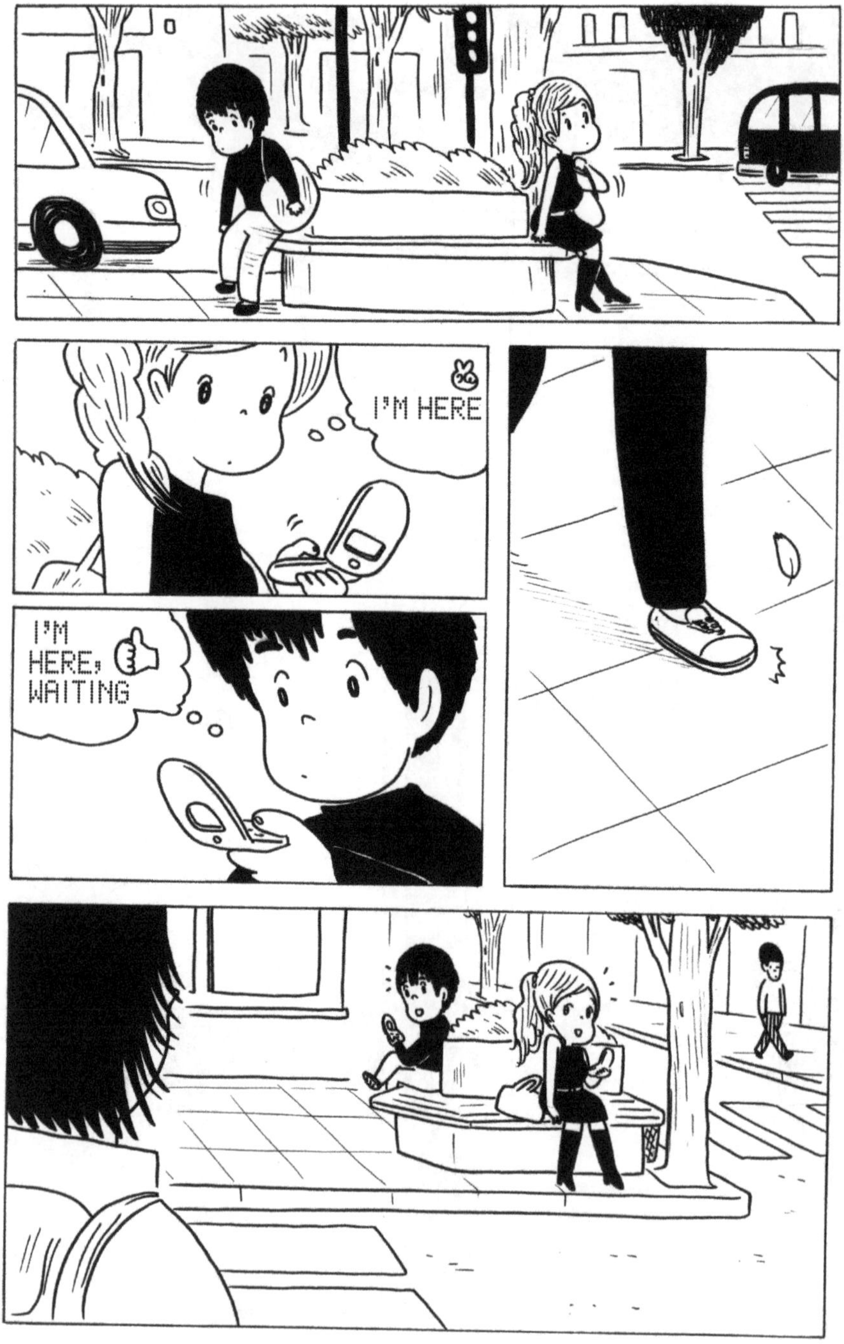
I'M HERE
I'M HERE, WAITING

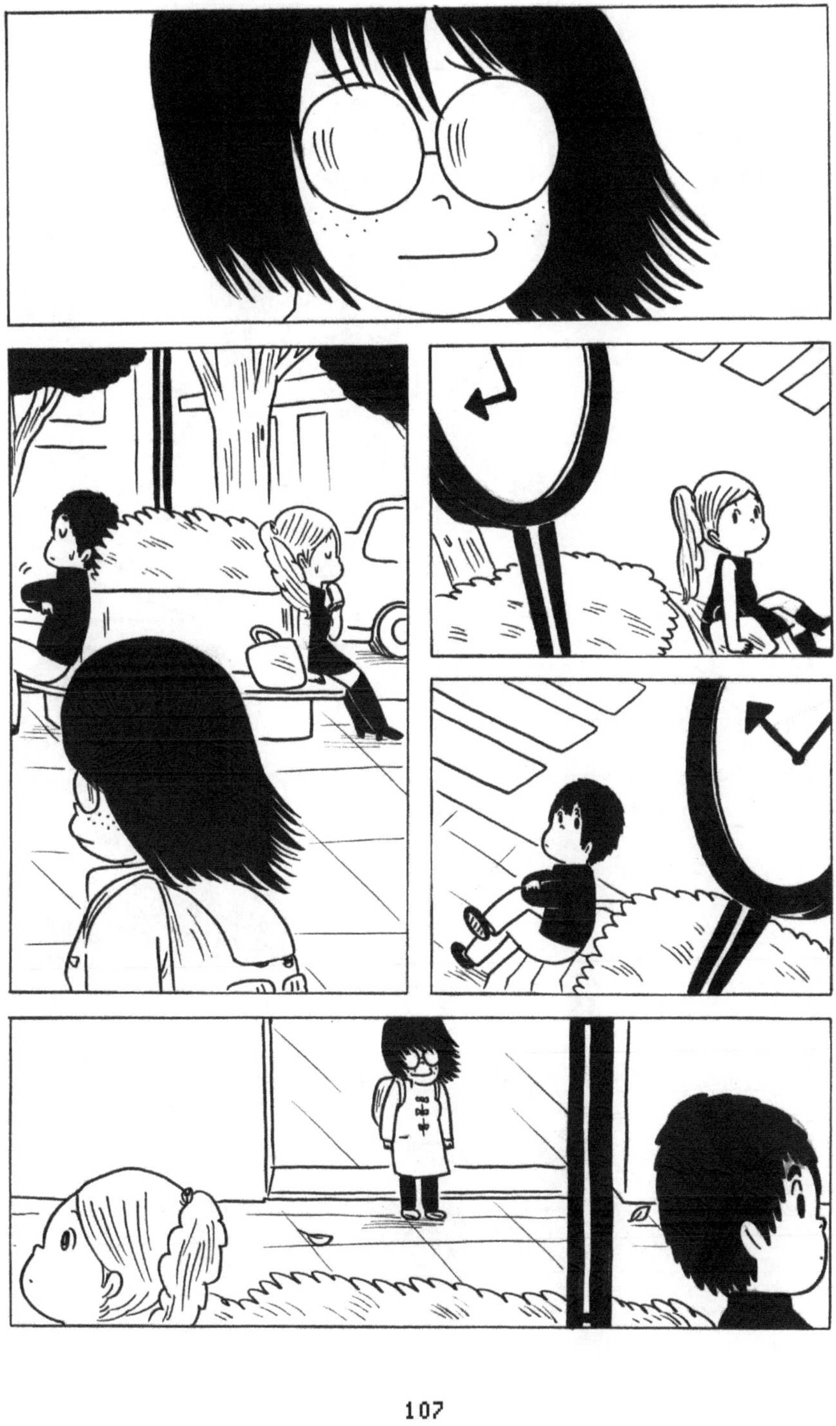

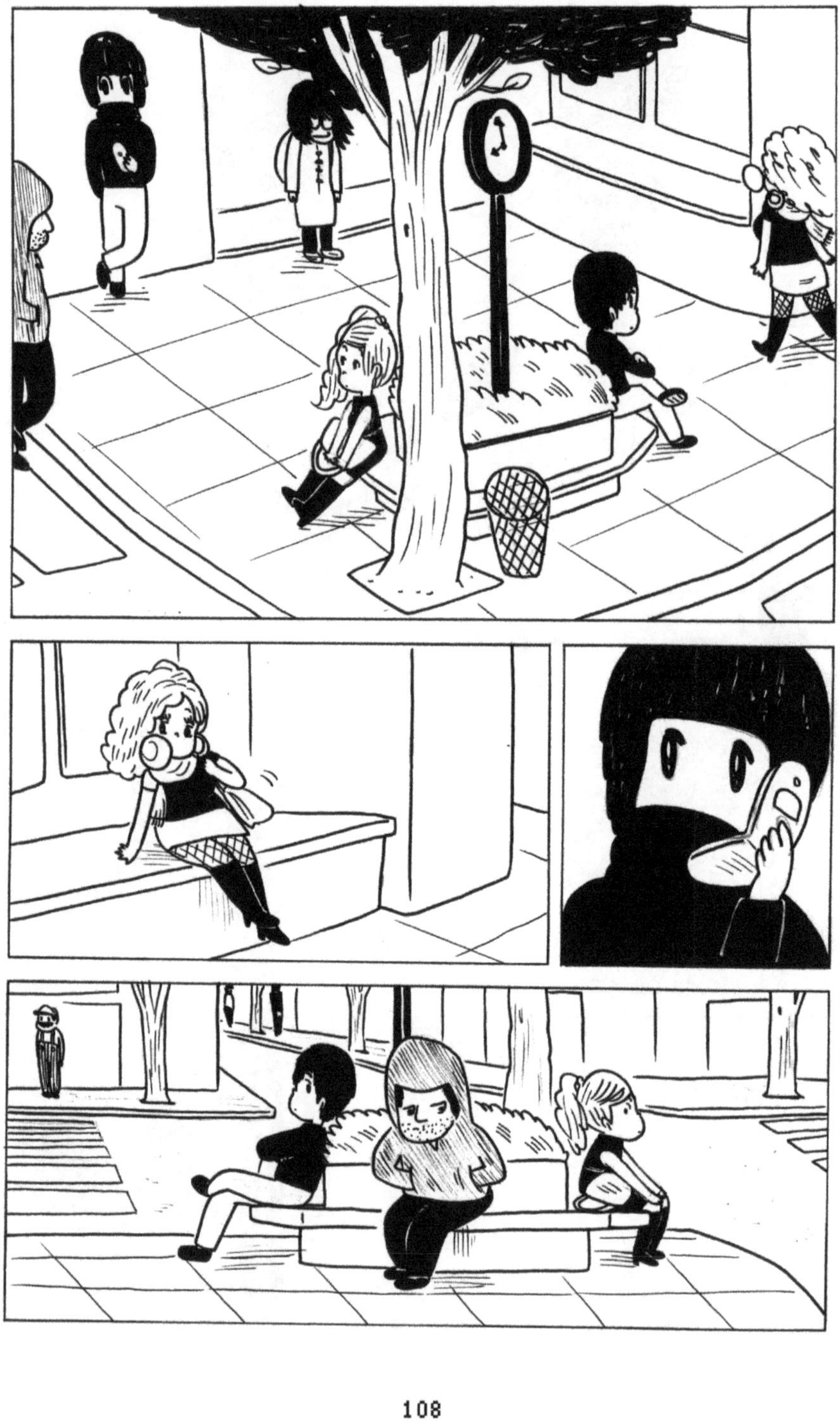

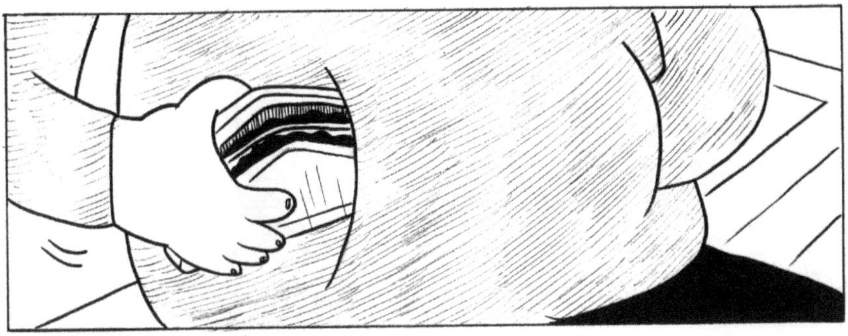
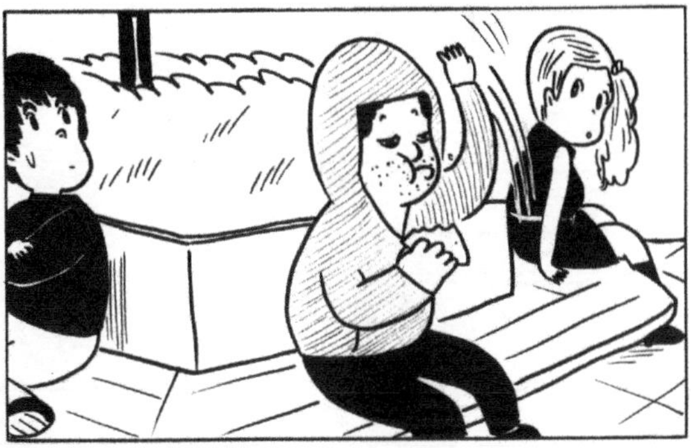
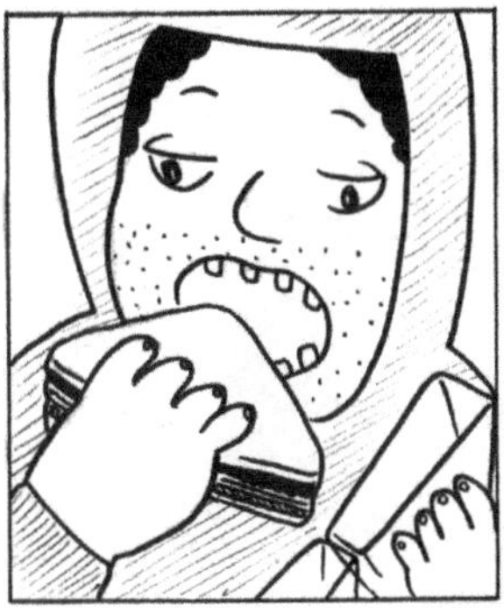
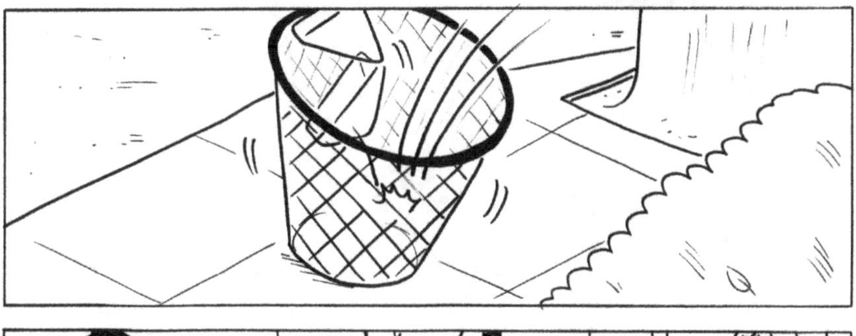
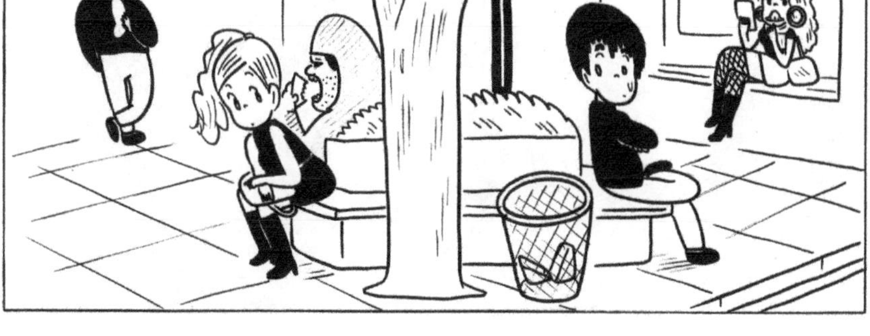

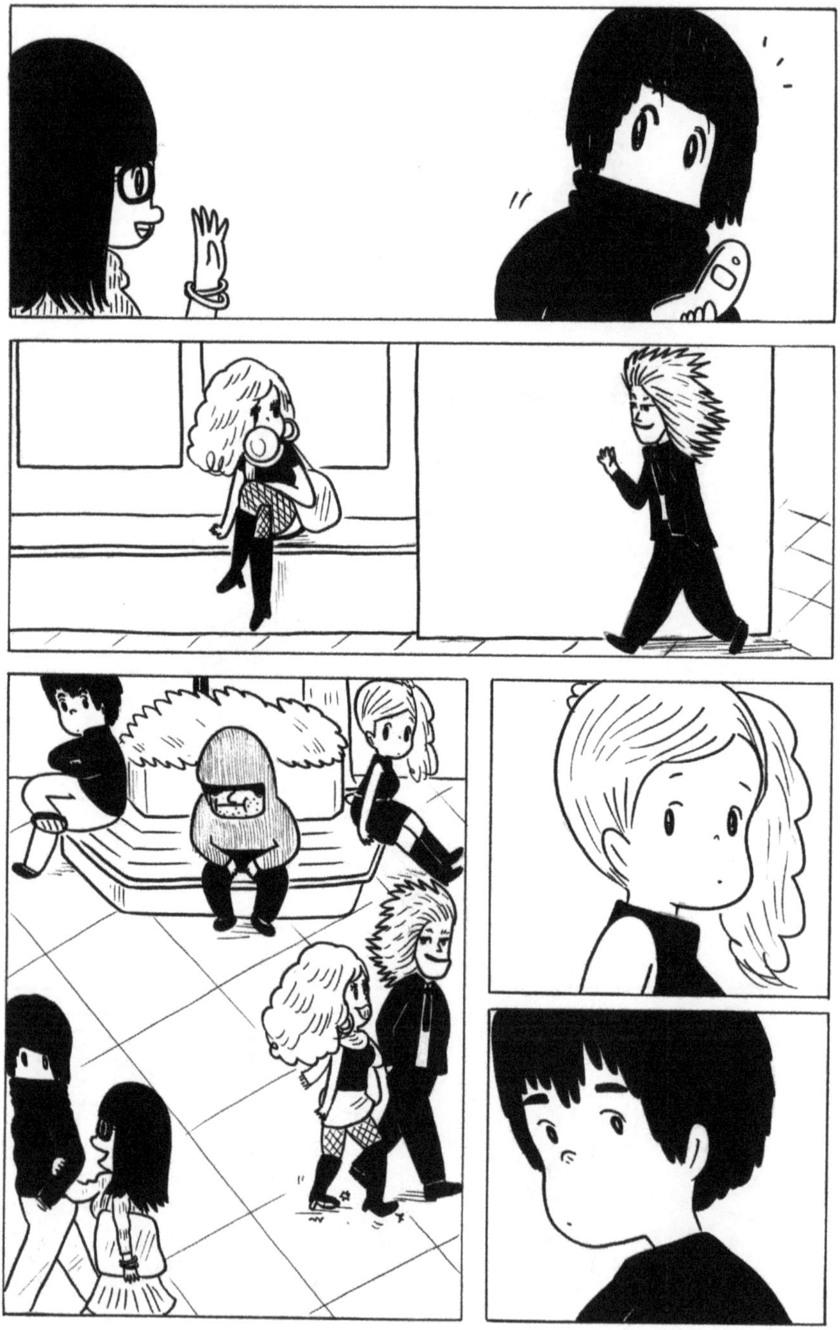

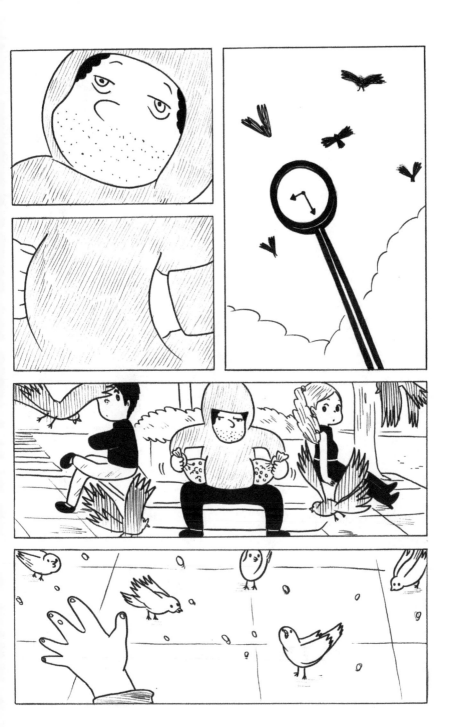

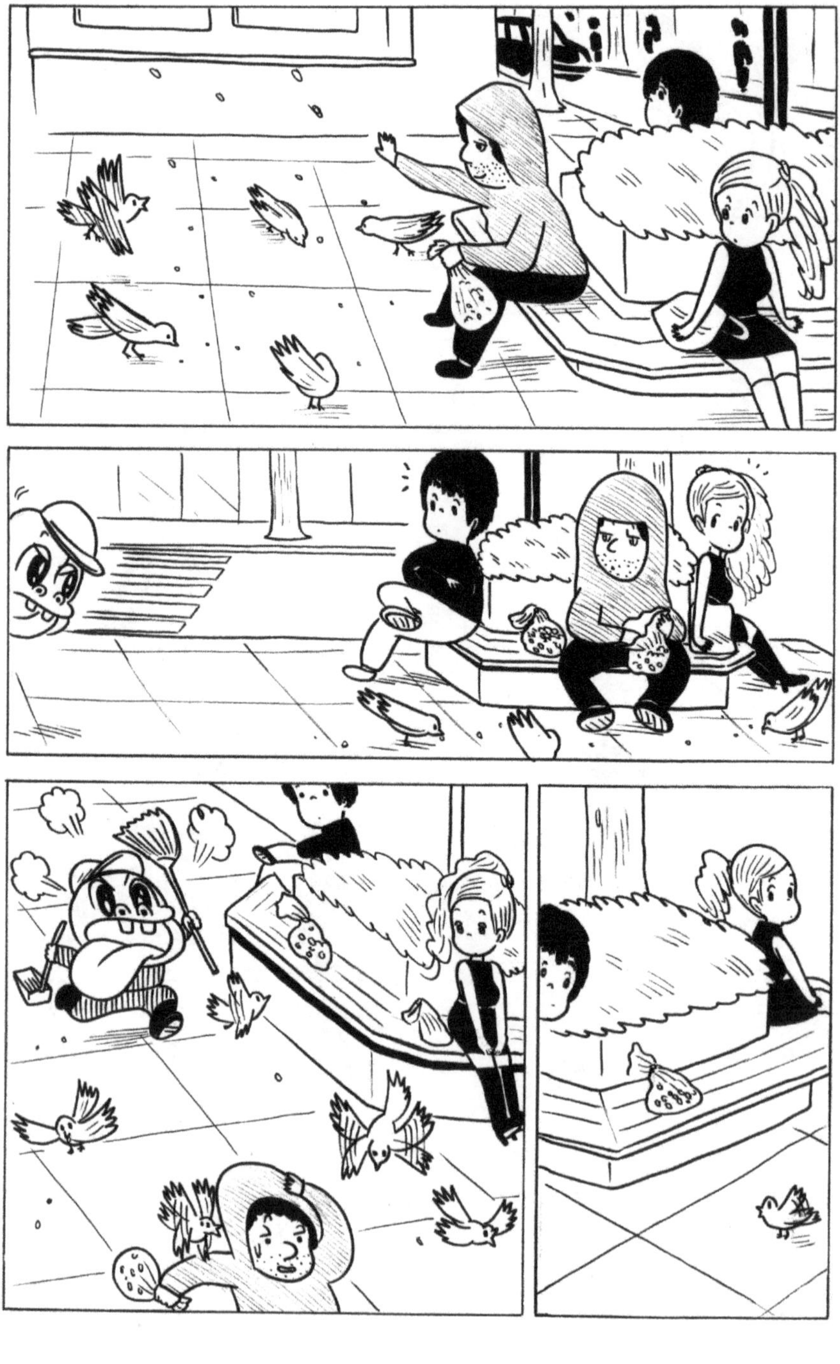

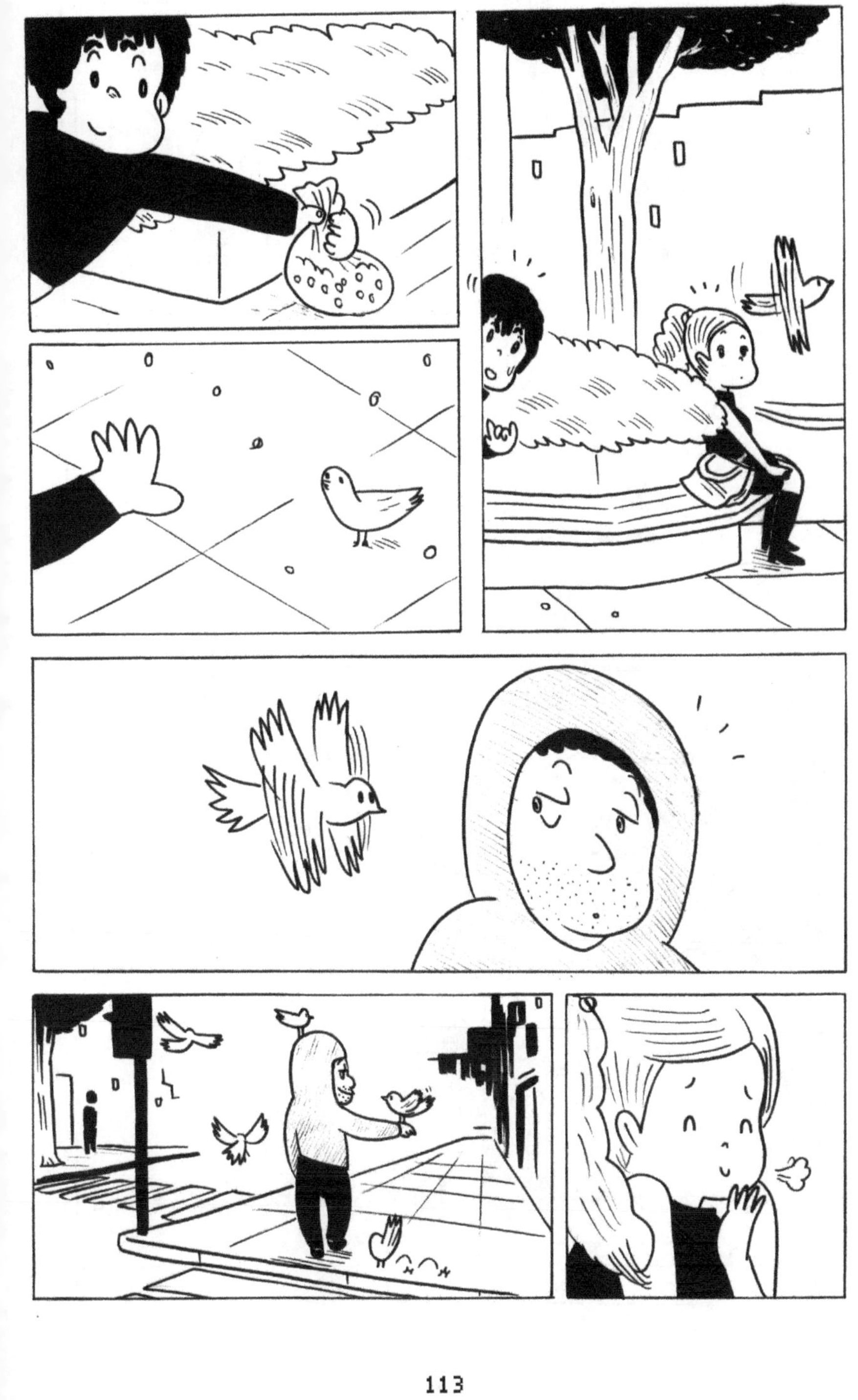

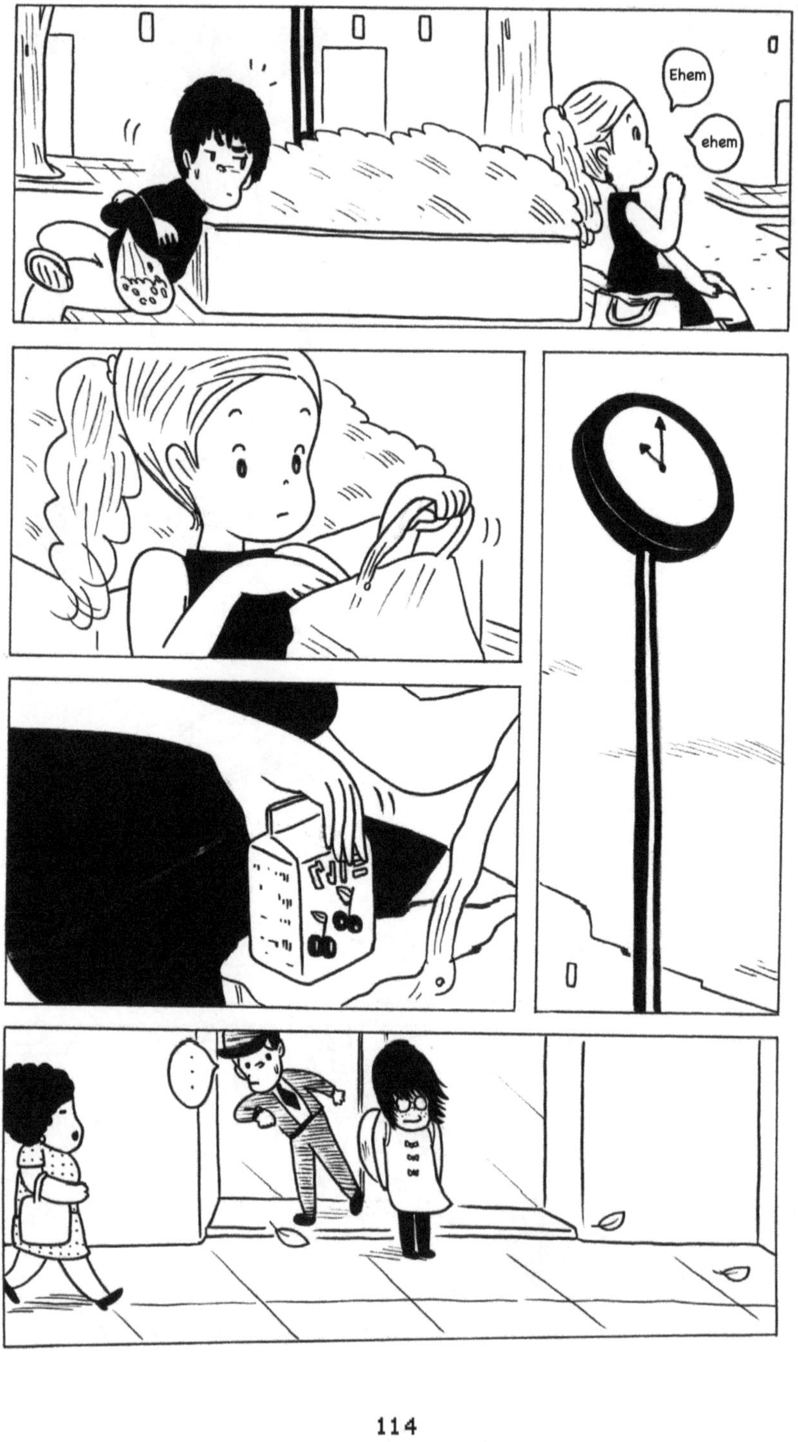
Ehem
ehem
...

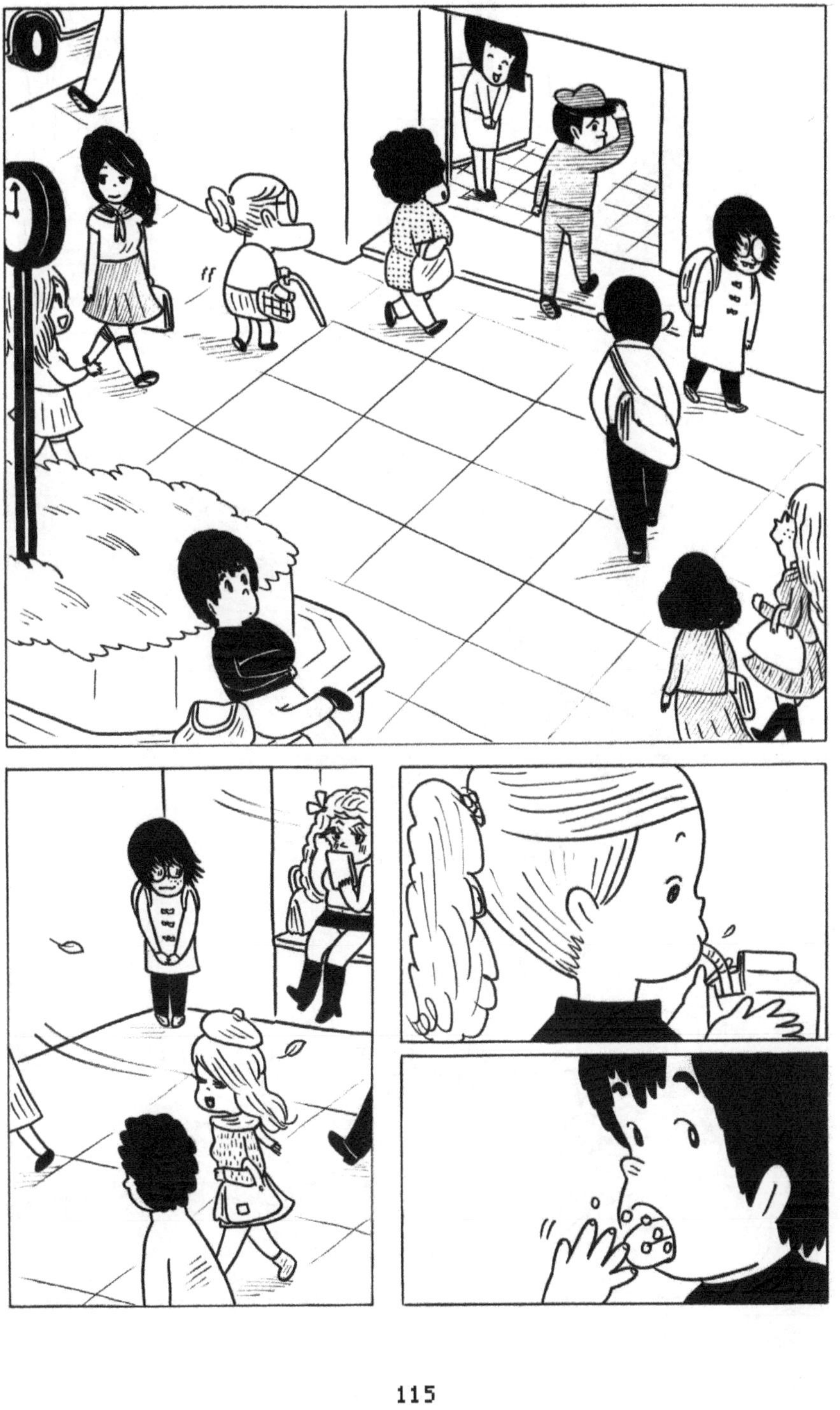

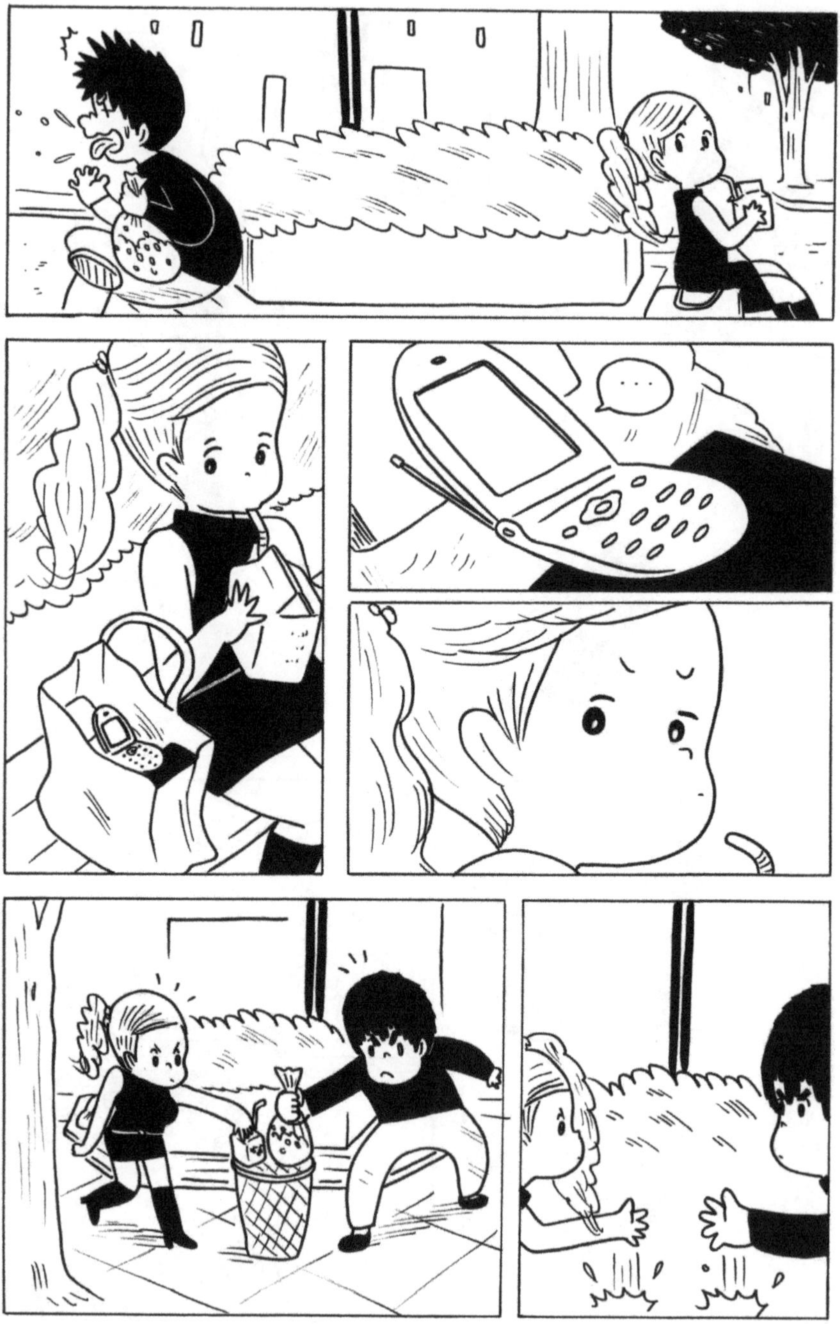
...

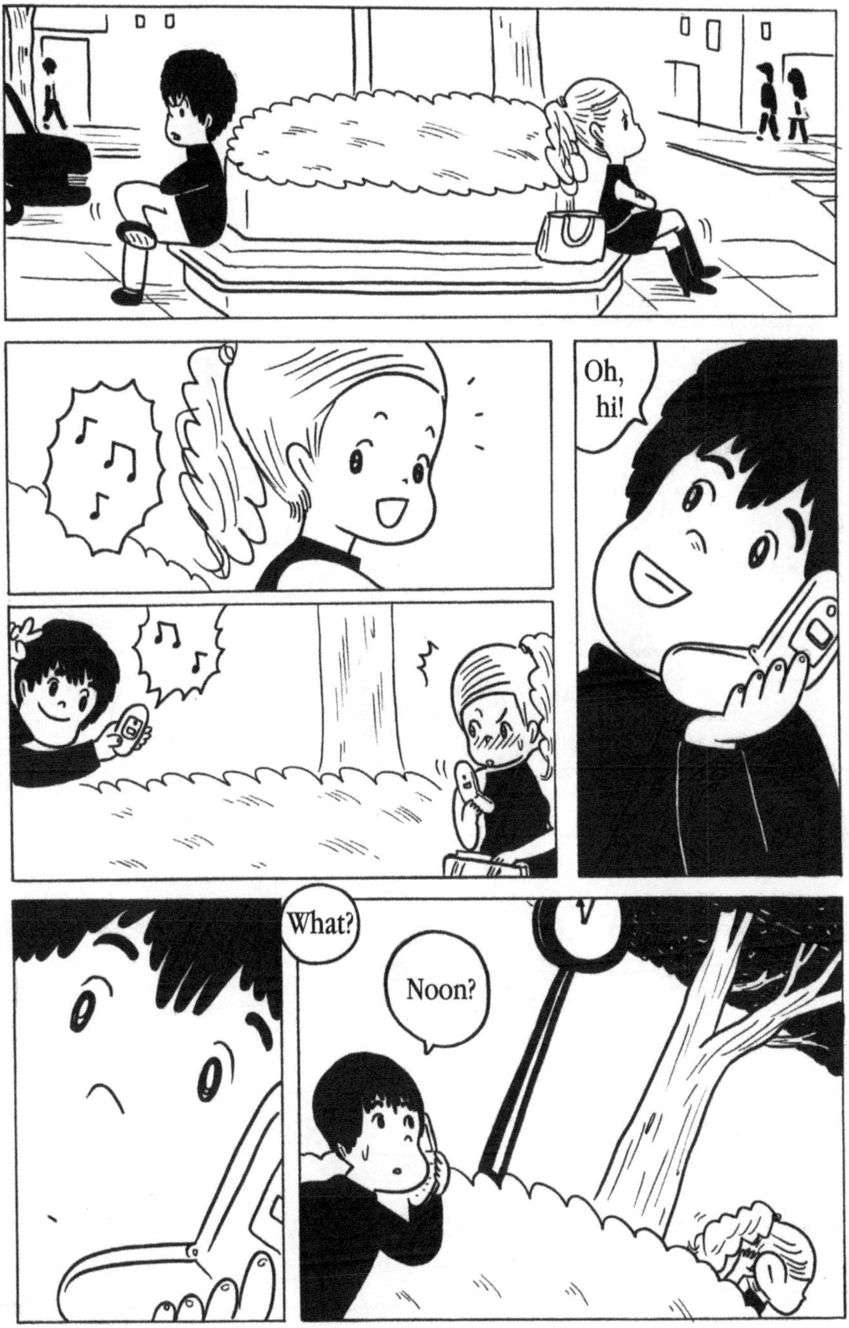
Oh, hi!
What?
Noon?

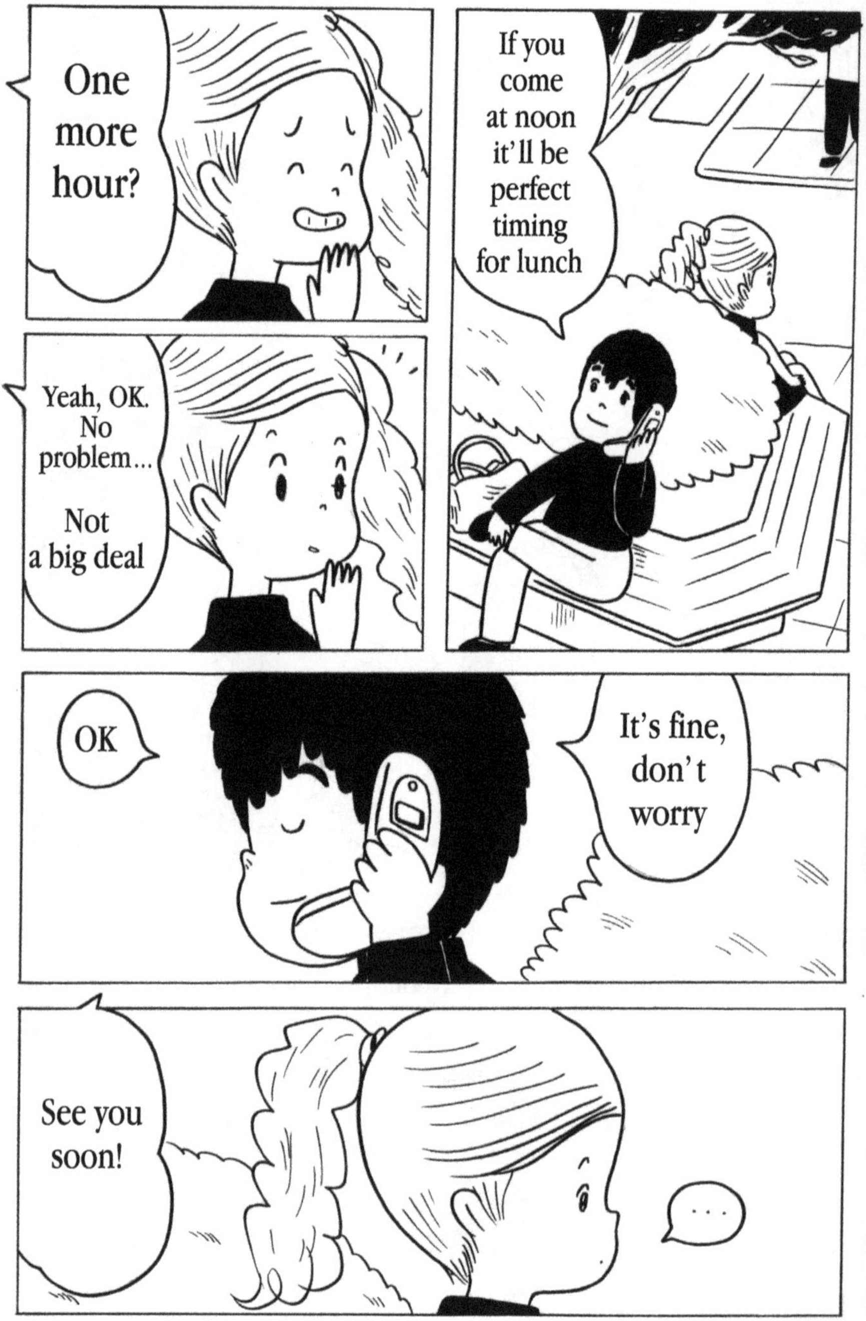
If you come at noon it'll be perfect timing for lunch
One more hour?
Yeah, OK. No problem...
Not a big deal
It's fine, don't worry
OK
See you soon!
...

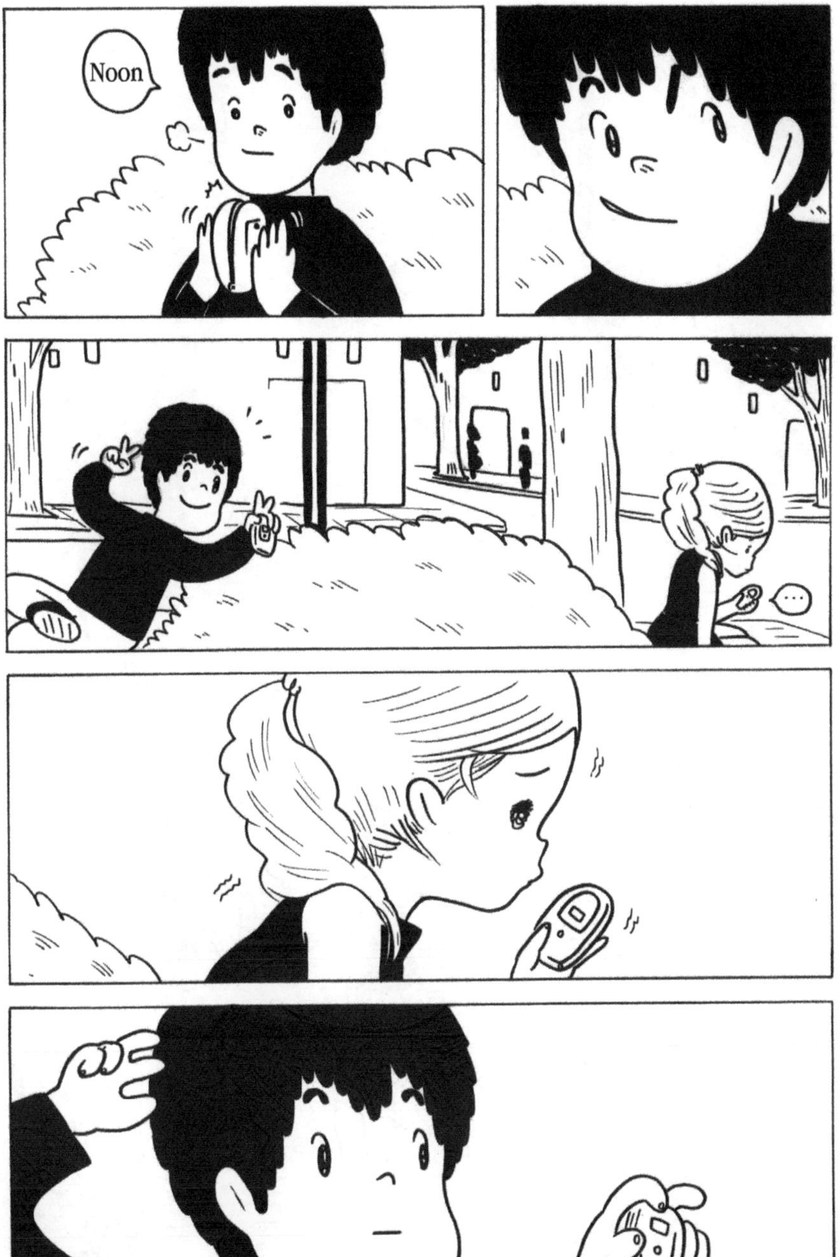
Noon
…

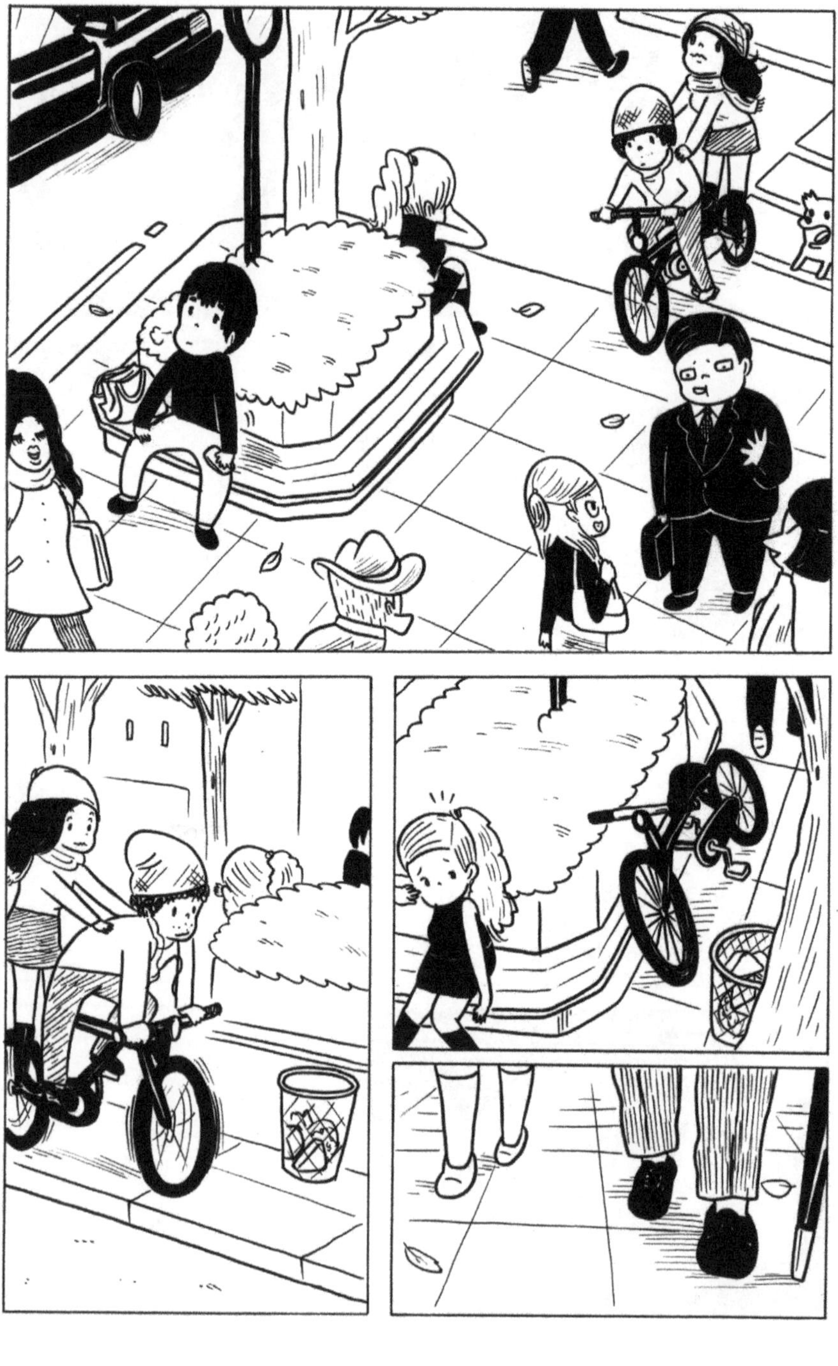

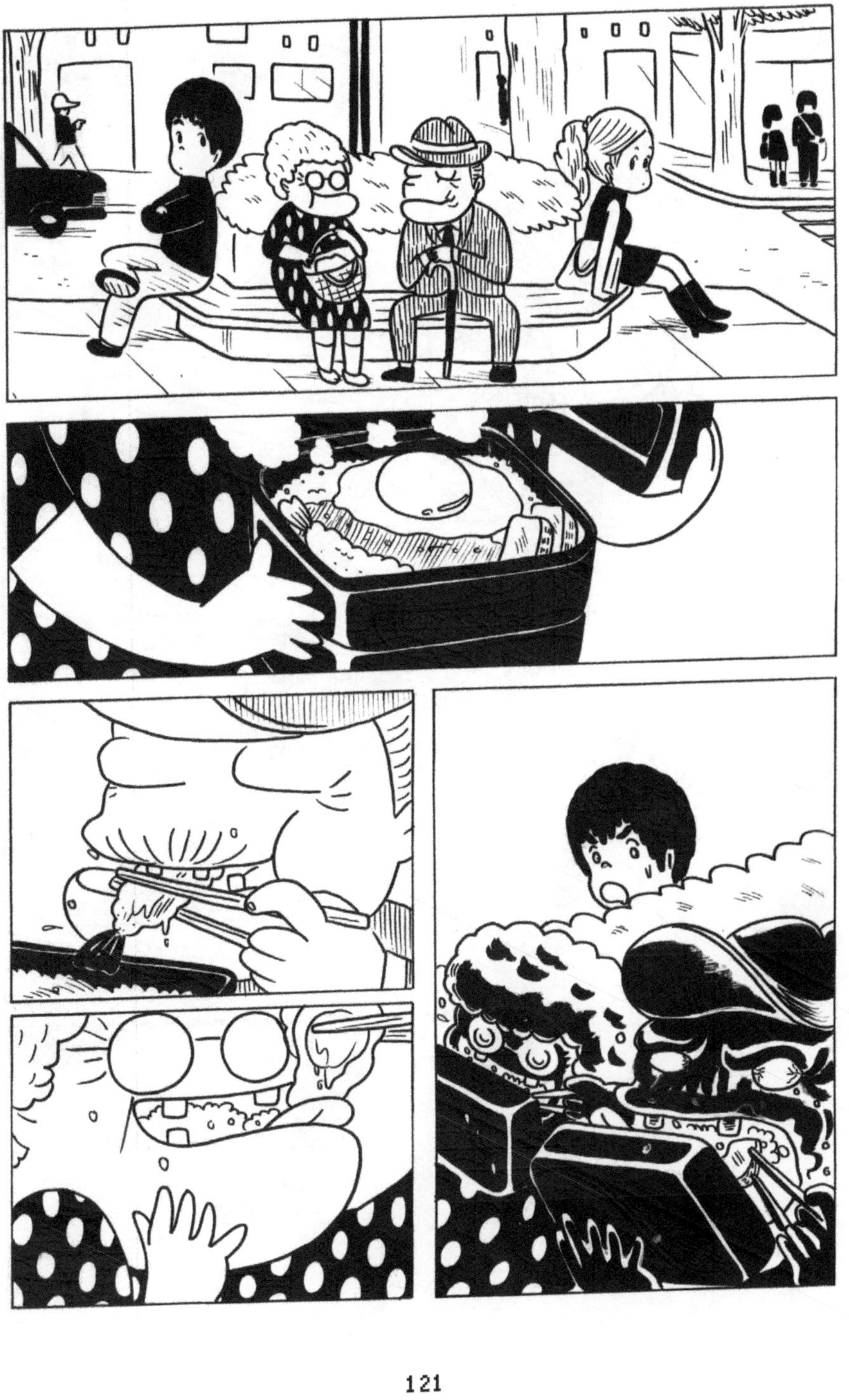

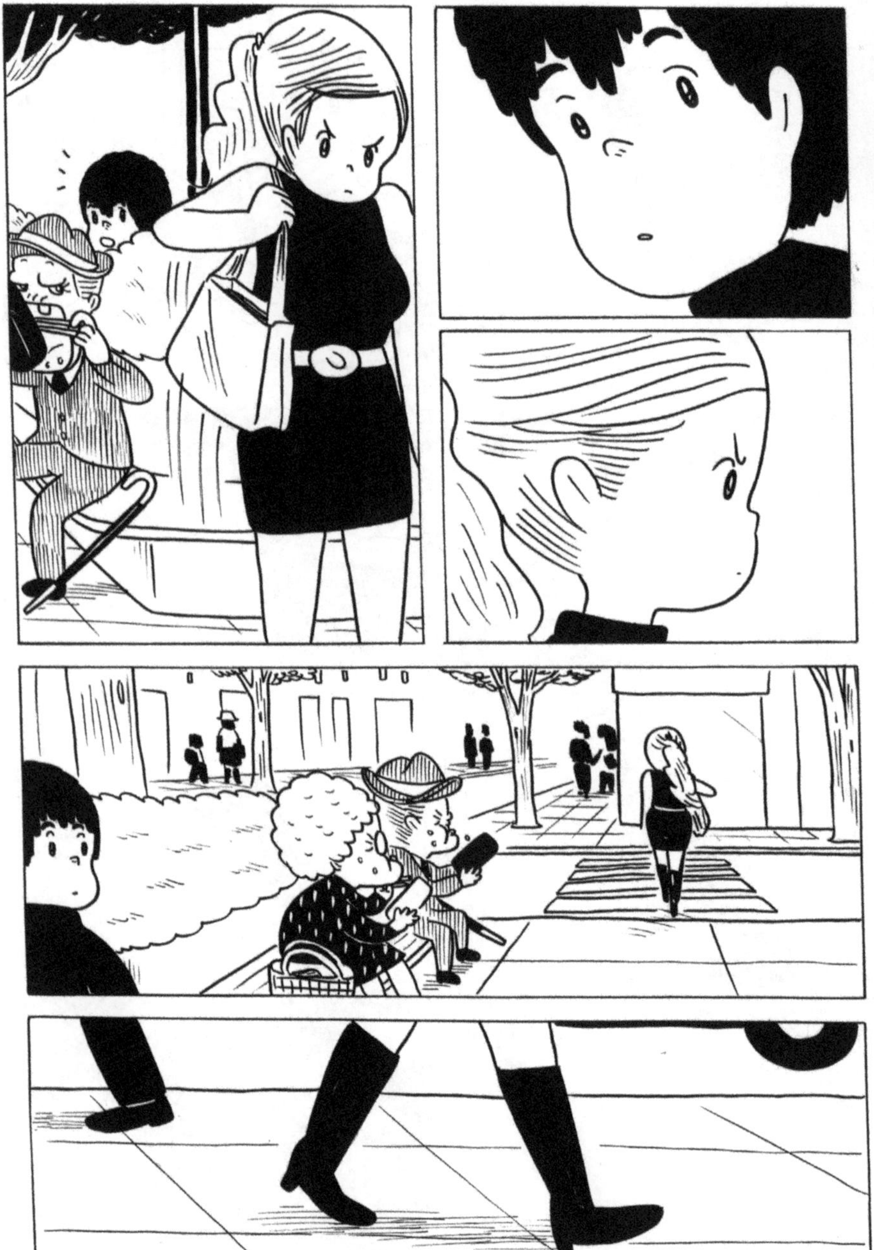

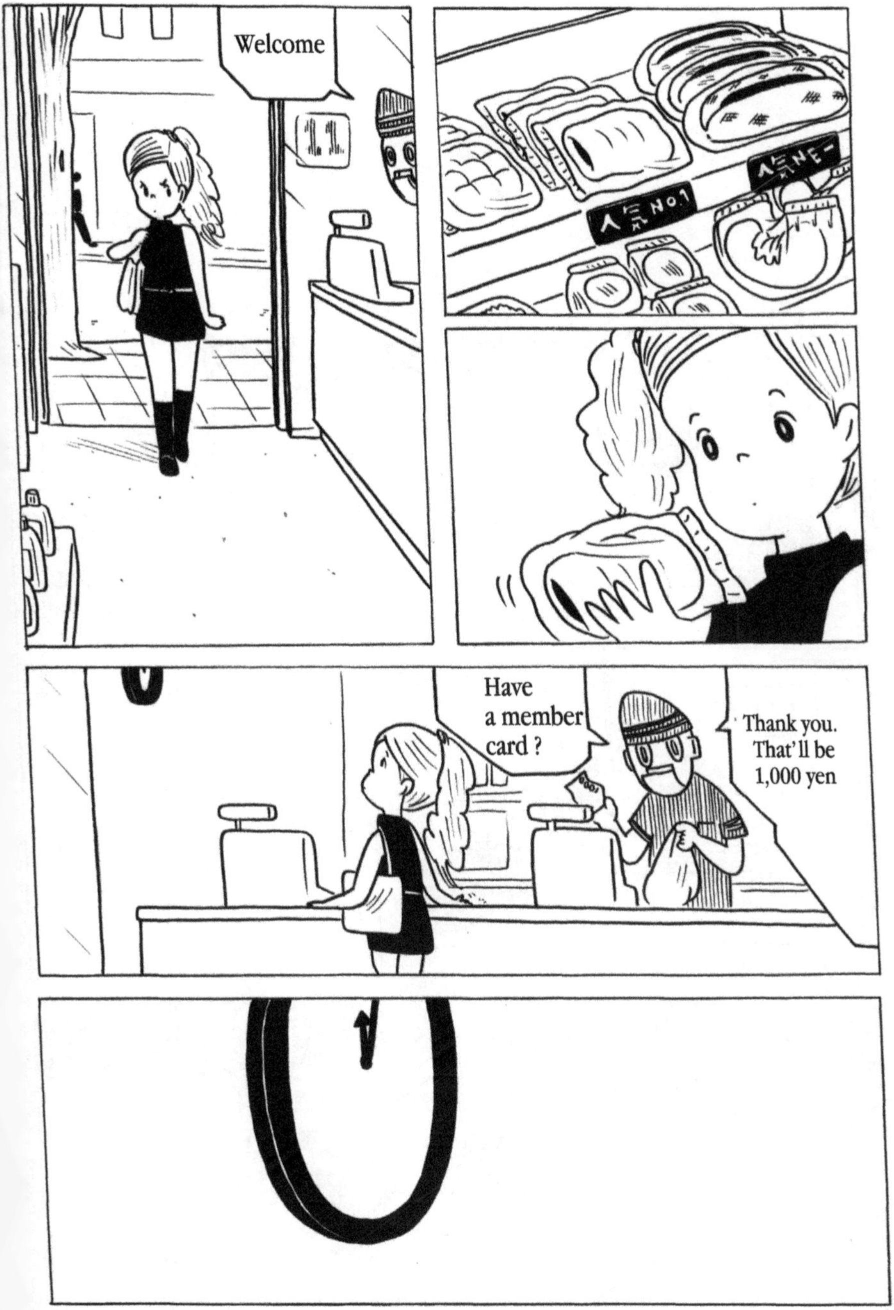
Welcome
Have a member card ?
Thank you. That'll be 1,000 yen

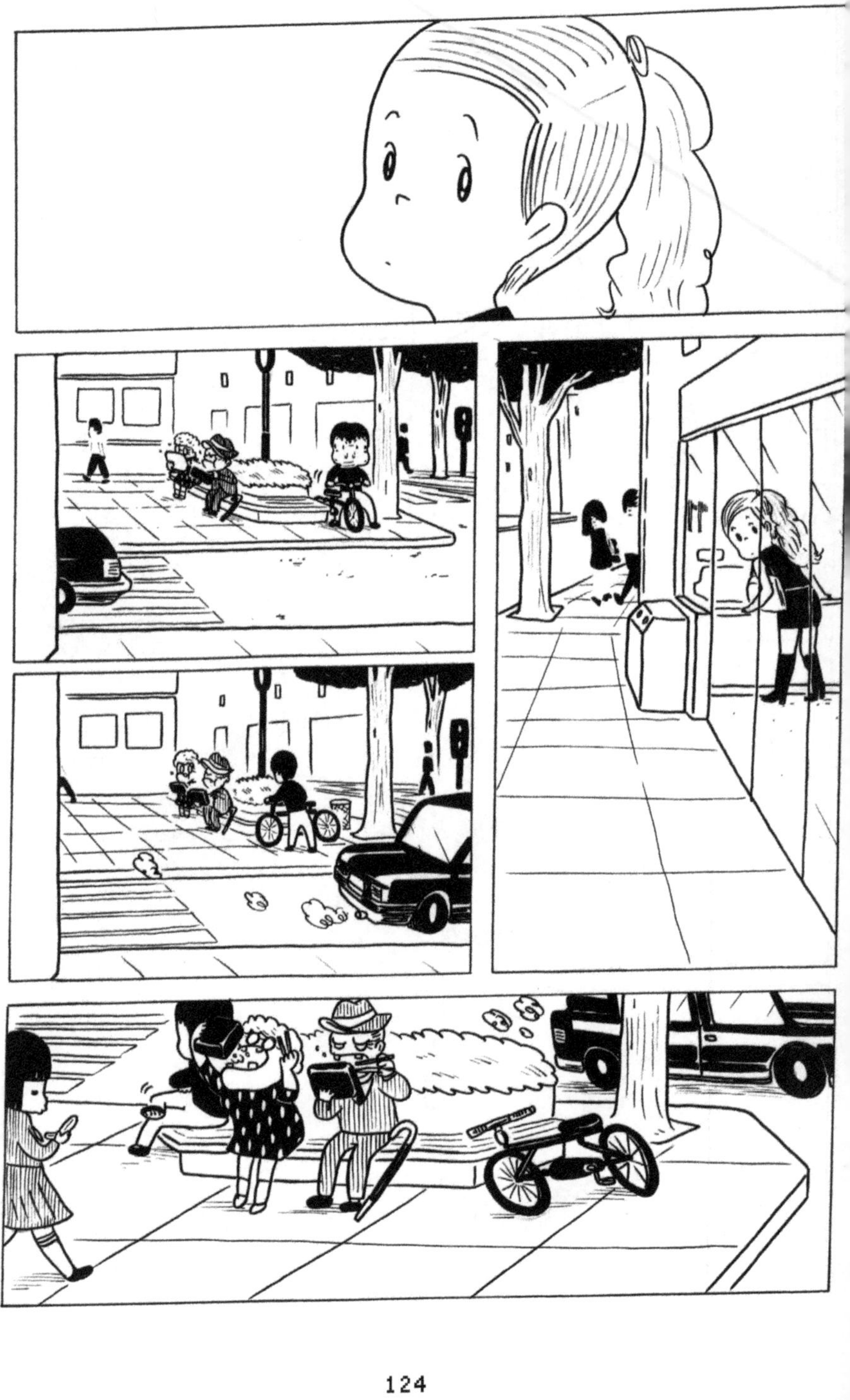

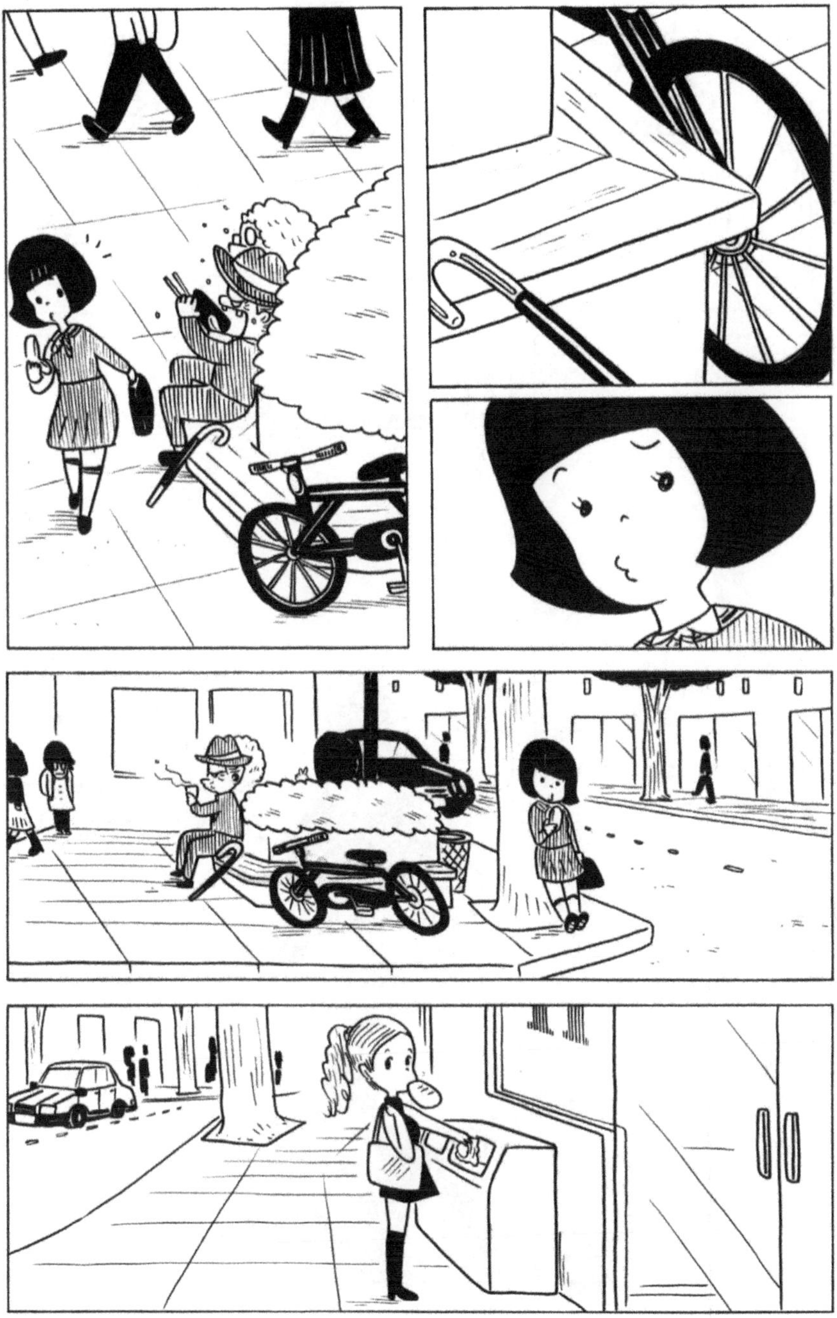

Hello again

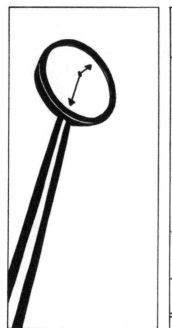

GROOWL~

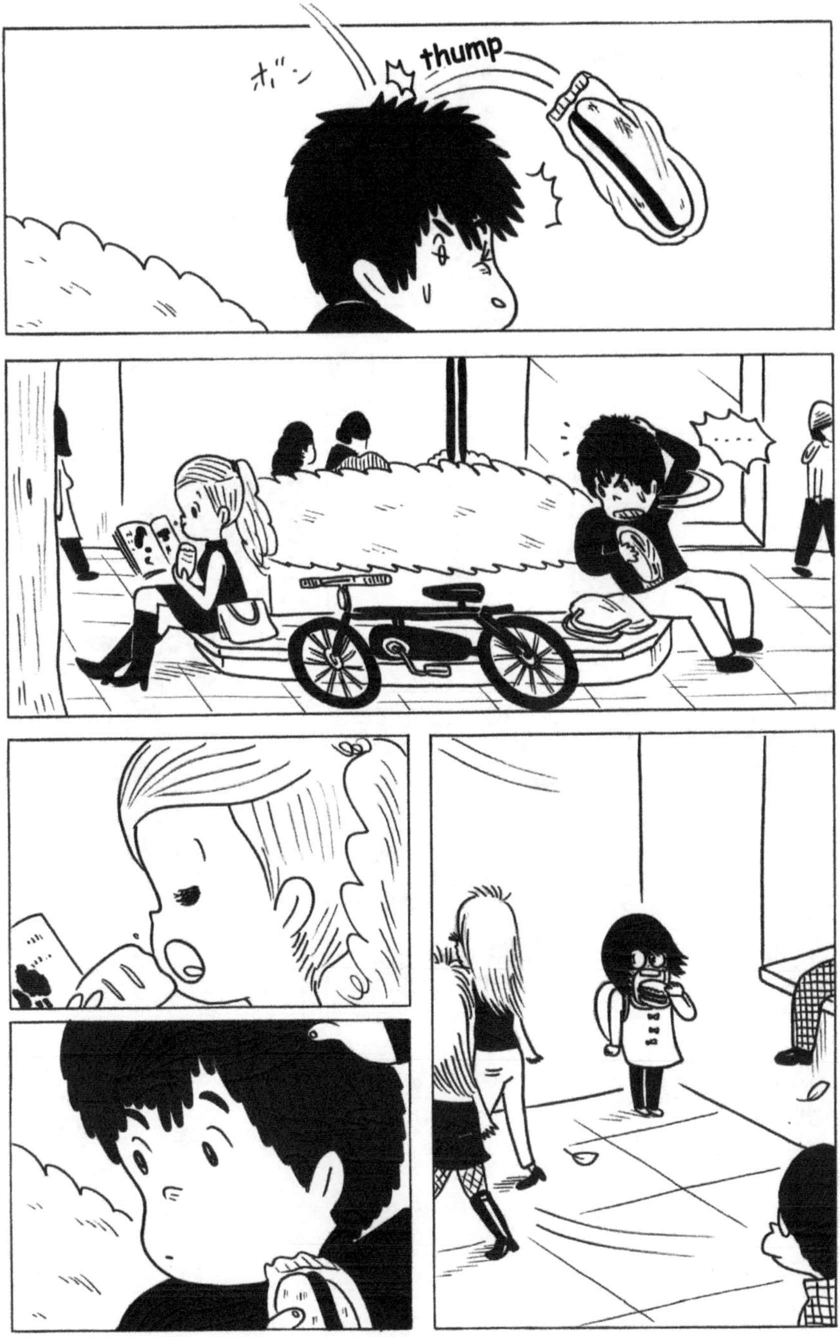
ボ゛ン
thump
. . . .

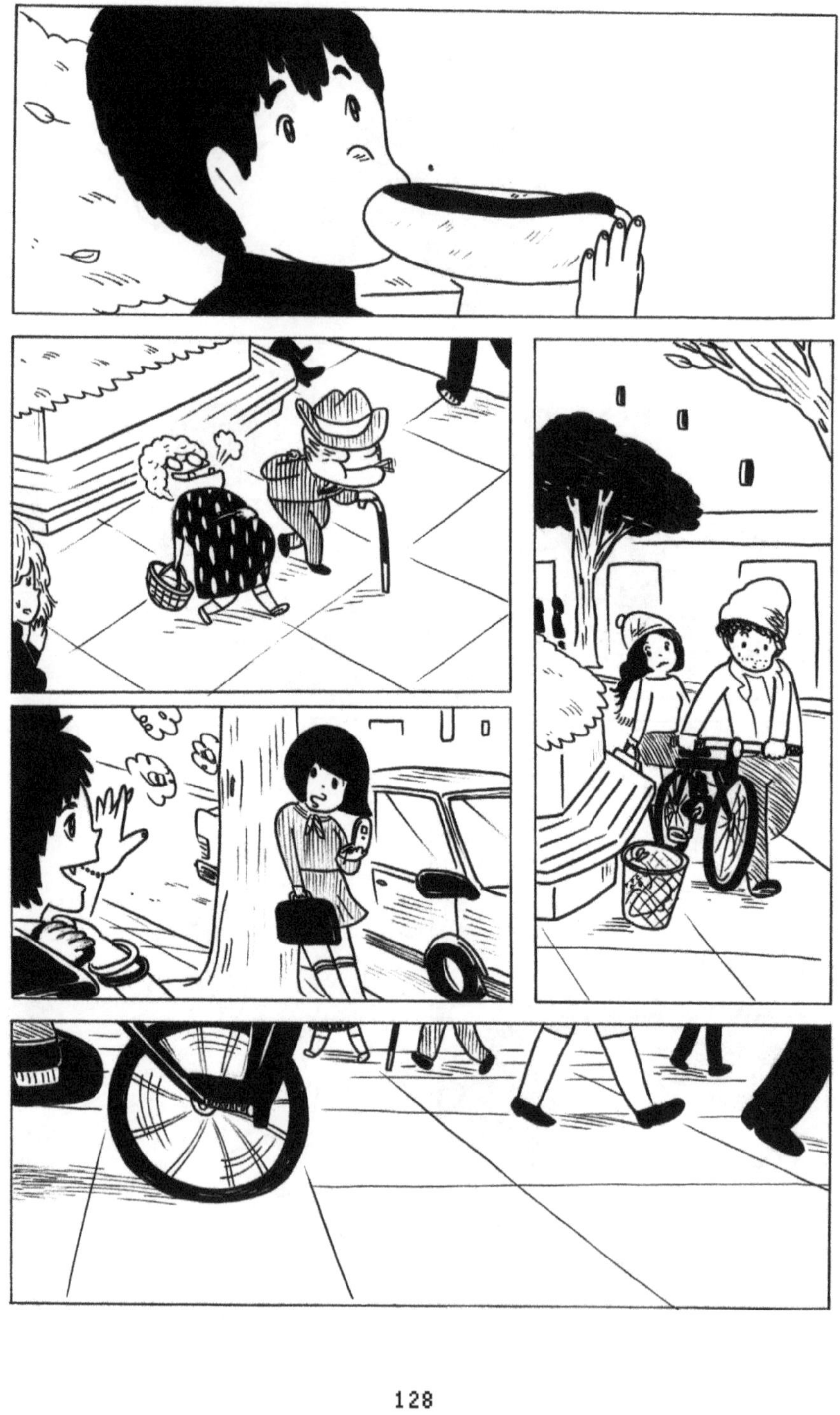

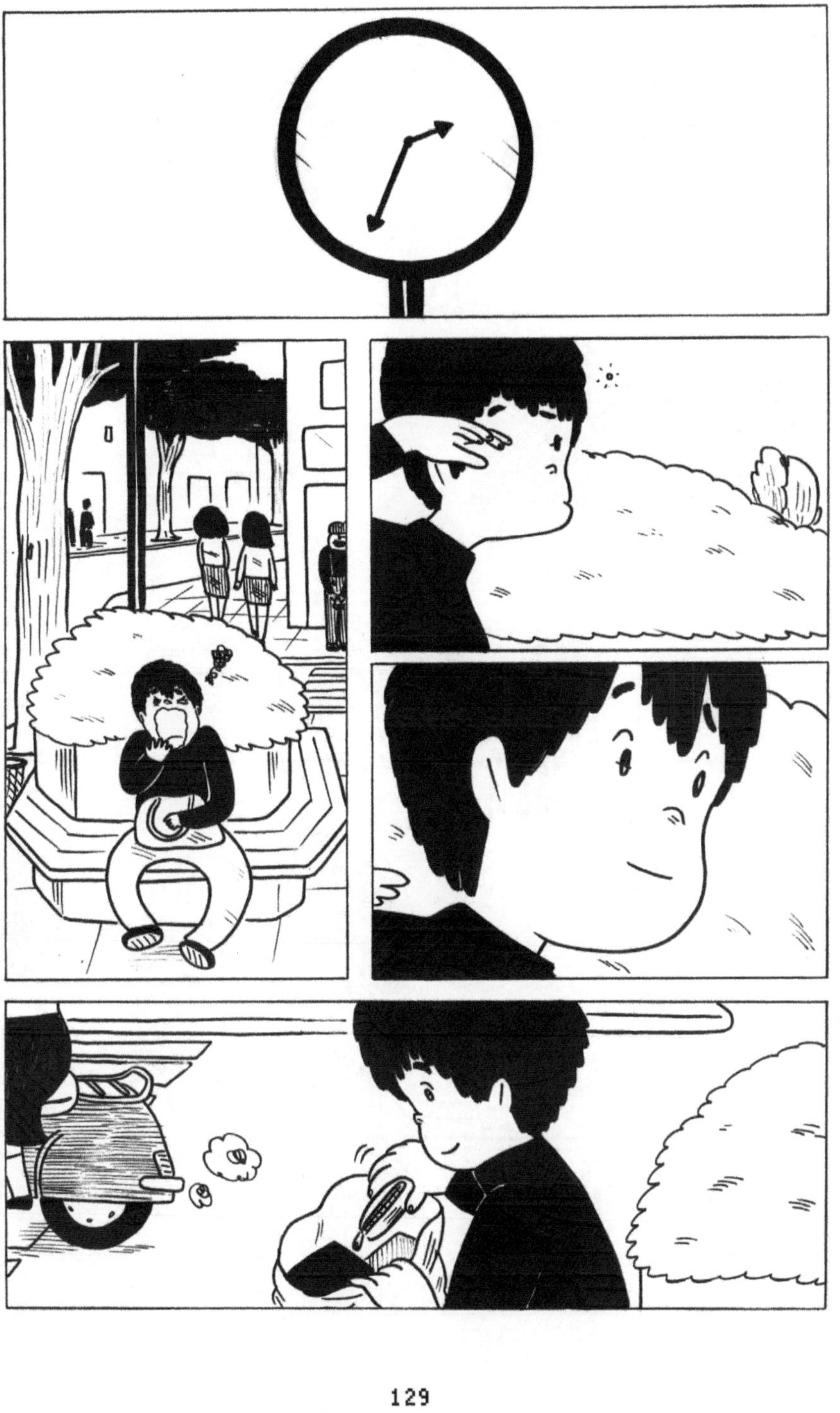

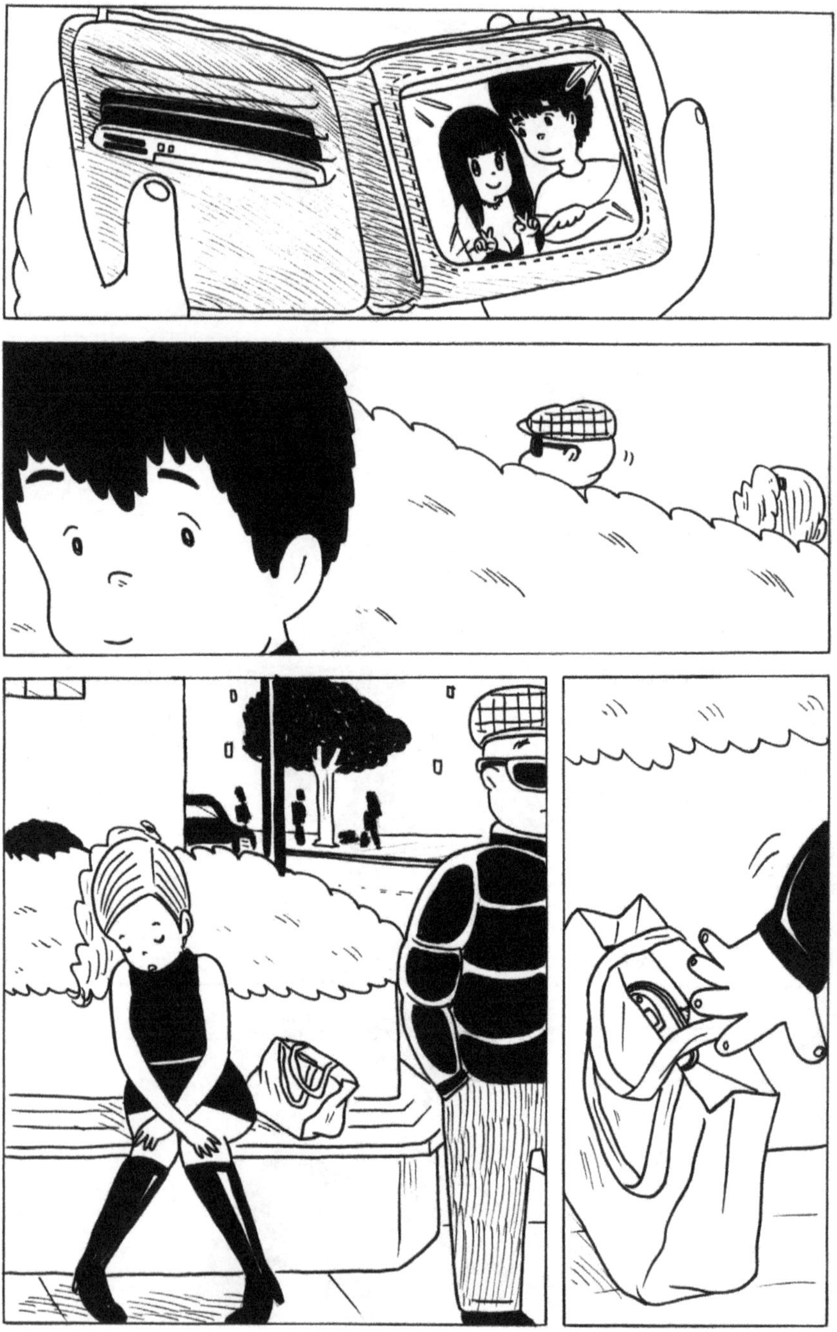

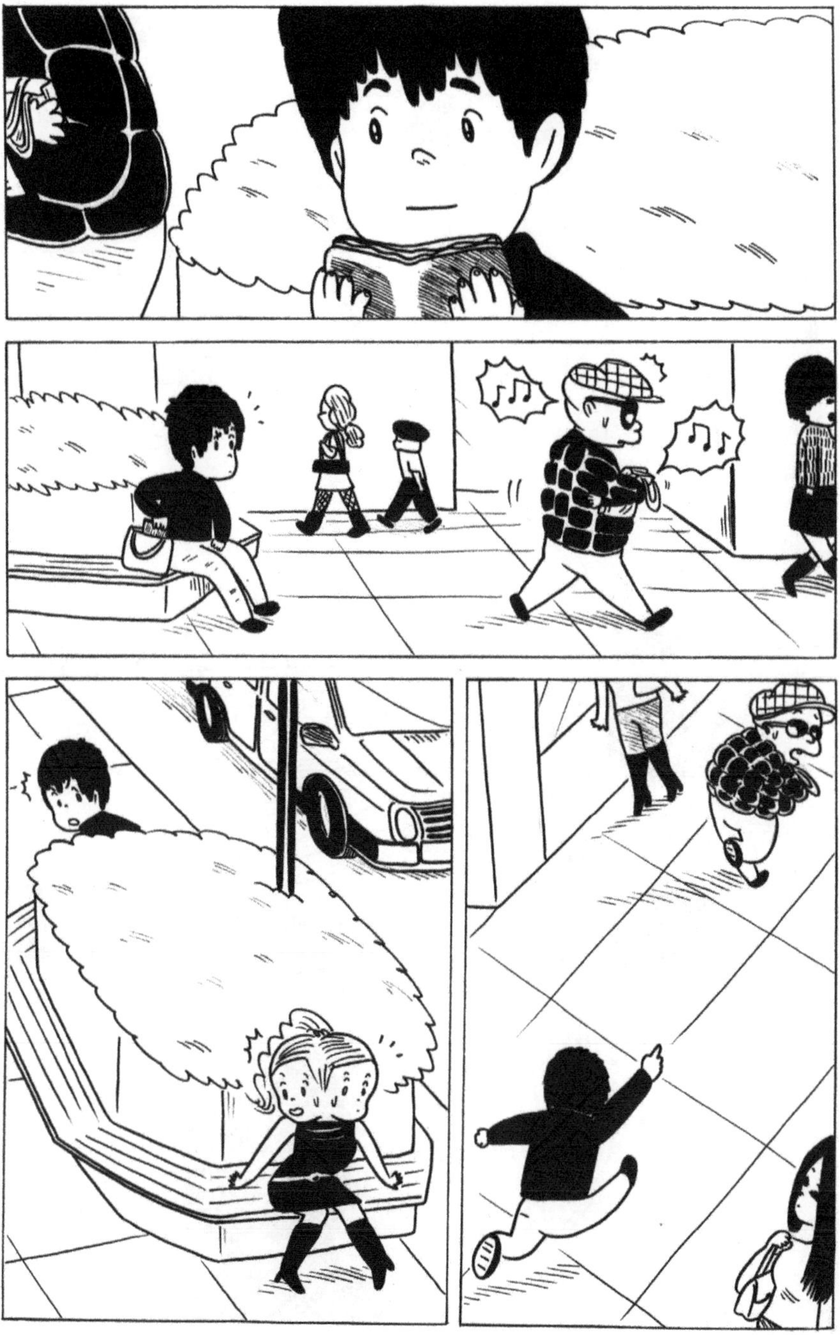

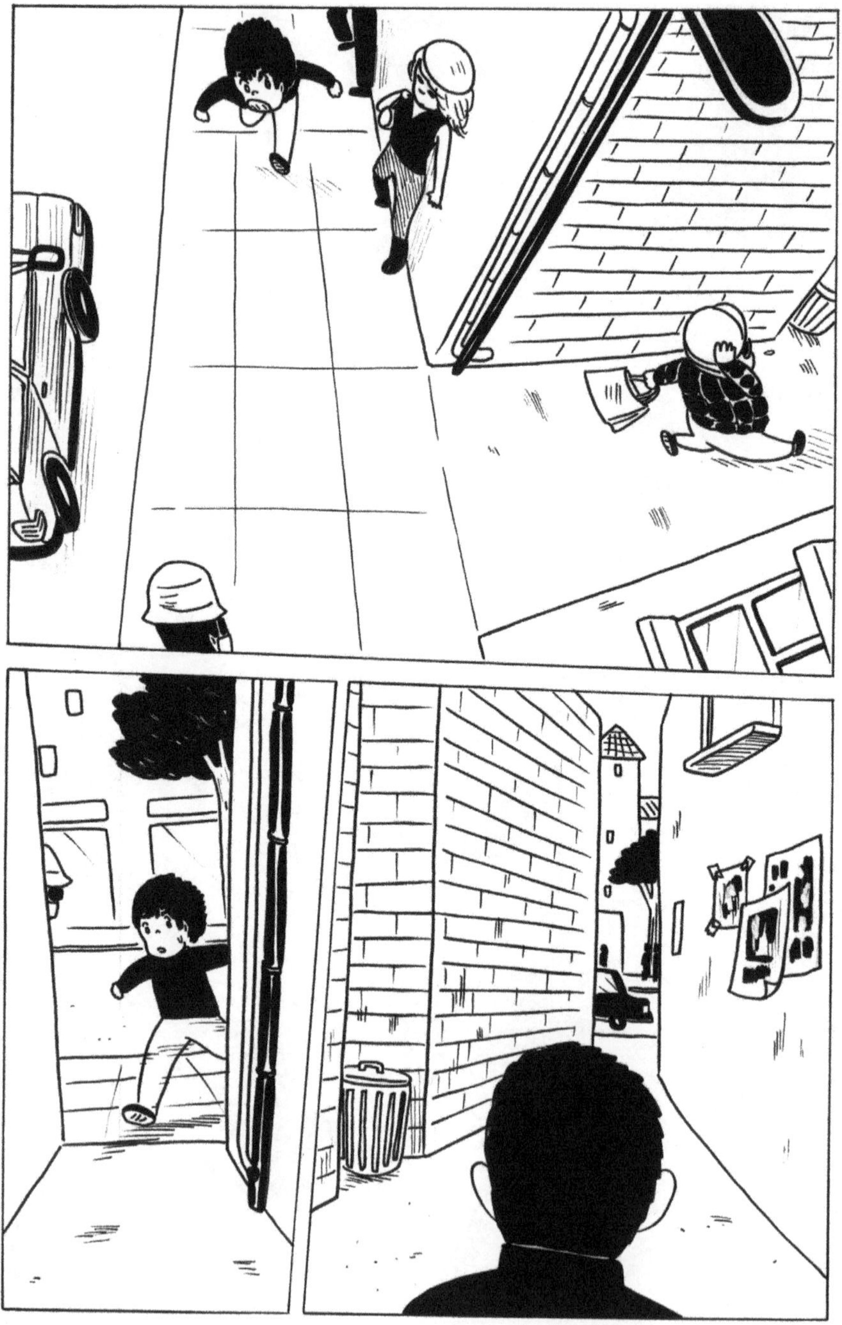

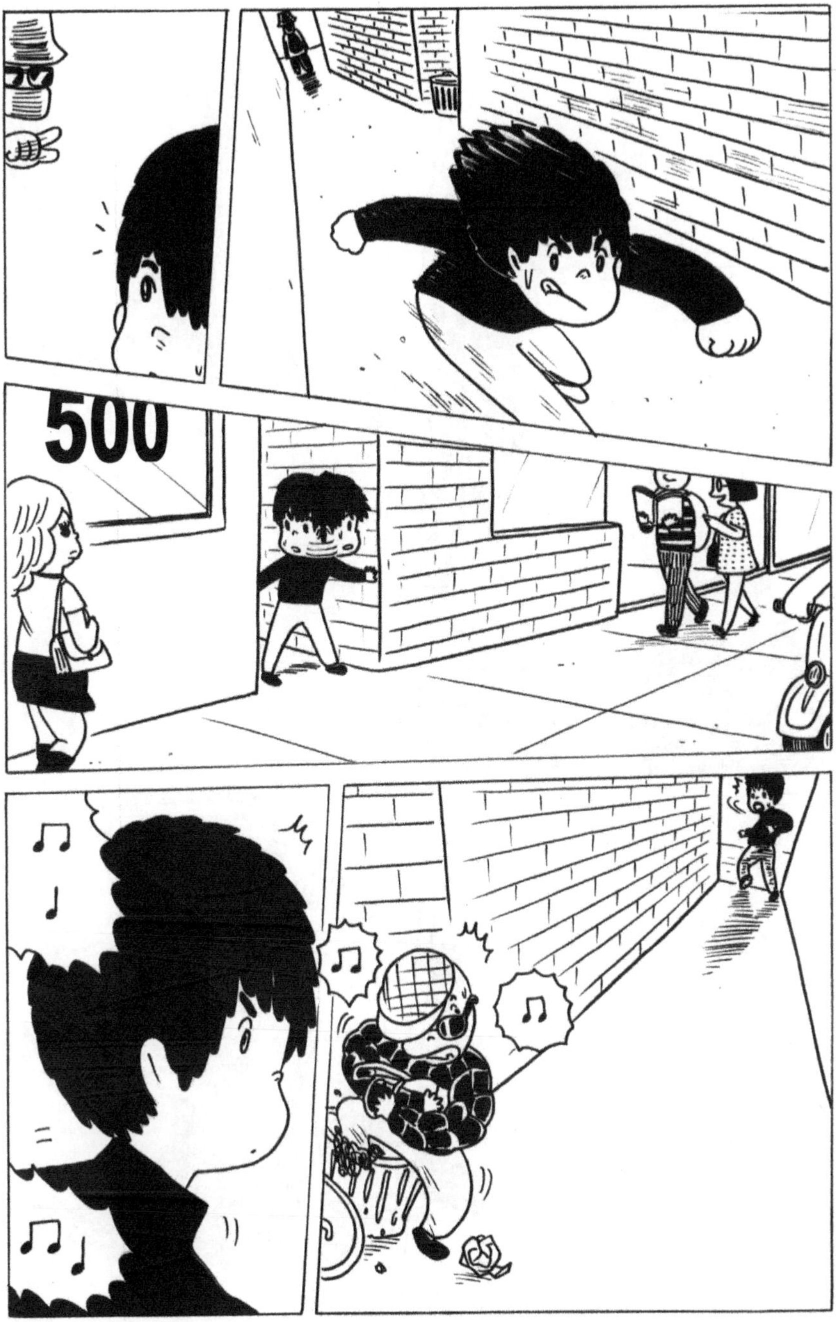
500

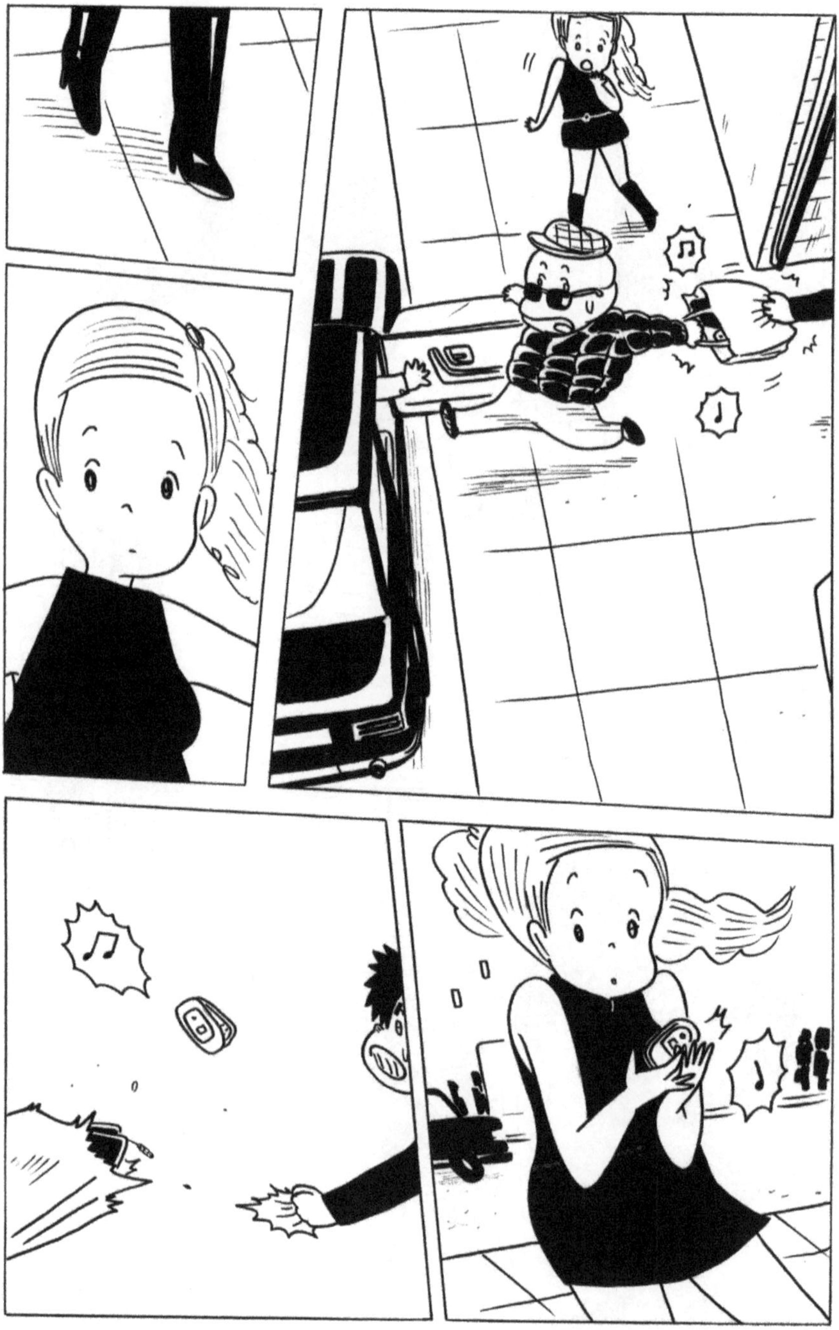

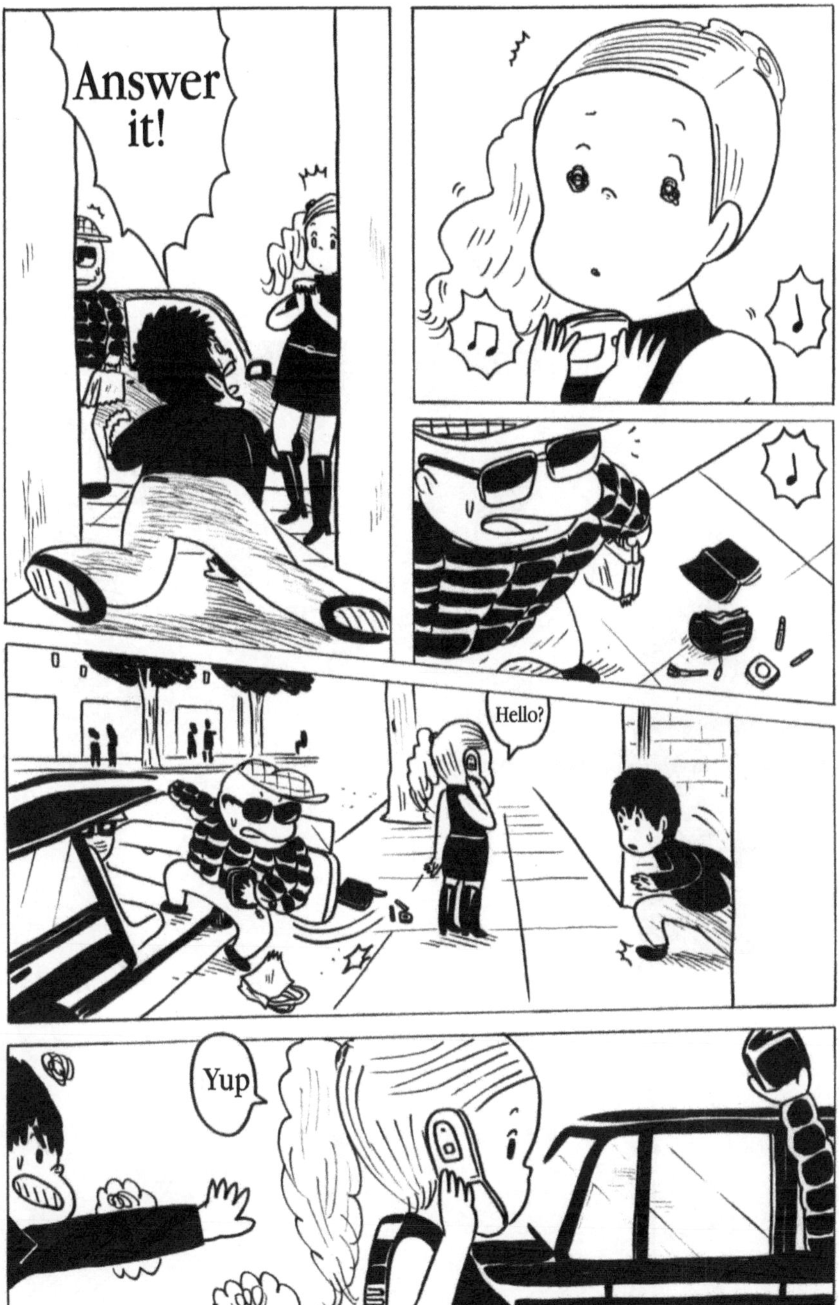
Answer it!
Hello?
Yup

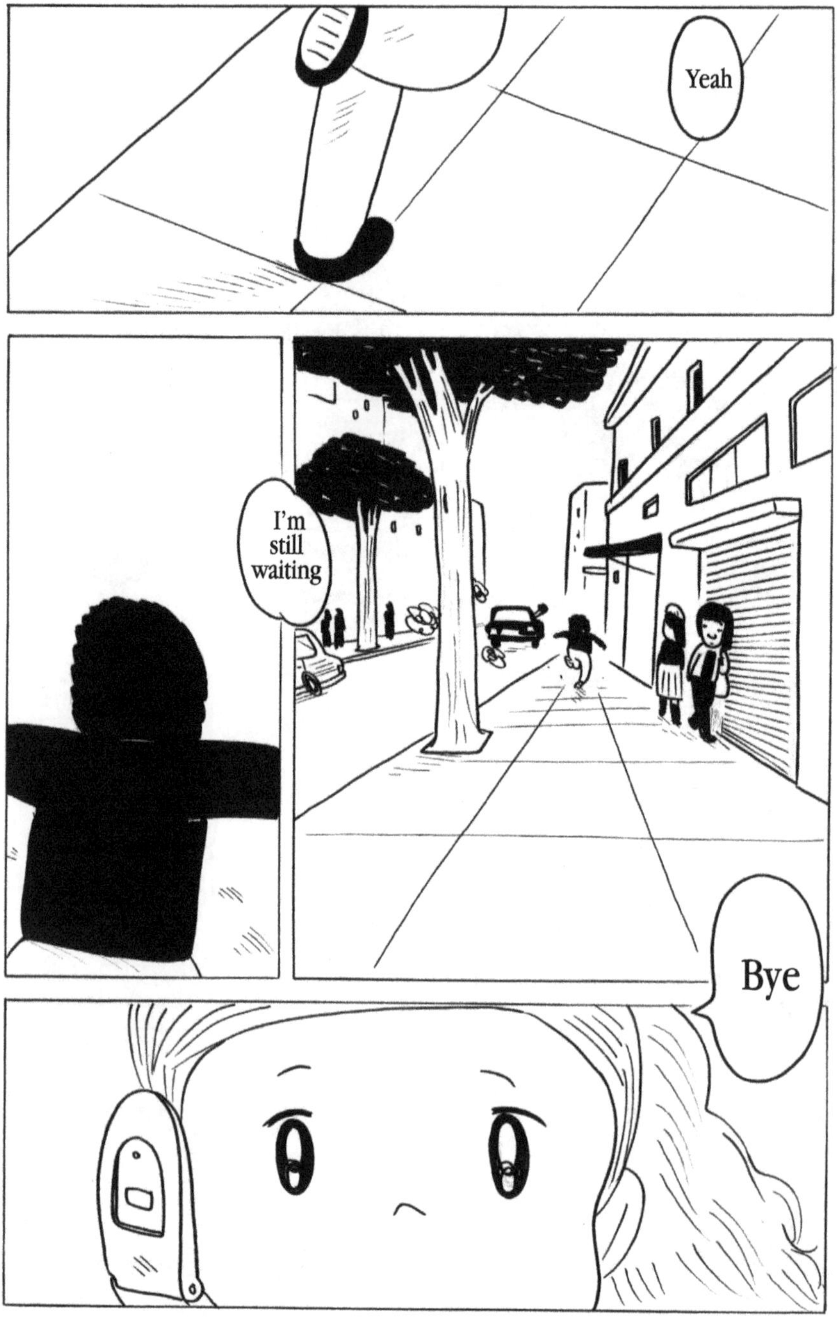
Yeah
I'm still waiting
Bye

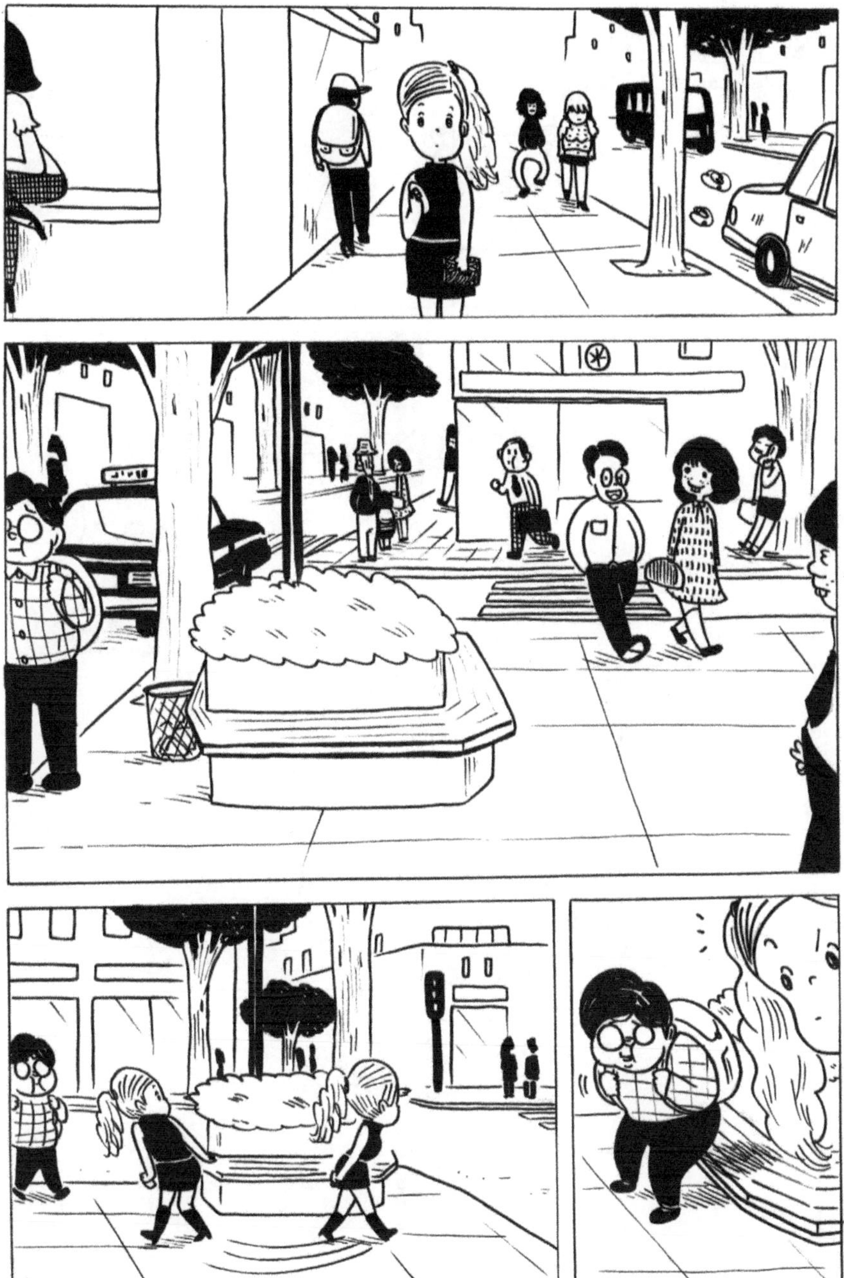

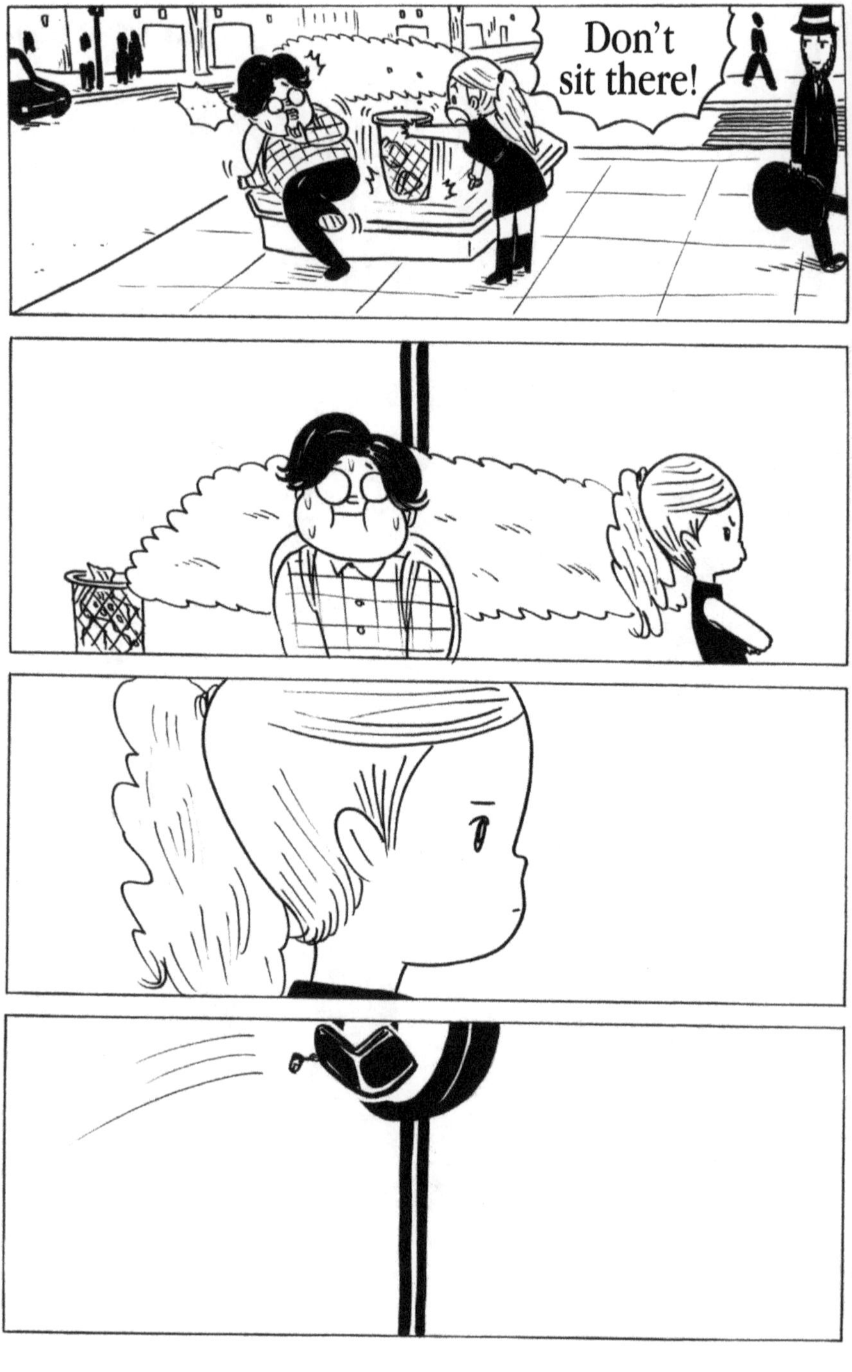
Don't sit there!

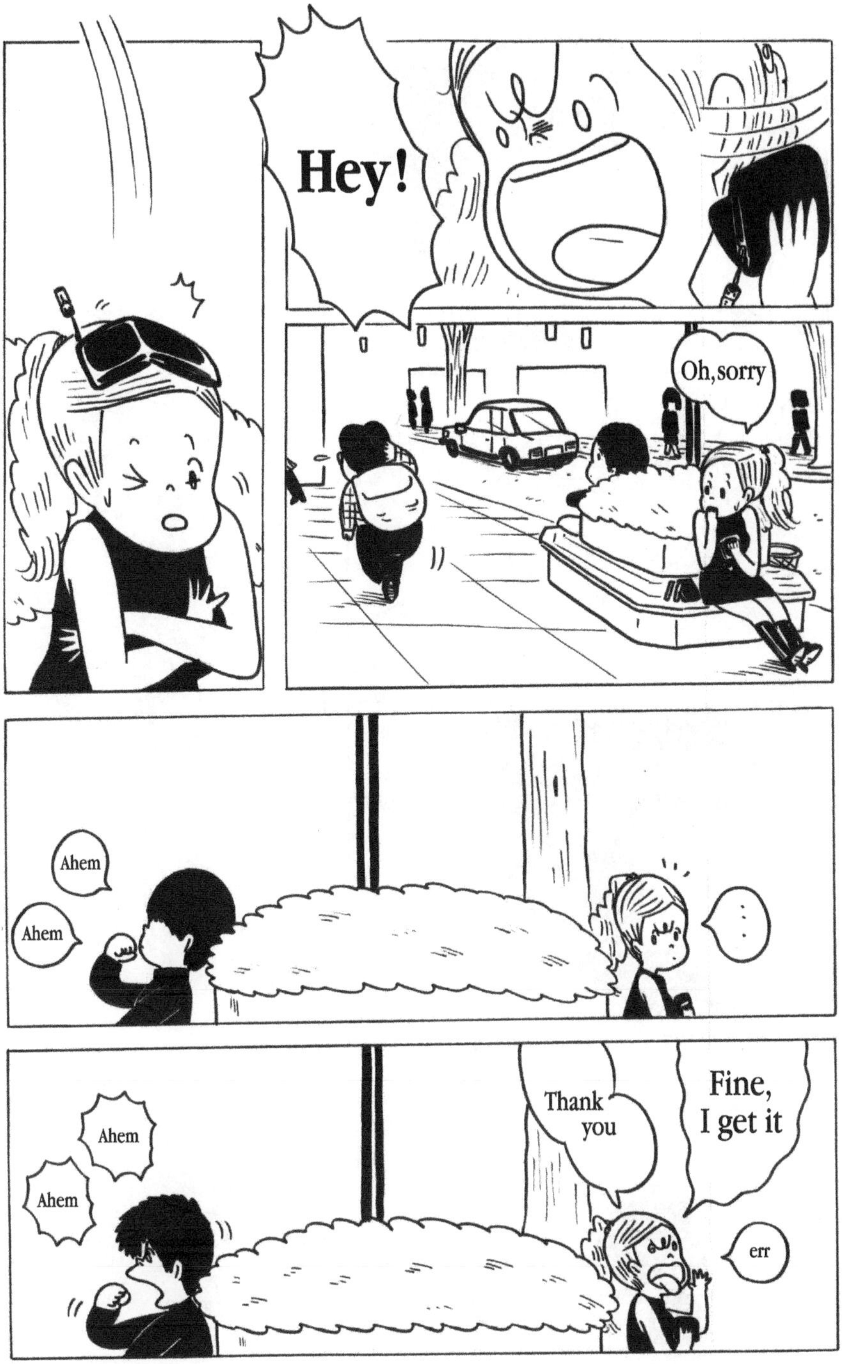
Hey!
Oh,sorry
...
Ahem
Ahem
Fine, I get it
Thank you
err
Ahem
Ahem

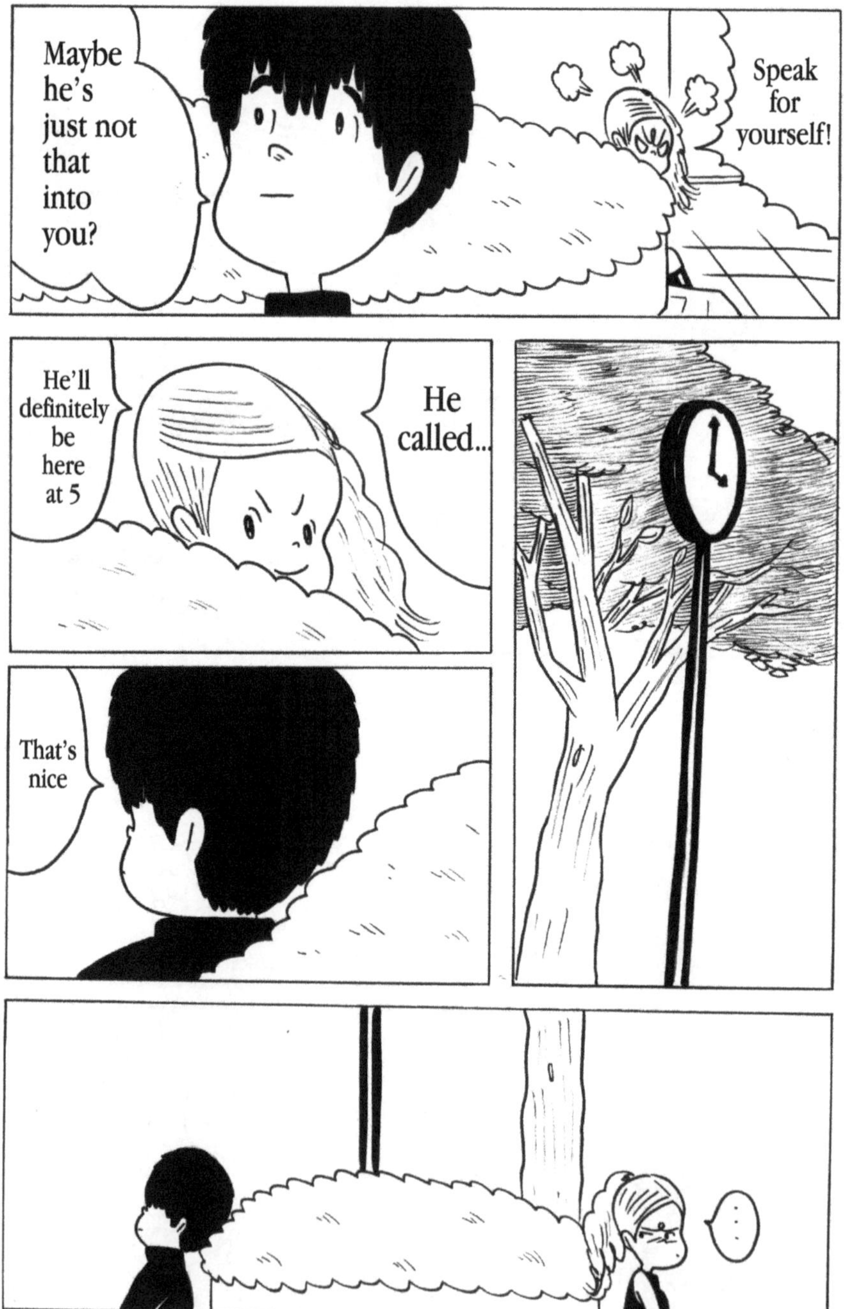
Speak for yourself!
Maybe he's just not that into you?
He called...
He'll definitely be here at 5
That's nice
. . .

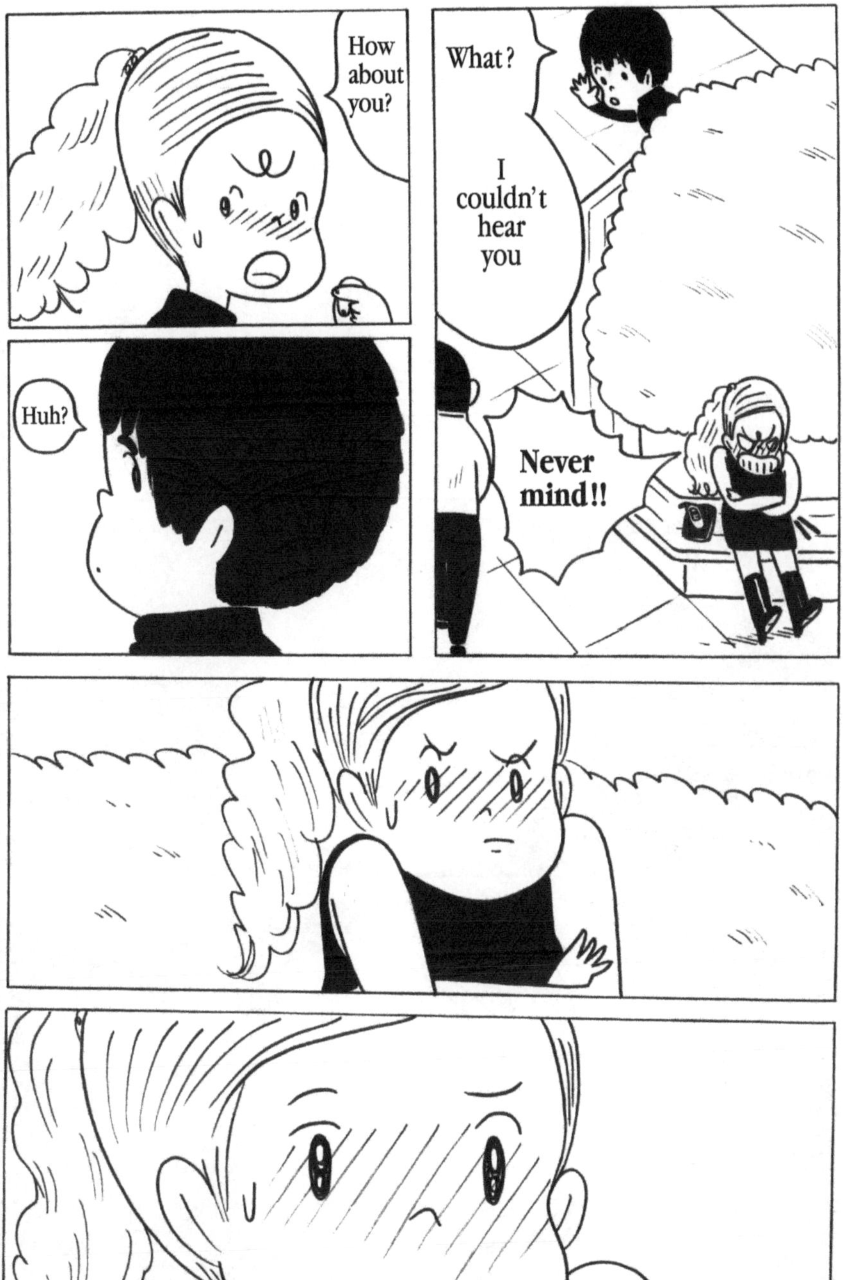
How about you?
Huh?
What?
I couldn't hear you
Never mind!!

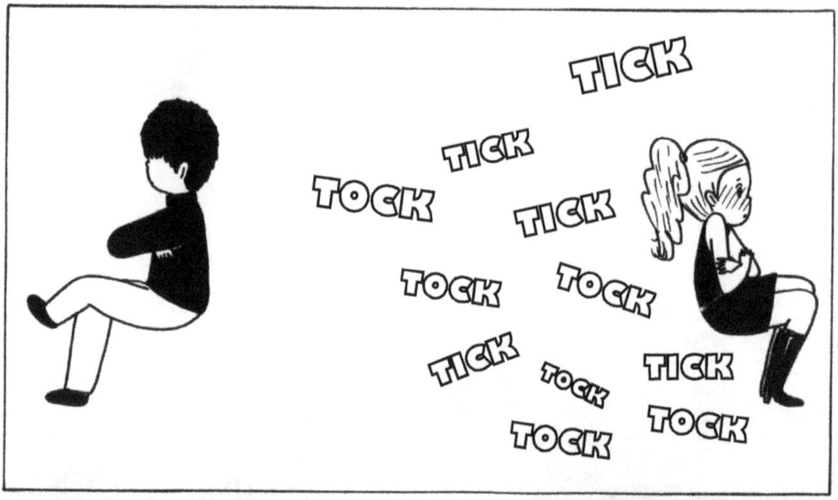
TICK
TICK
TICK
TOCK
TOCK
TOCK
TICK
TICK
TOCK
TOCK
TOCK

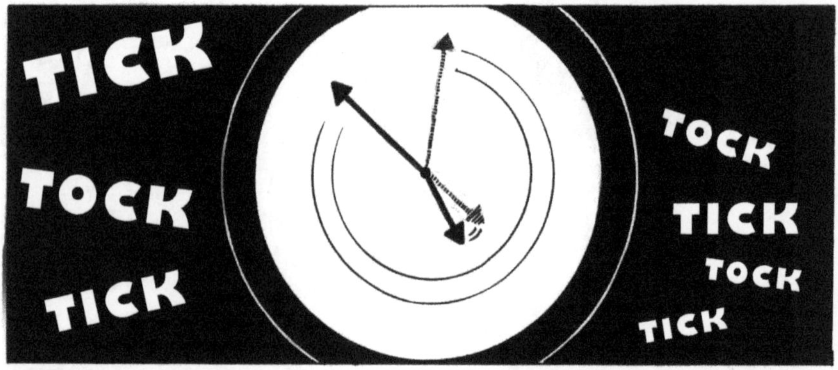
TOCK
TICK
TOCK
TICK
TICK
TOCK
TICK

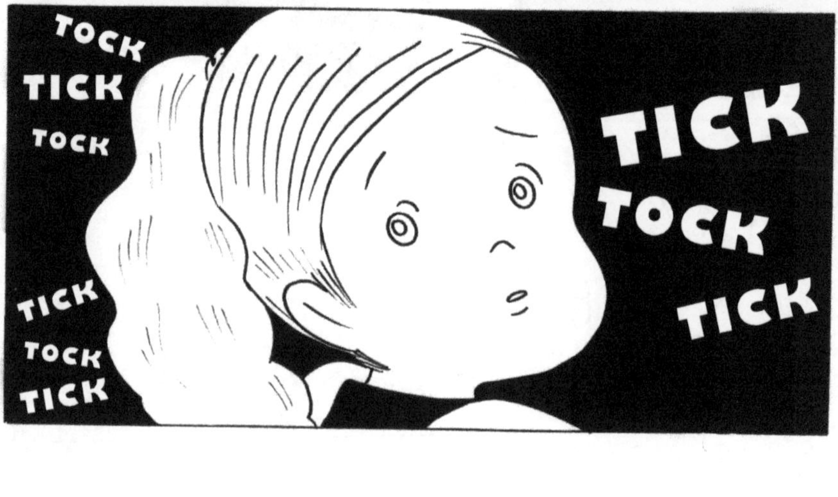
TICK
TOCK
TICK
TOCK
TICK
TOCK
TICK
TOCK
TICK

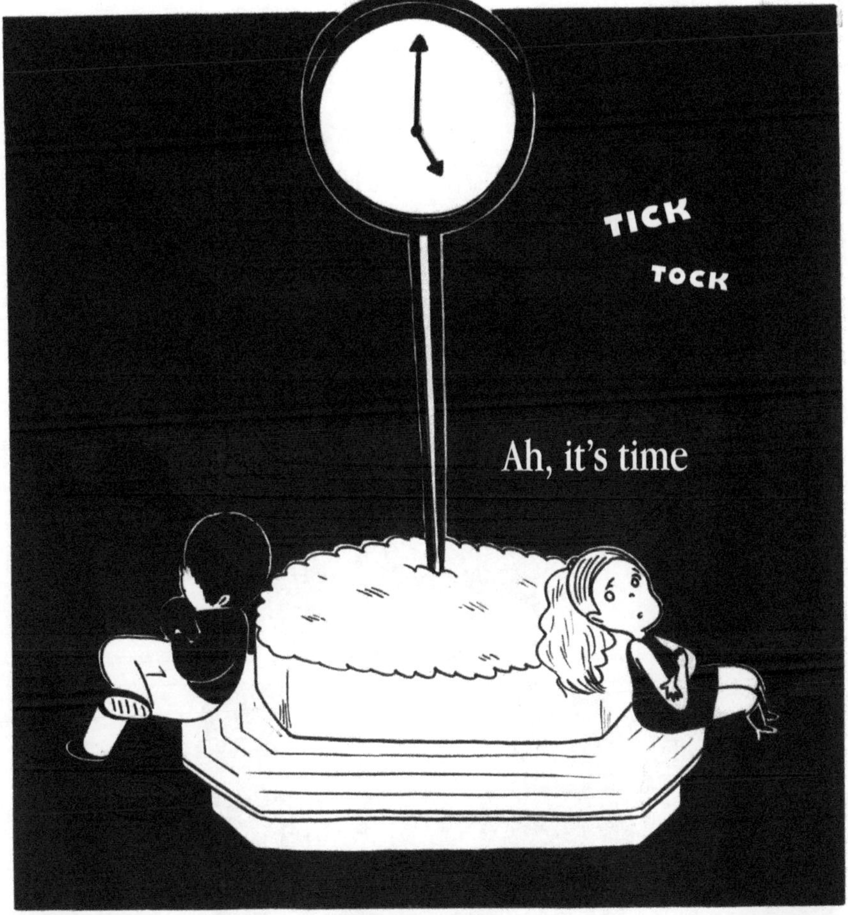
TICK
TOCK
Ah, it's time

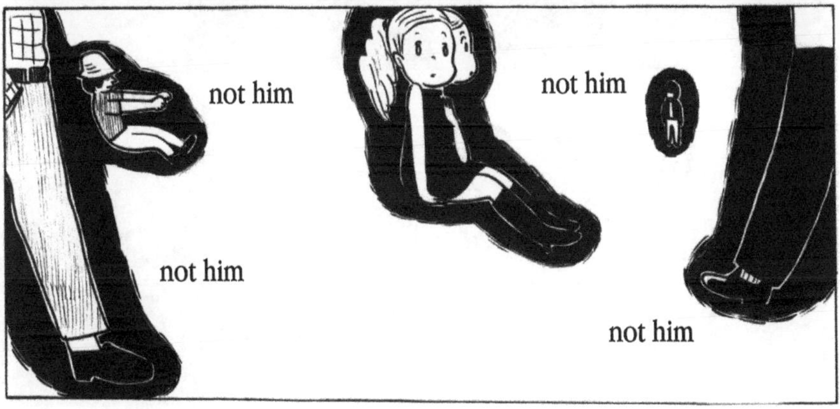
not him
not him
not him
not him

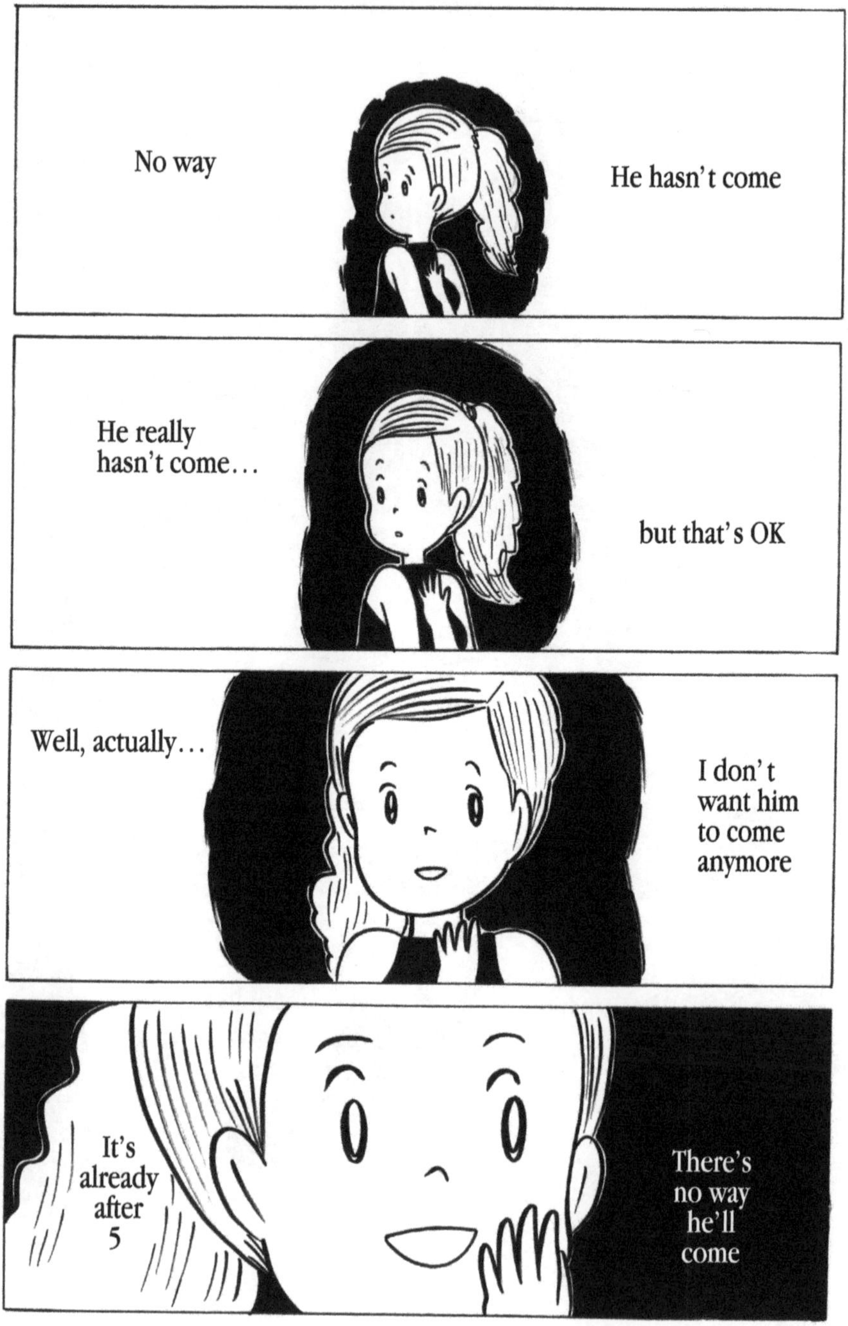
No way
He hasn't come
He really hasn't come…
but that's OK
Well, actually…
I don't want him to come anymore
It's already after 5
There's no way he'll come

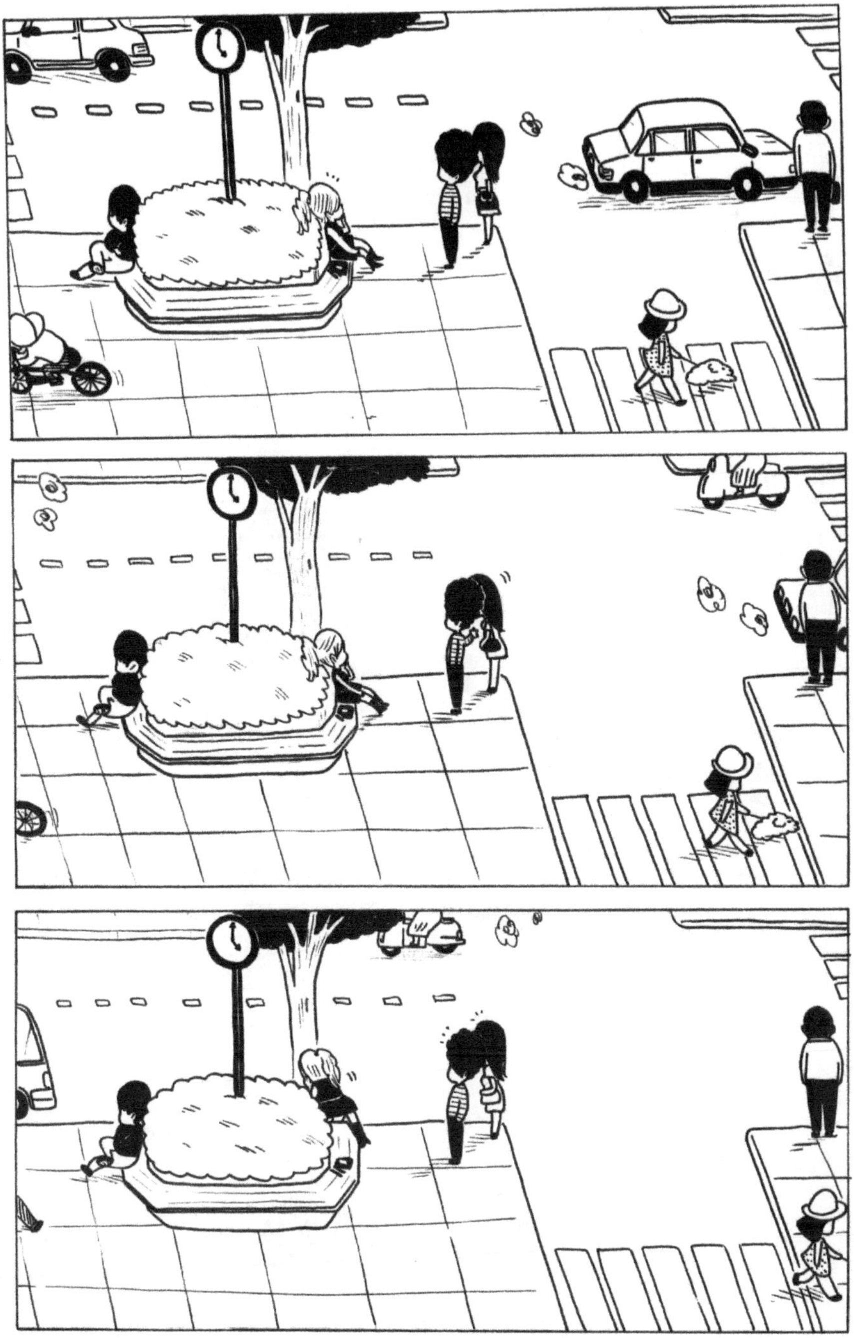

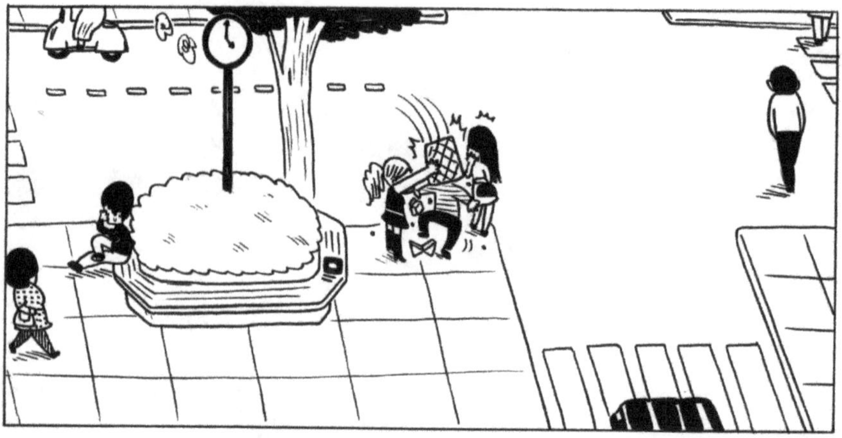
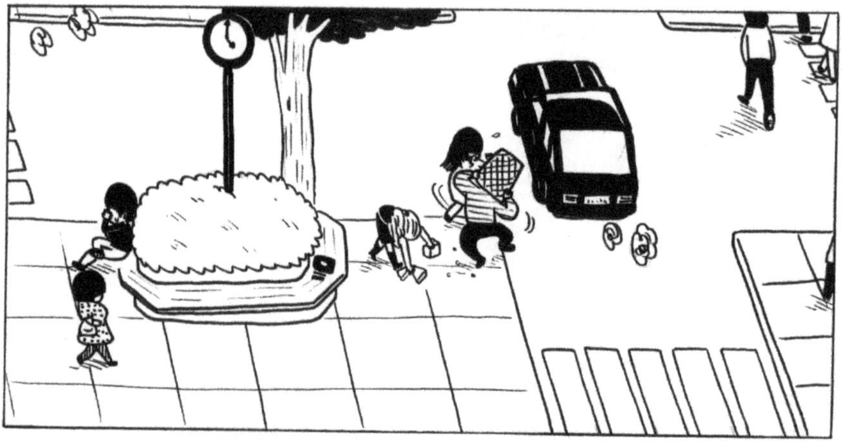
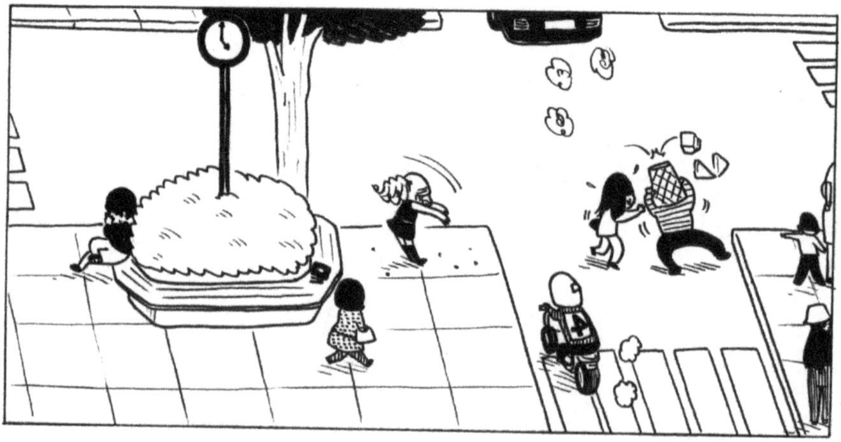

So!?
Your boyfriend came, right?
Yeah, ha-ha
So.... what are you waiting for now?
For your girlfriend, of course

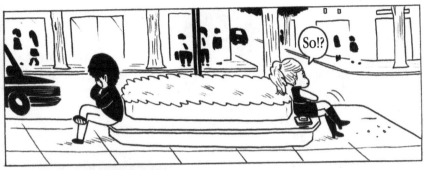

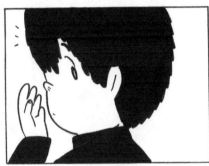

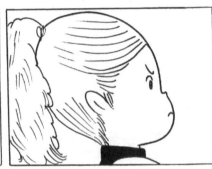

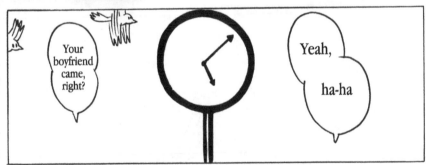

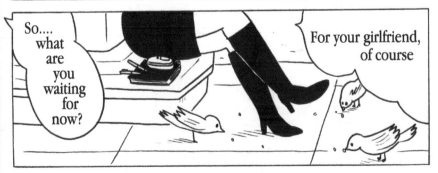

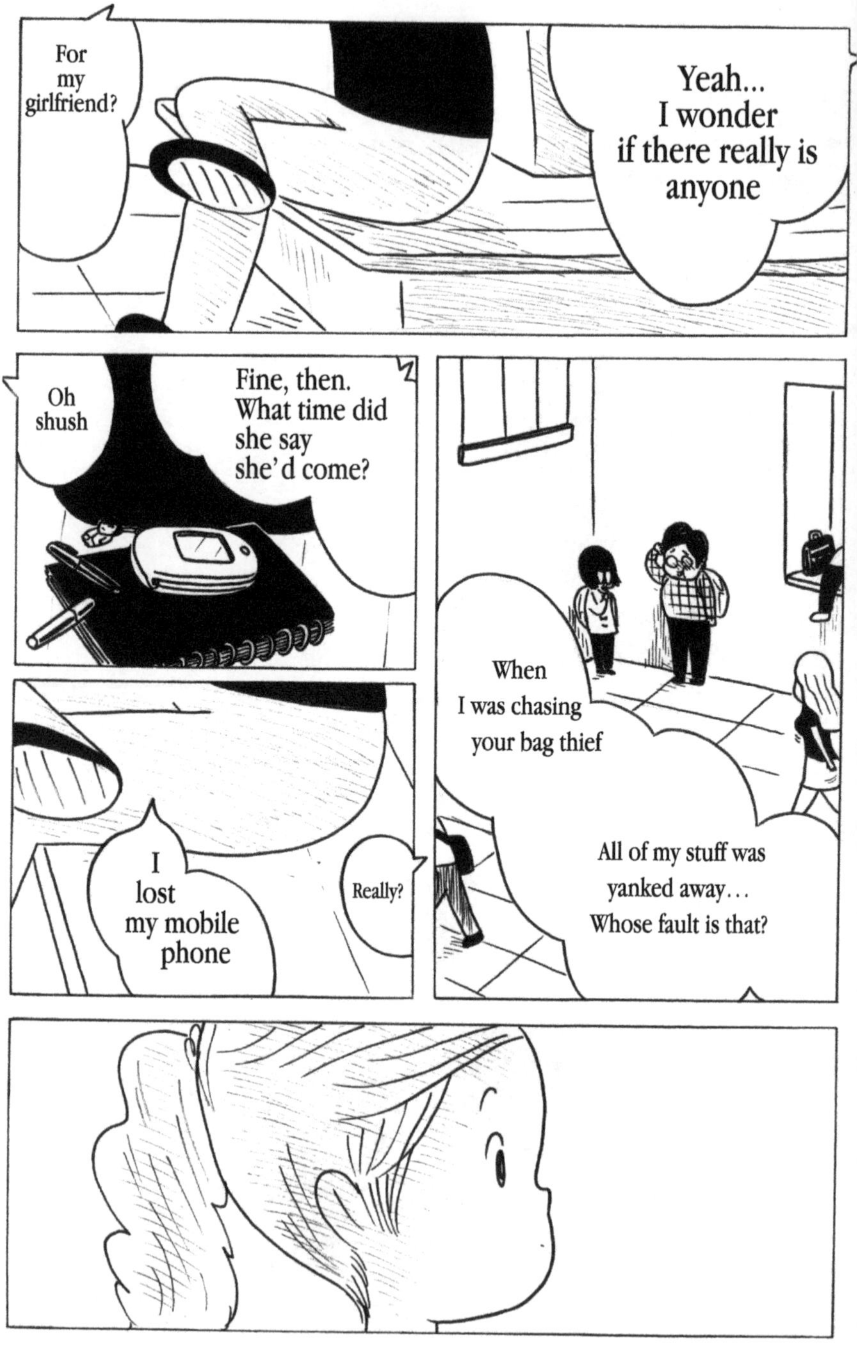
For my girlfriend?
Yeah... I wonder if there really is anyone
Oh shush
Fine, then. What time did she say she'd come?
I lost my mobile phone
Really?
When I was chasing your bag thief
All of my stuff was yanked away... Whose fault is that?

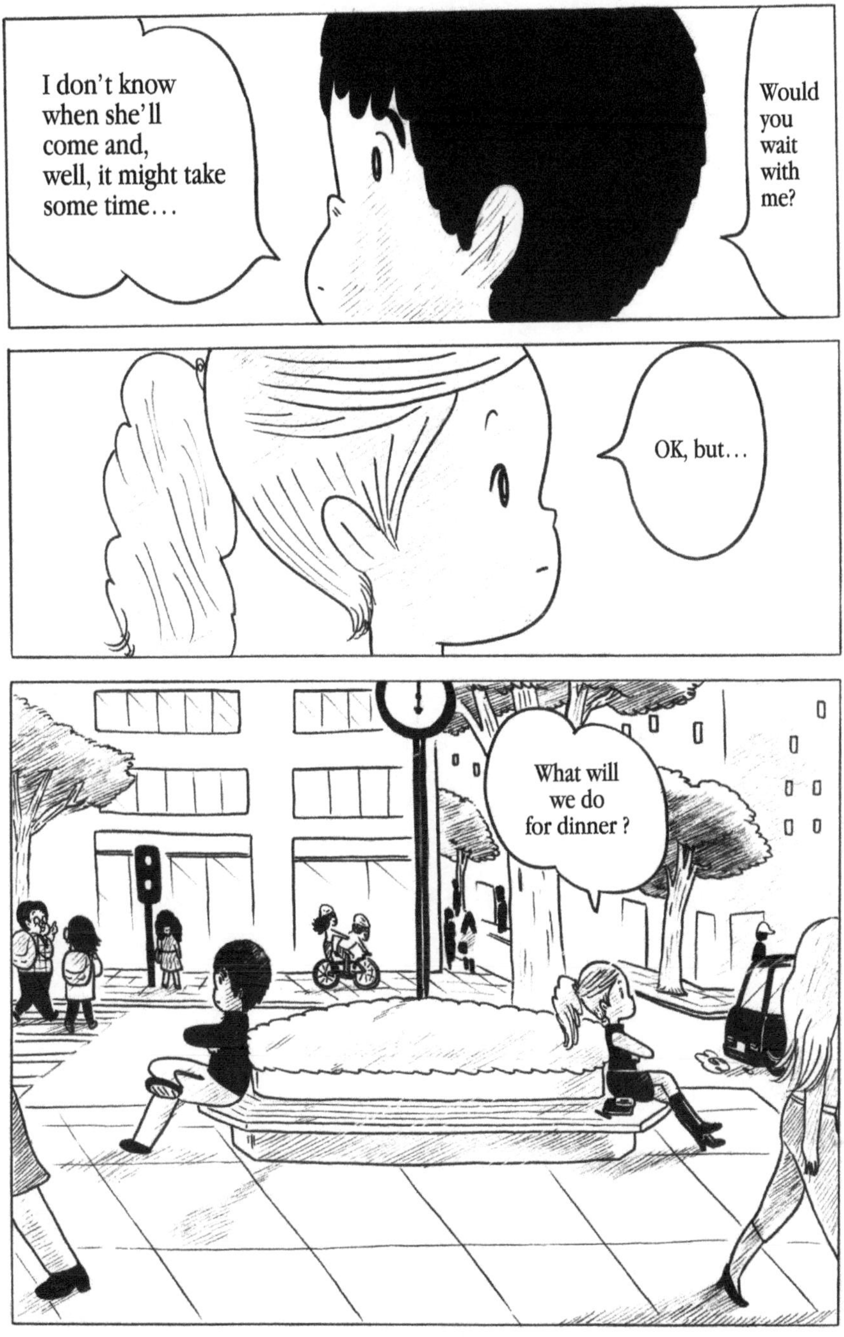
I don't know when she'll come and, well, it might take some time…
Would you wait with me?
OK, but…
What will we do for dinner ?

Eye Sickness

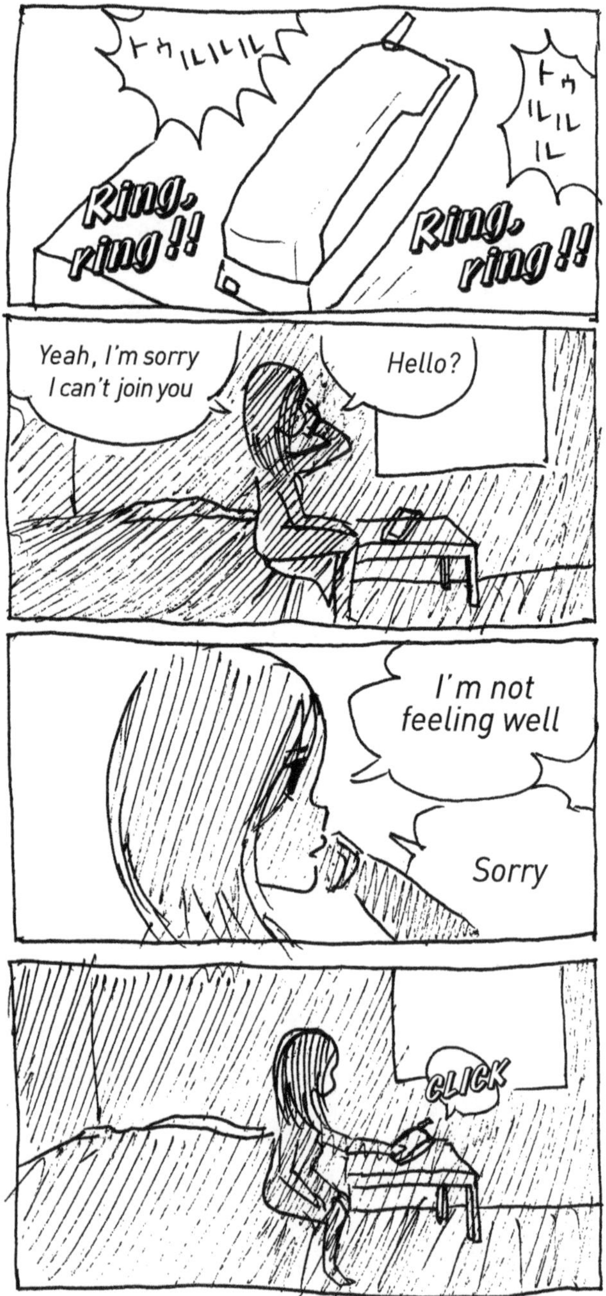
トゥルルル
Ring, ring!!
トゥルルル
Ring, ring!!
Hello?
Yeah, I'm sorry I can't join you
I'm not feeling well
Sorry
CLICK

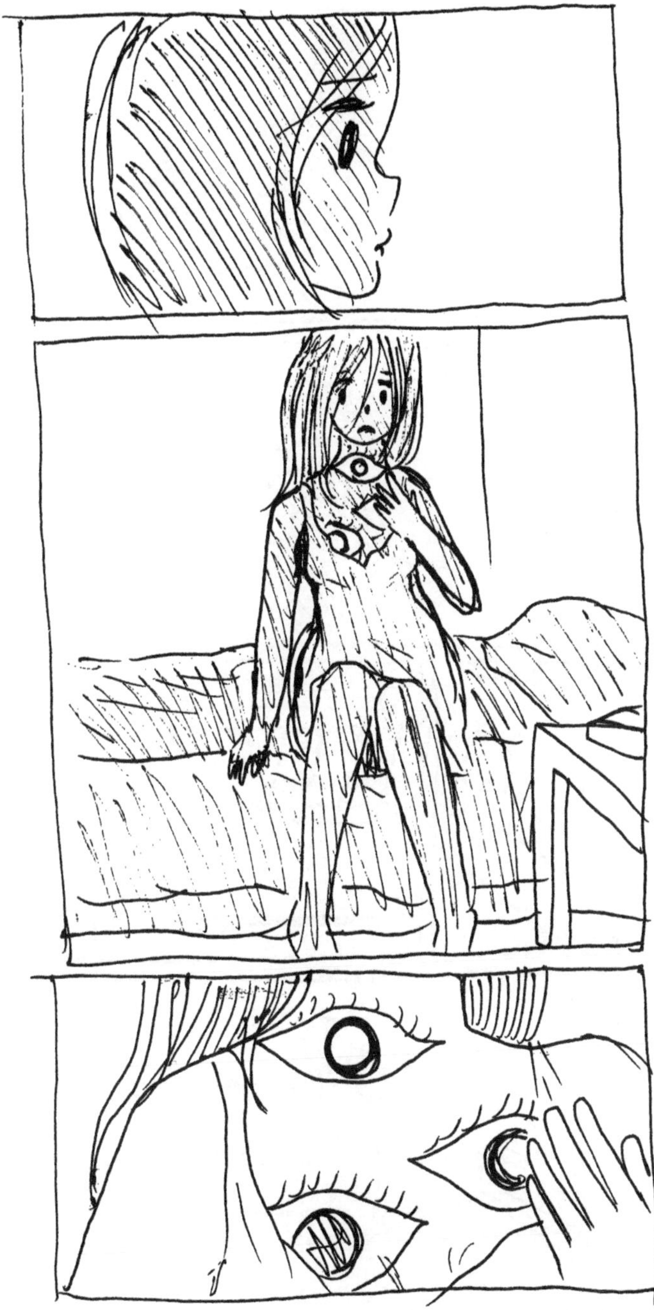

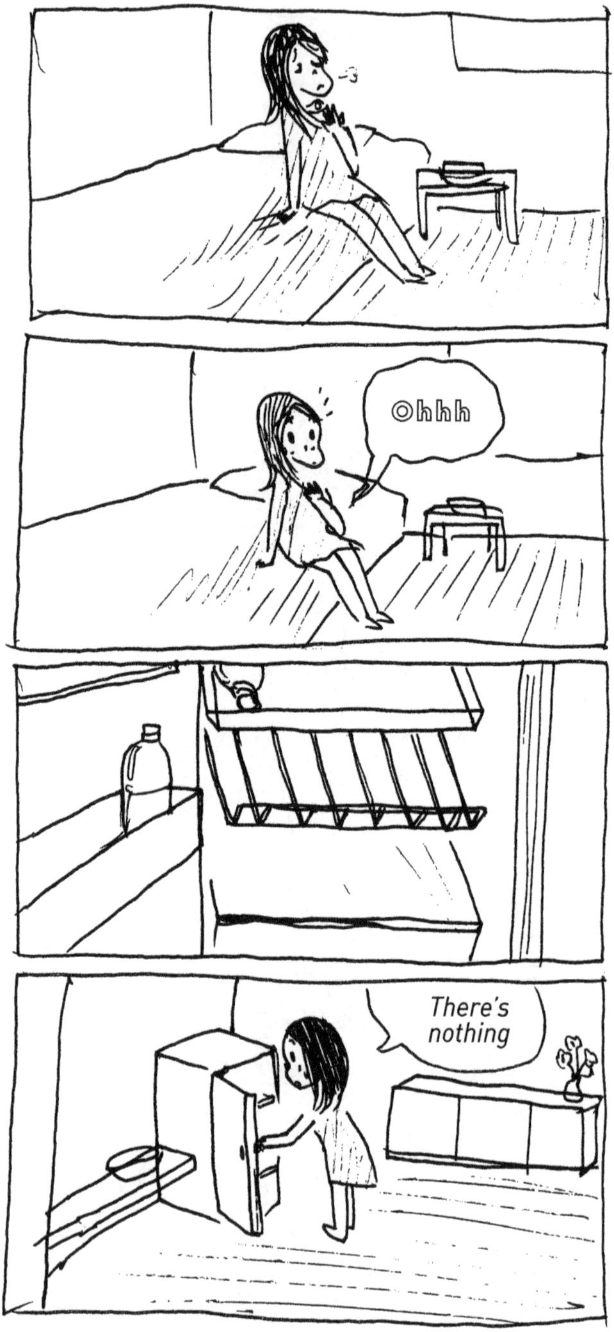
Ohhh
There's nothing

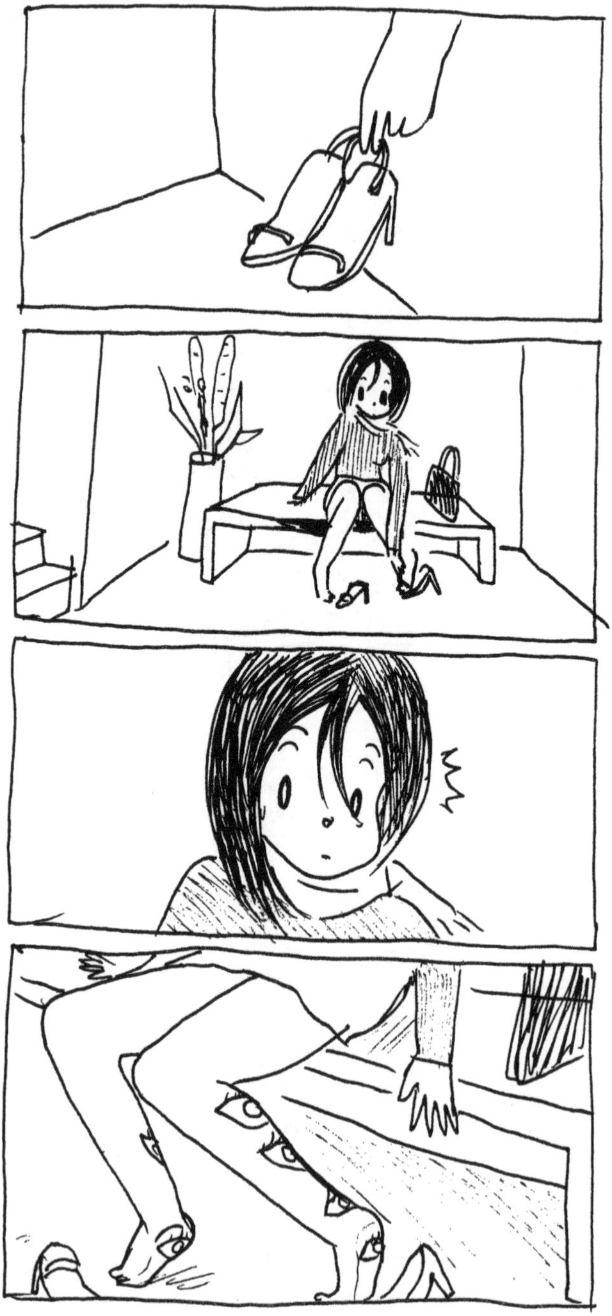

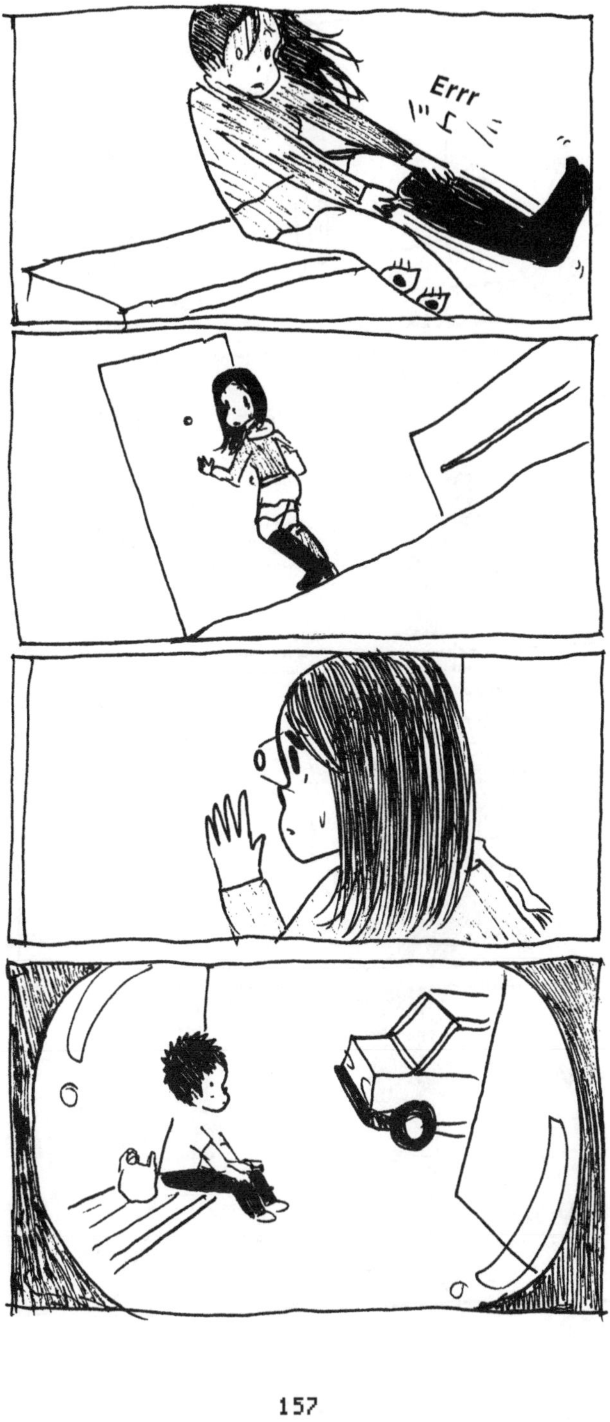
Errr

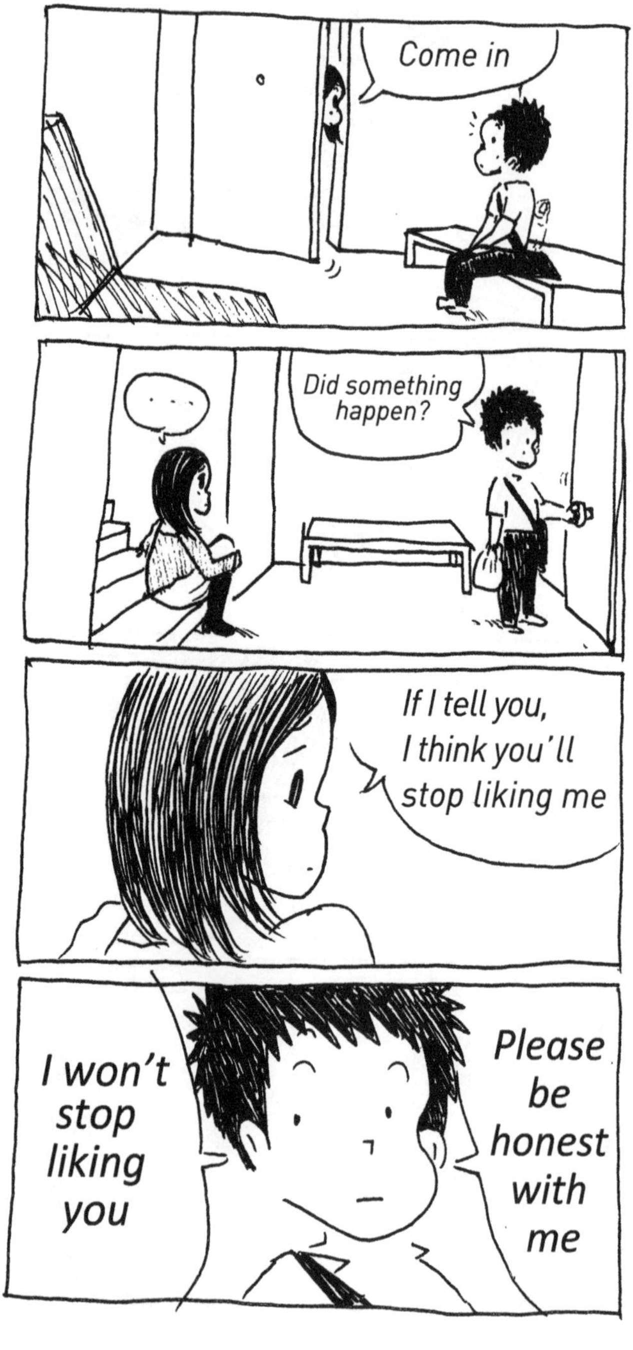
Come in
Did something happen?
...
If I tell you, I think you'll stop liking me
Please be honest with me
I won't stop liking you

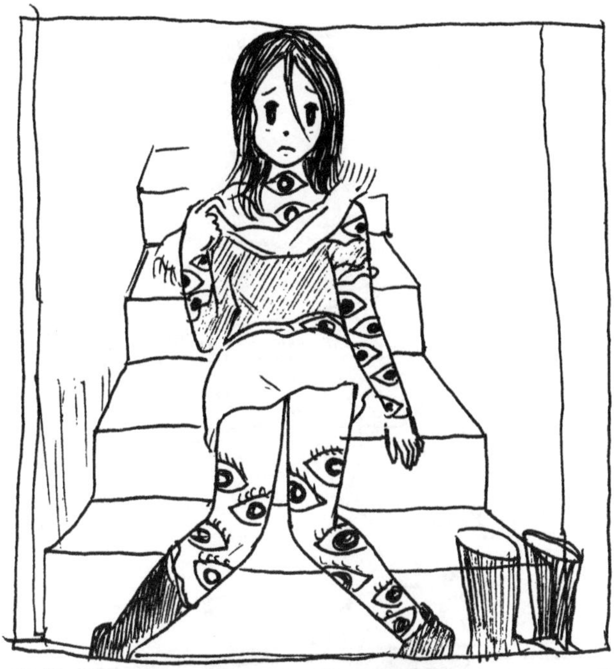

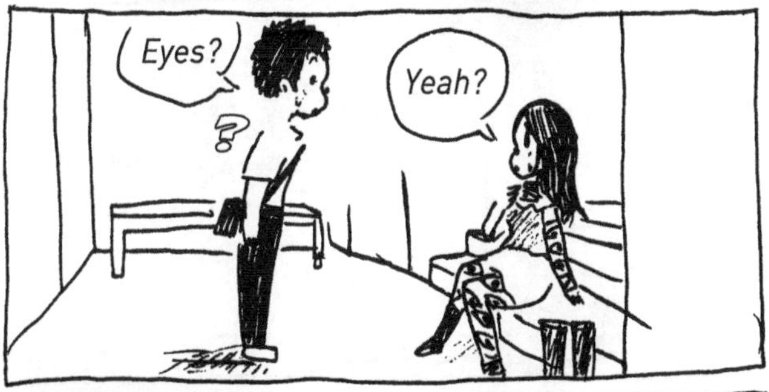
Eyes?
Yeah?

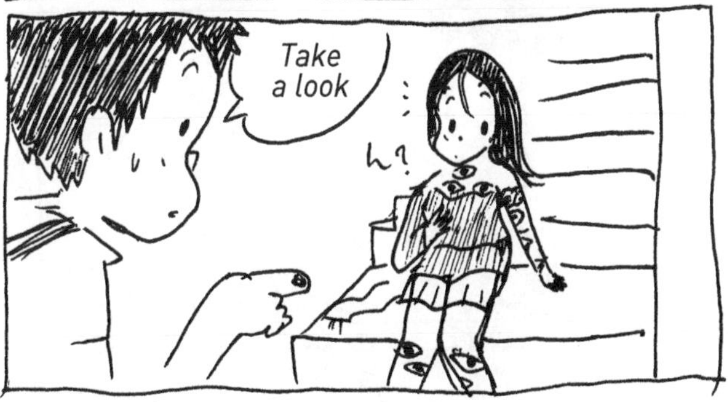
Take a look
ん?

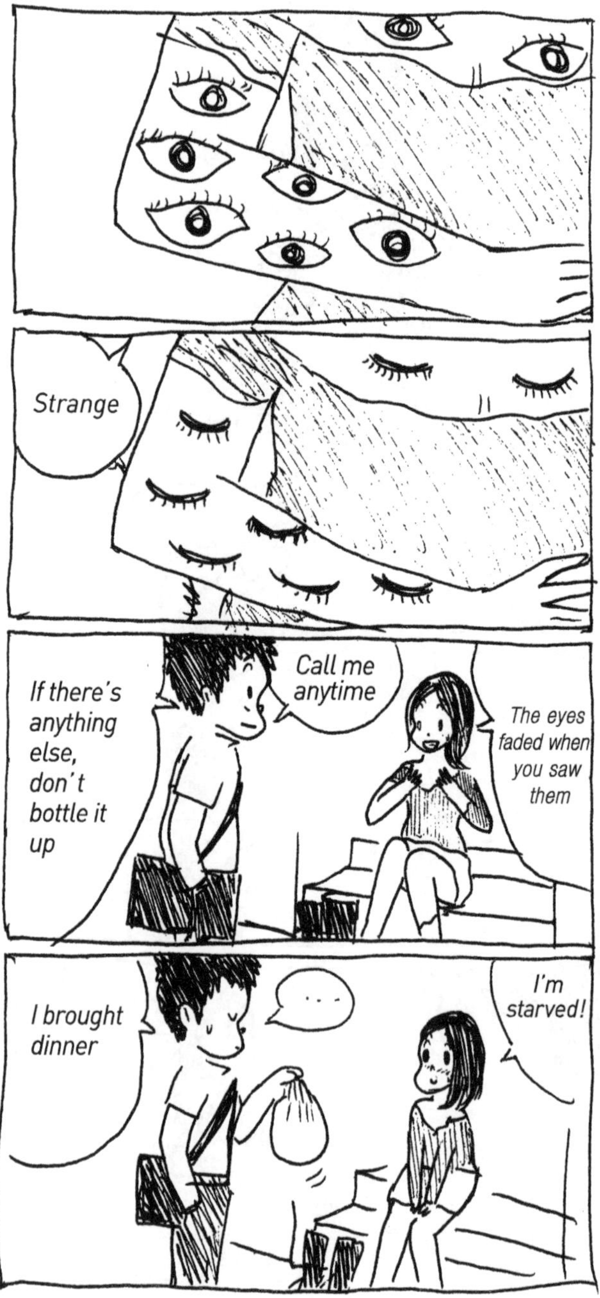
Strange
If there's anything else, don't bottle it up
Call me anytime
The eyes faded when you saw them
I brought dinner
. . .
I'm starved!

romance
continued

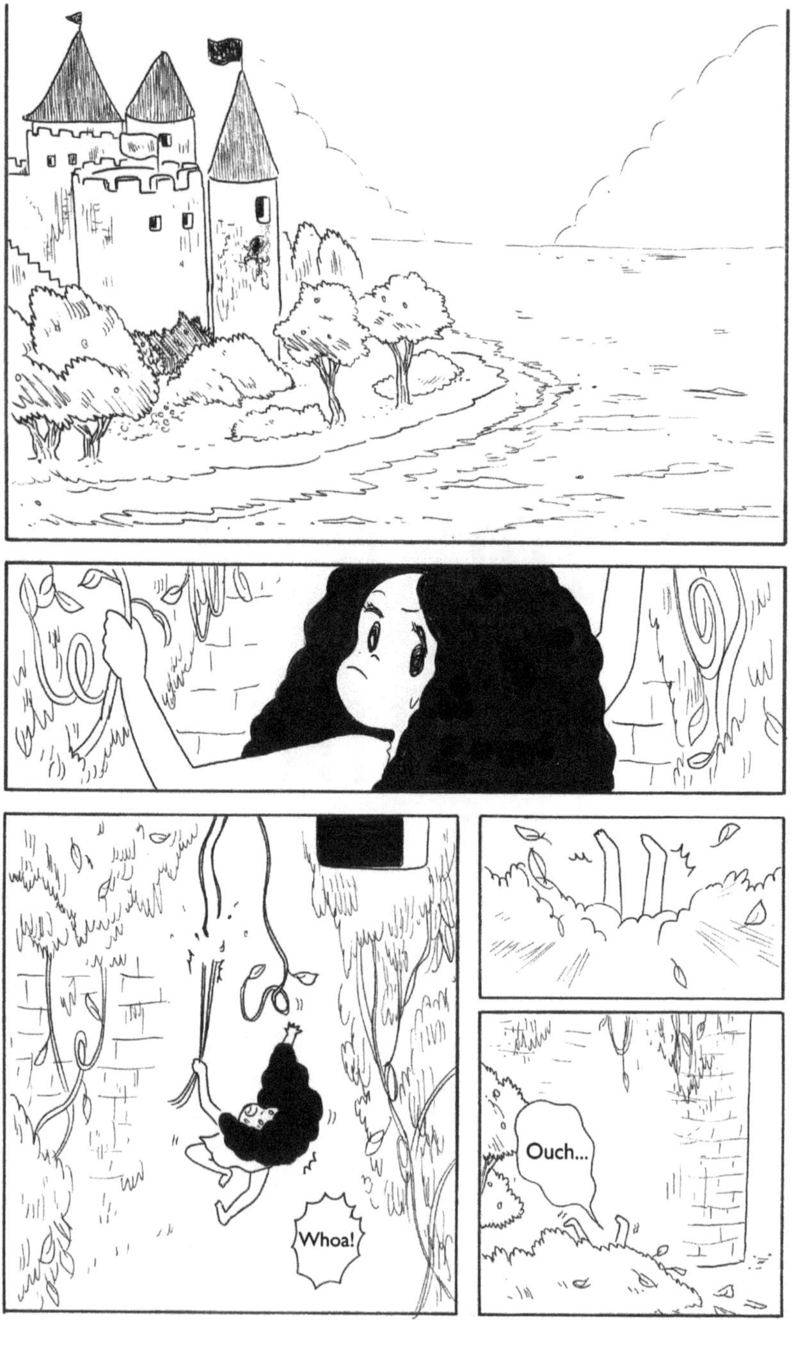
Whoa!
Ouch...

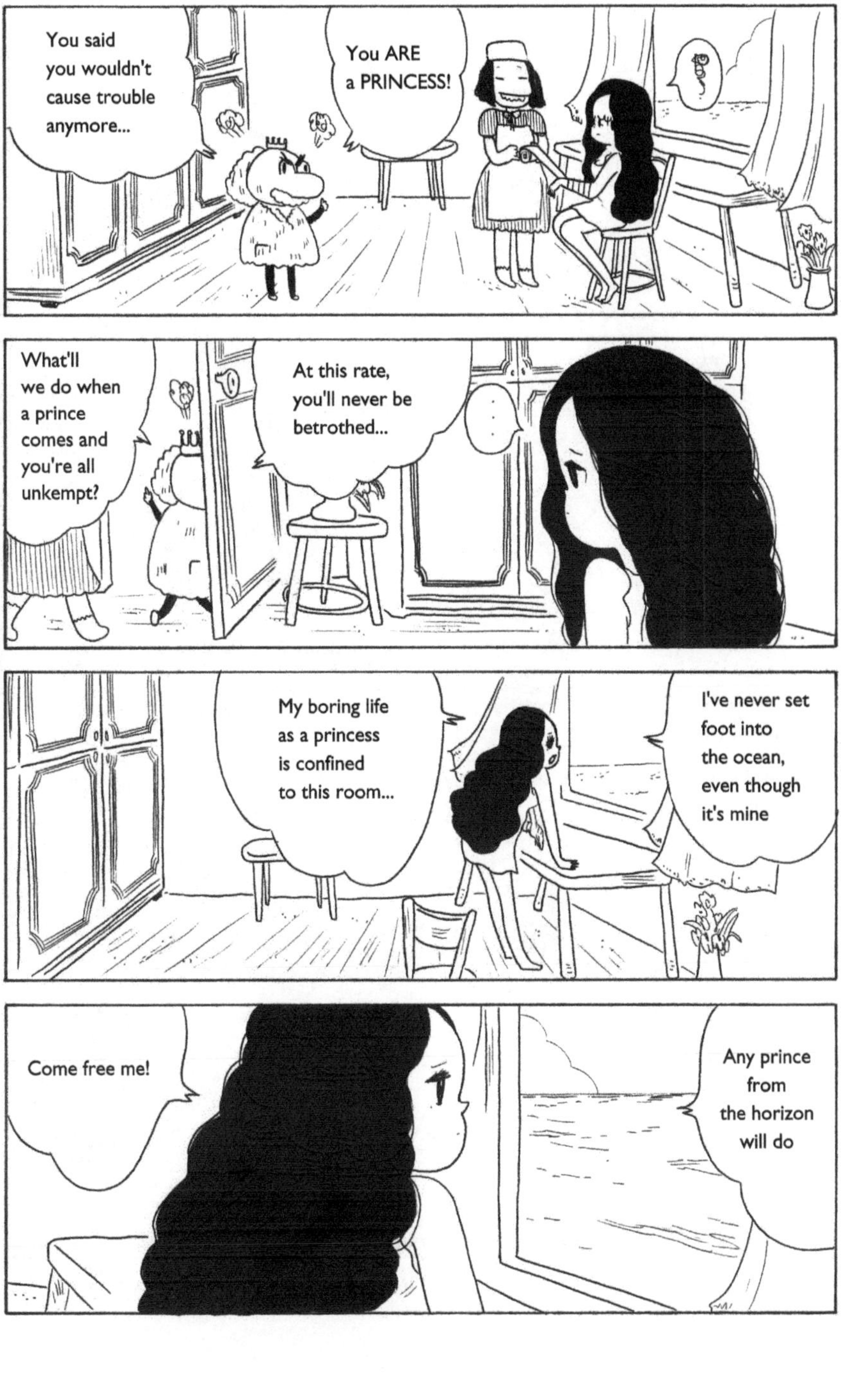
You said you wouldn't cause trouble anymore...
You ARE a PRINCESS!
What'll we do when a prince comes and you're all unkempt?
At this rate, you'll never be betrothed...
...
My boring life as a princess is confined to this room...
I've never set foot into the ocean, even though it's mine
Come free me!
Any prince from the horizon will do

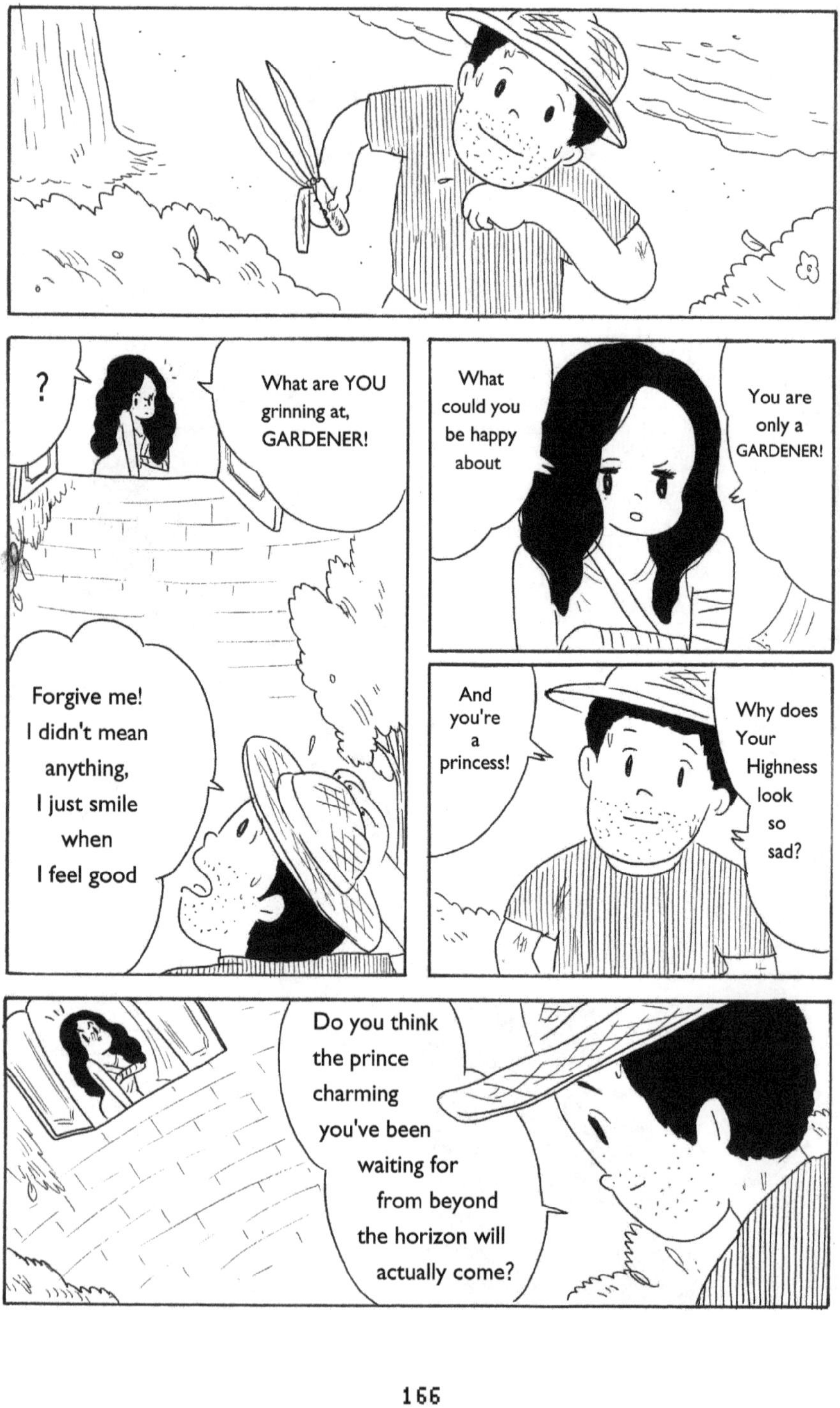
?
What are YOU grinning at, GARDENER!
Forgive me! I didn't mean anything, I just smile when I feel good
What could you be happy about
You are only a GARDENER!
And you're a princess!
Why does Your Highness look so sad?
Do you think the prince charming you've been waiting for from beyond the horizon will actually come?

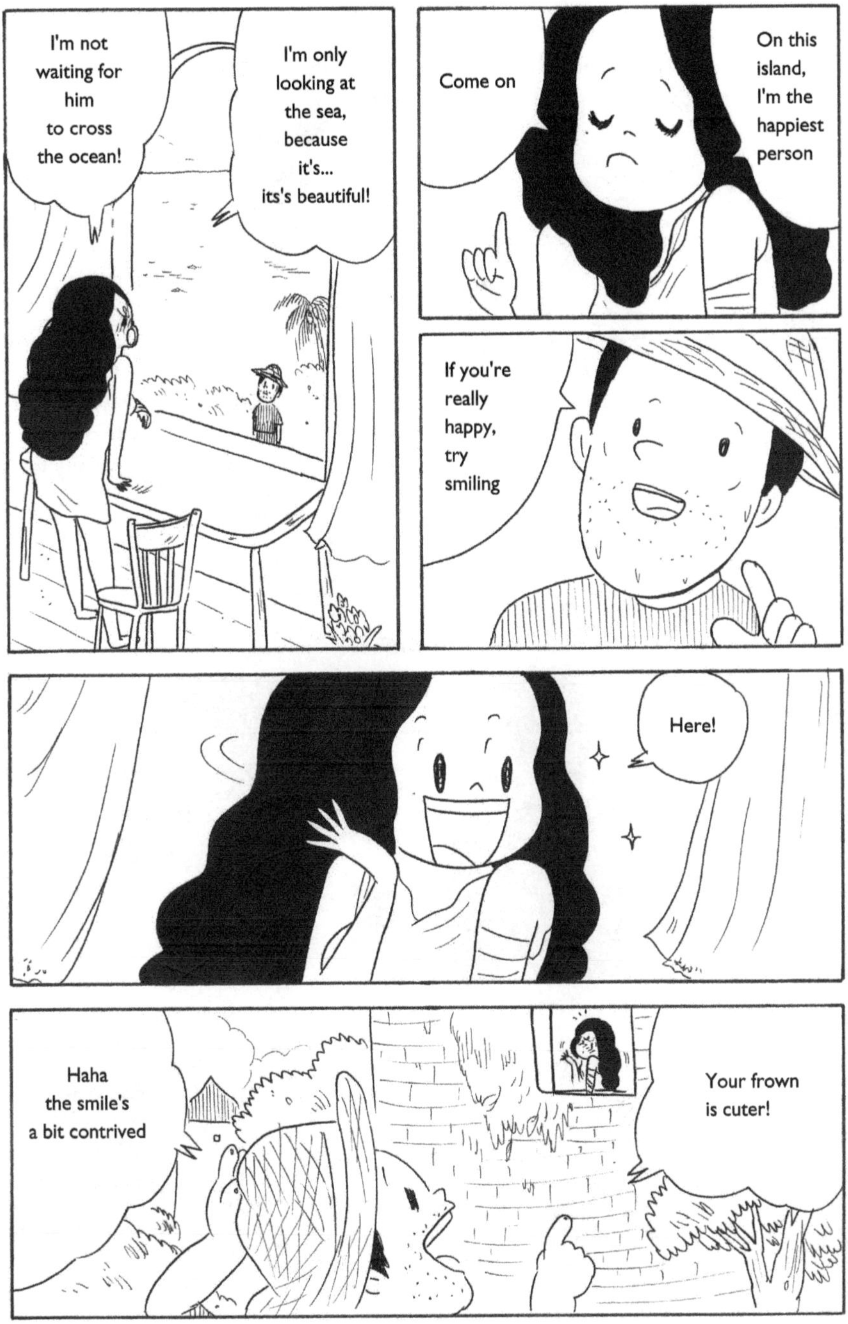
I'm not waiting for him to cross the ocean!
I'm only looking at the sea, because it's... its's beautiful!
Come on
On this island, I'm the happiest person
If you're really happy, try smiling
Here!
Haha the smile's a bit contrived
Your frown is cuter!

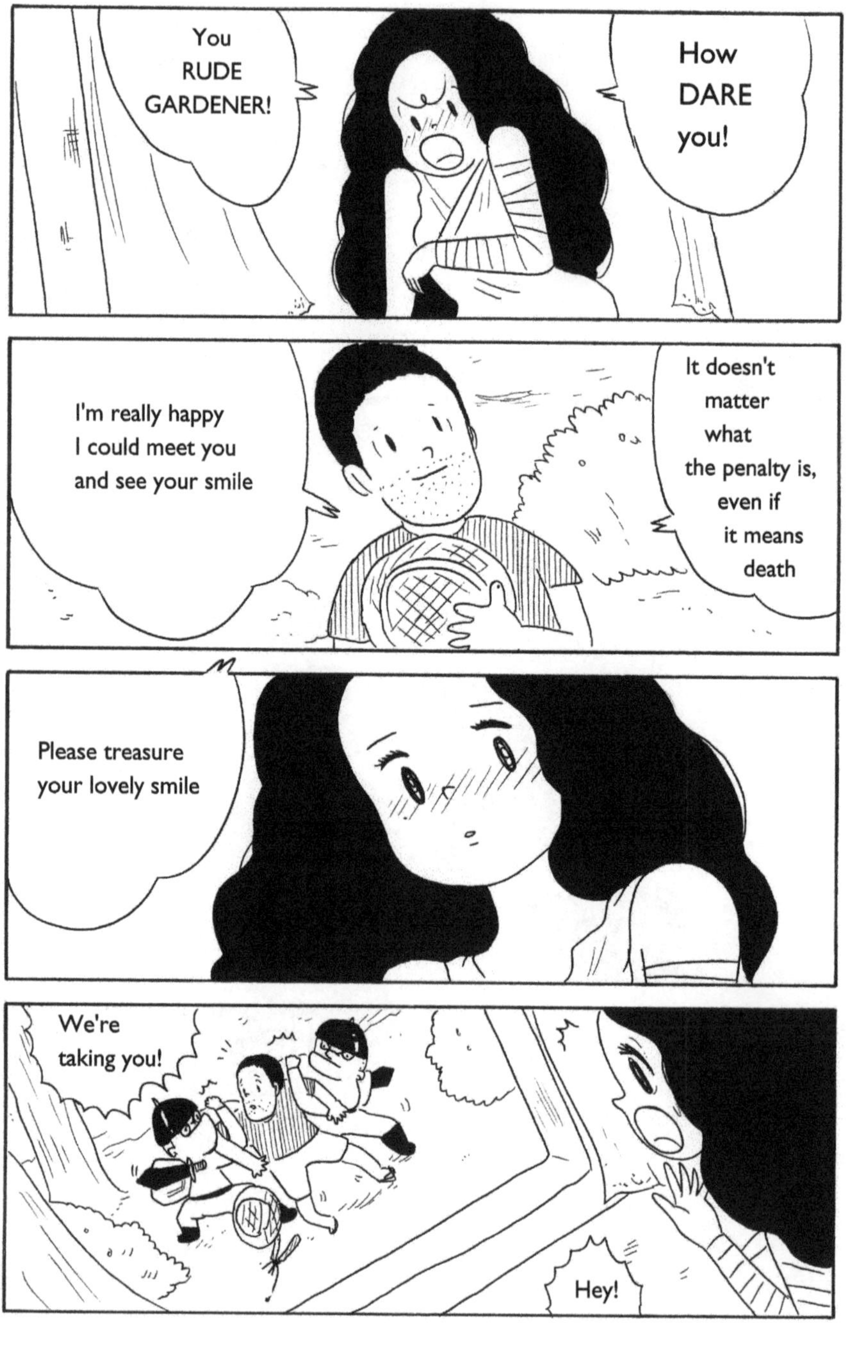
How DARE you!
You RUDE GARDENER!
It doesn't matter what the penalty is, even if it means death
I'm really happy I could meet you and see your smile
Please treasure your lovely smile
We're taking you!
Hey!

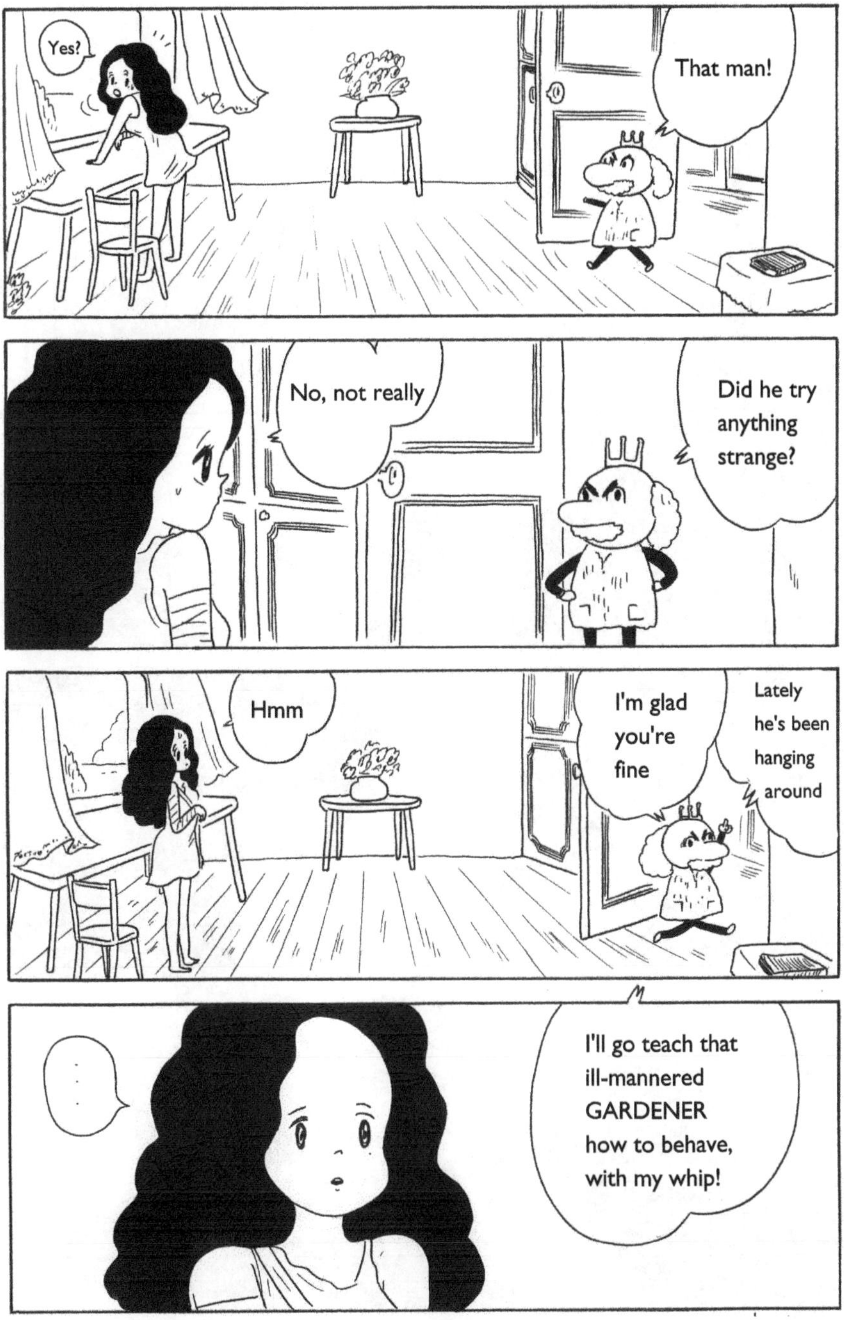
That man!
Yes?
Did he try anything strange?
No, not really
Lately he's been hanging around
I'm glad you're fine
Hmm
I'll go teach that ill-mannered GARDENER how to behave, with my whip!
. . .

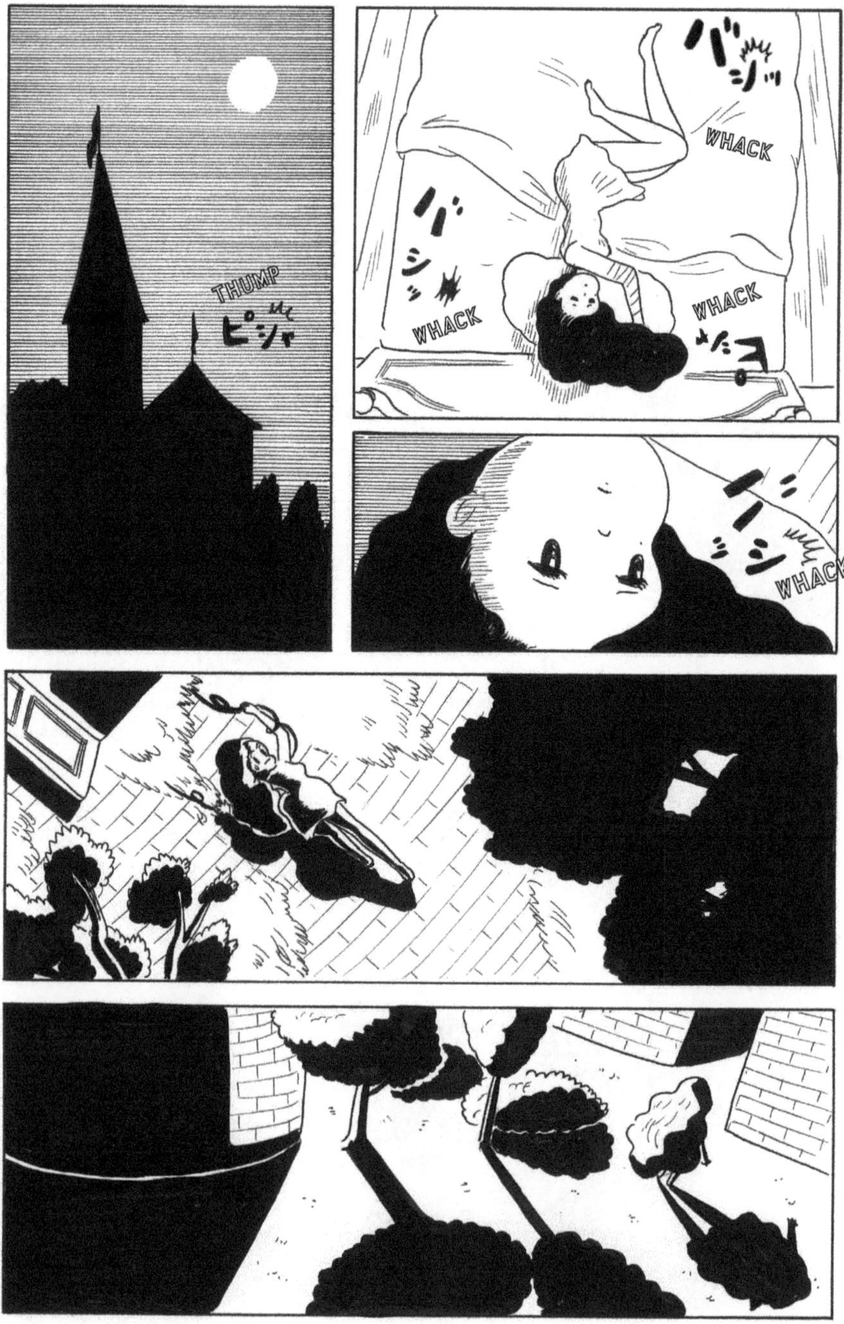
バシッ
WHACK
バシッ
WHACK
WHACK
バシッ
WHACK
THUMP
ピシャ

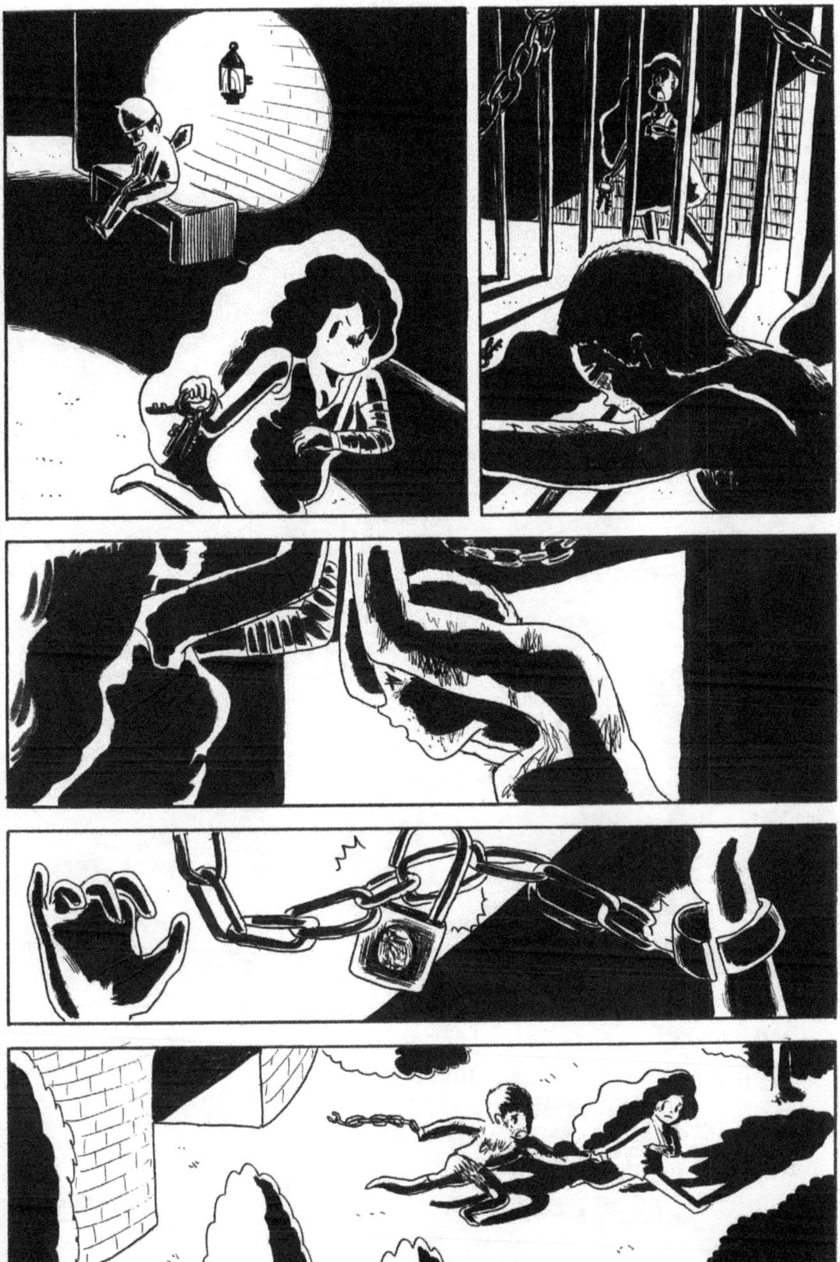

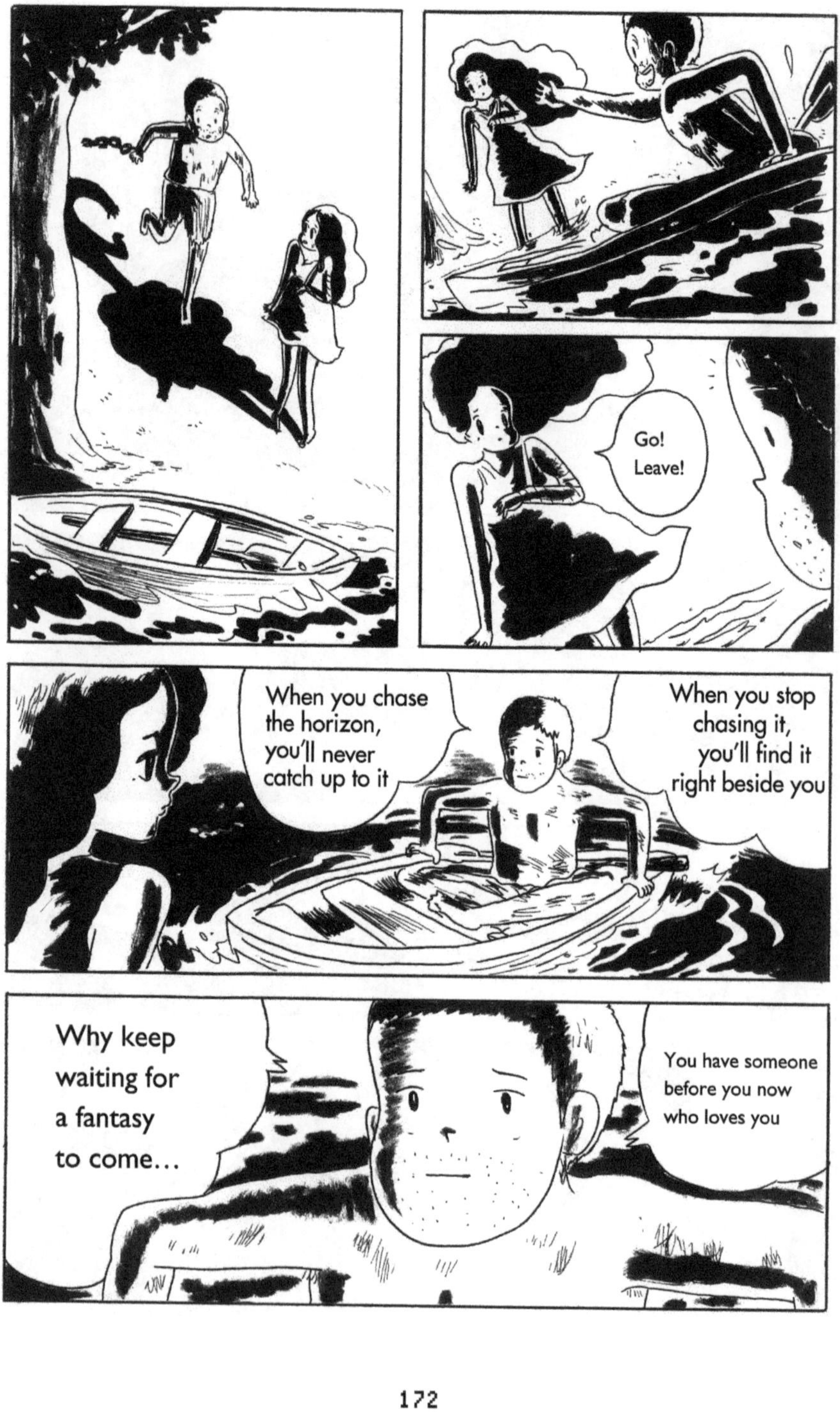
Go! Leave!
When you chase the horizon, you'll never catch up to it
When you stop chasing it, you'll find it right beside you
Why keep waiting for a fantasy to come...
You have someone before you now who loves you

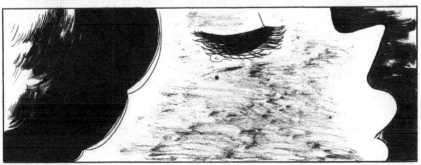

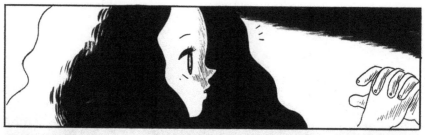

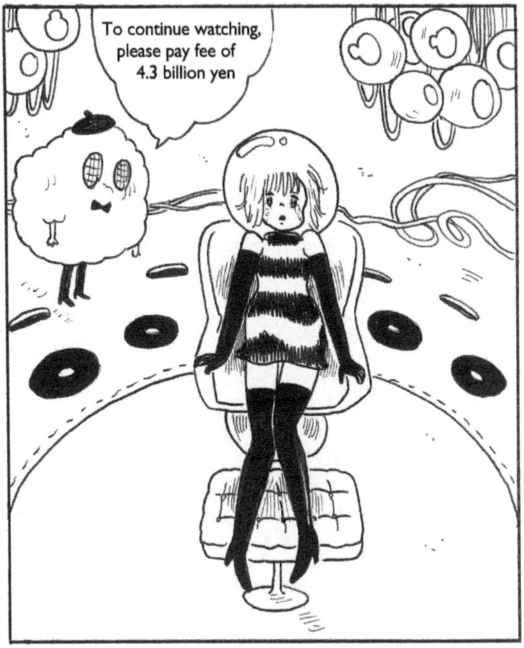
To continue watching, please pay fee of 4.3 billion yen

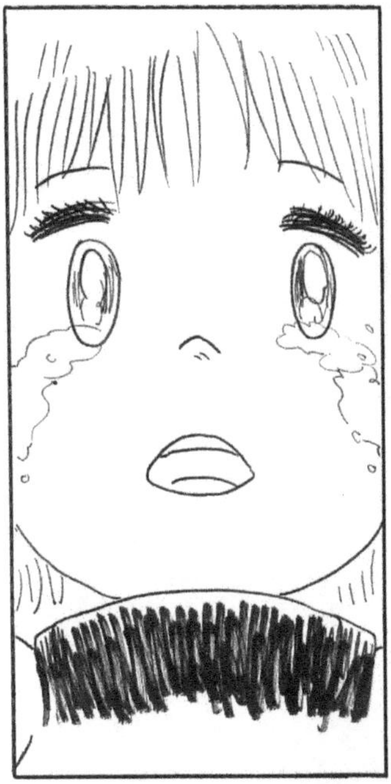

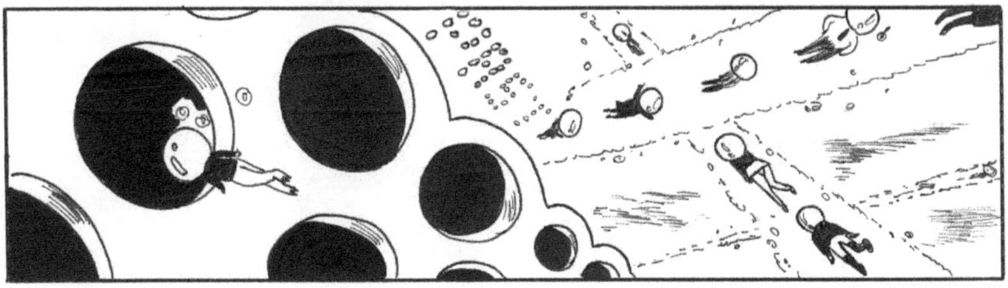

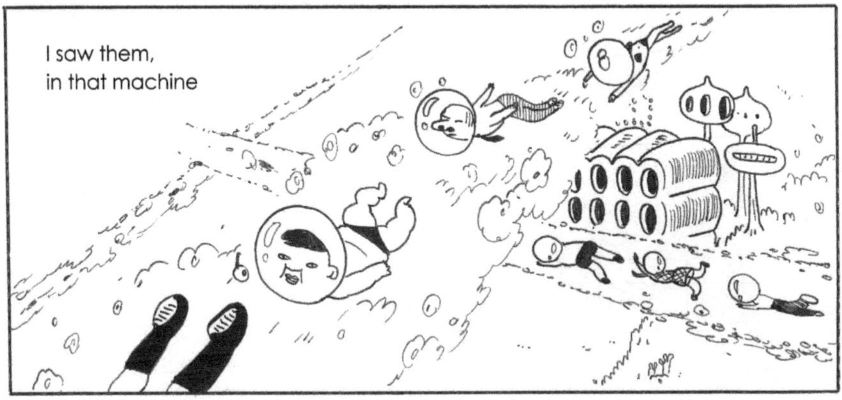
I saw them,
in that machine

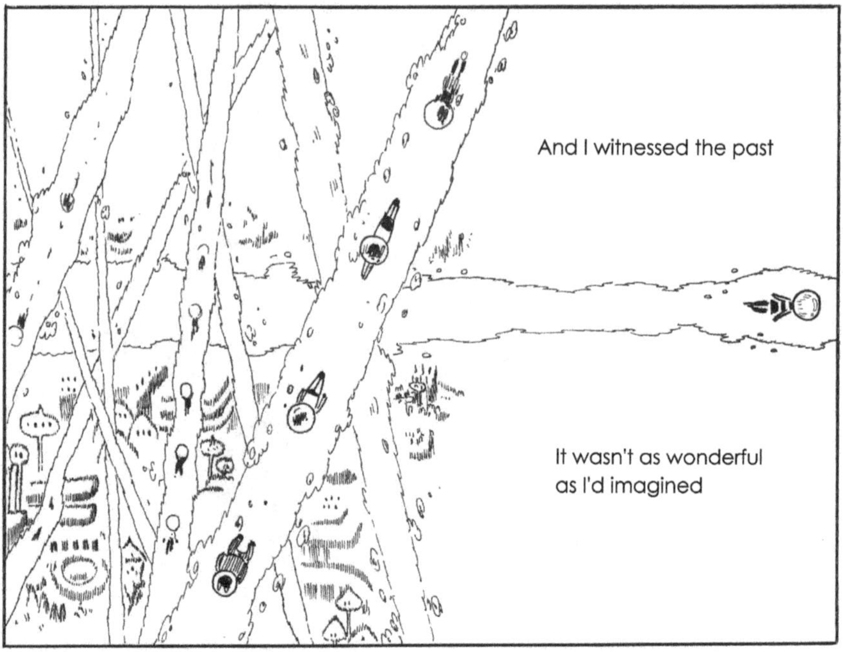
And I witnessed the past
It wasn't as wonderful as I'd imagined

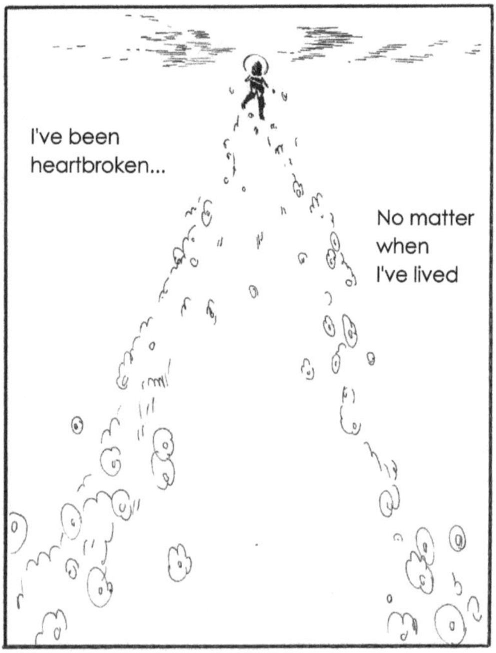
No matter when I've lived
I've been heartbroken...

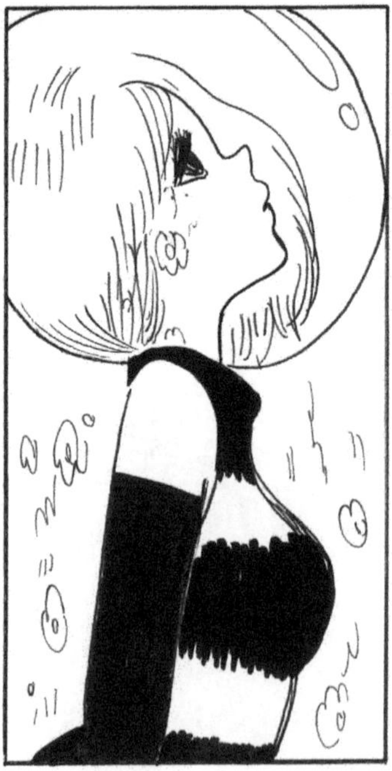

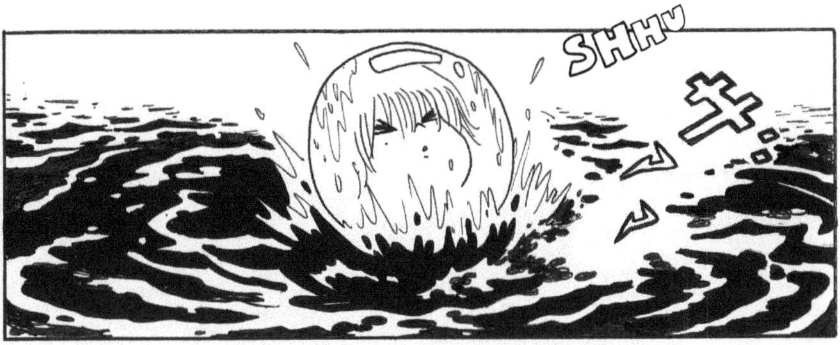
SHHU

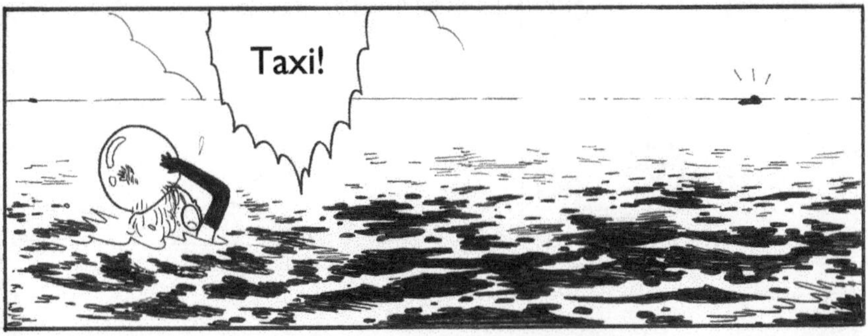
Taxi!

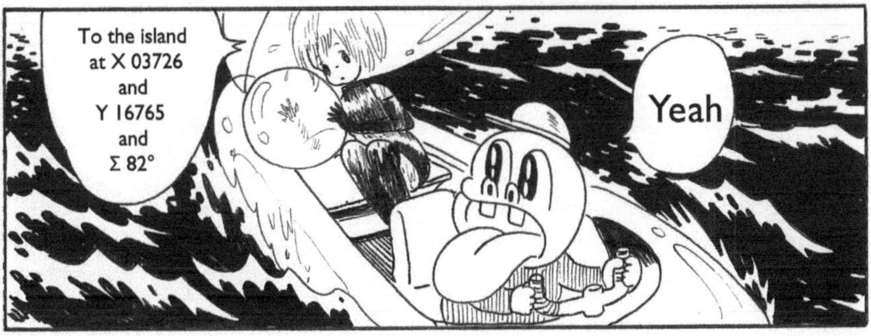
To the island at X 03726 and Y 16765 and Σ 82°
Yeah

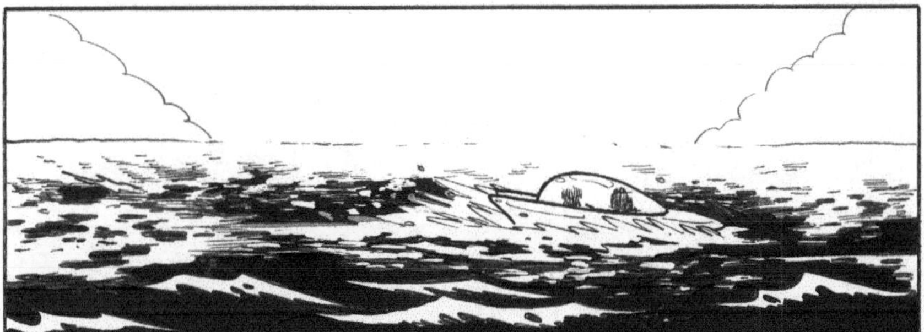

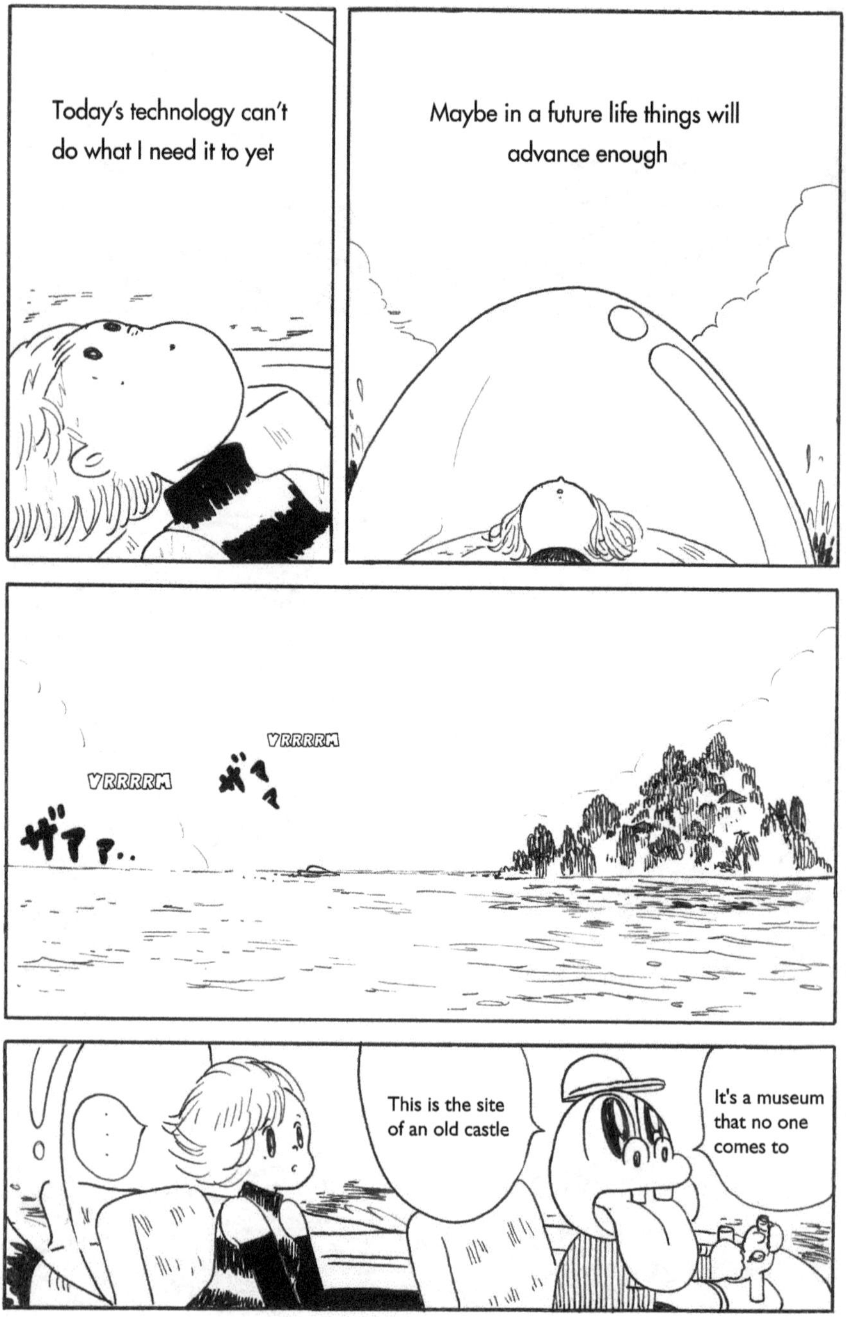
Today's technology can't do what I need it to yet
Maybe in a future life things will advance enough
VRRRRM
ザァァ..
VRRRRM
ザァァ
This is the site of an old castle
It's a museum that no one comes to

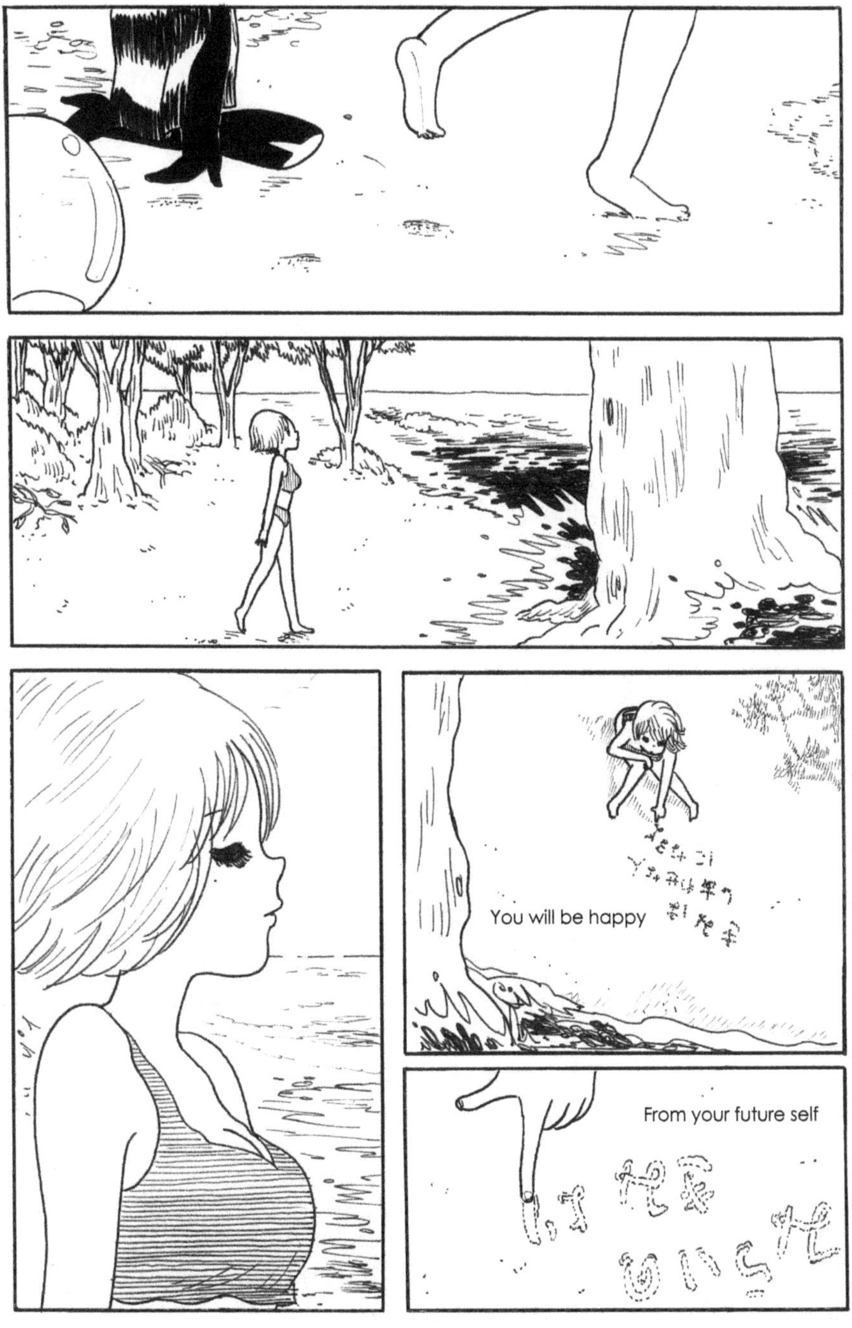
You will be happy
From your future self

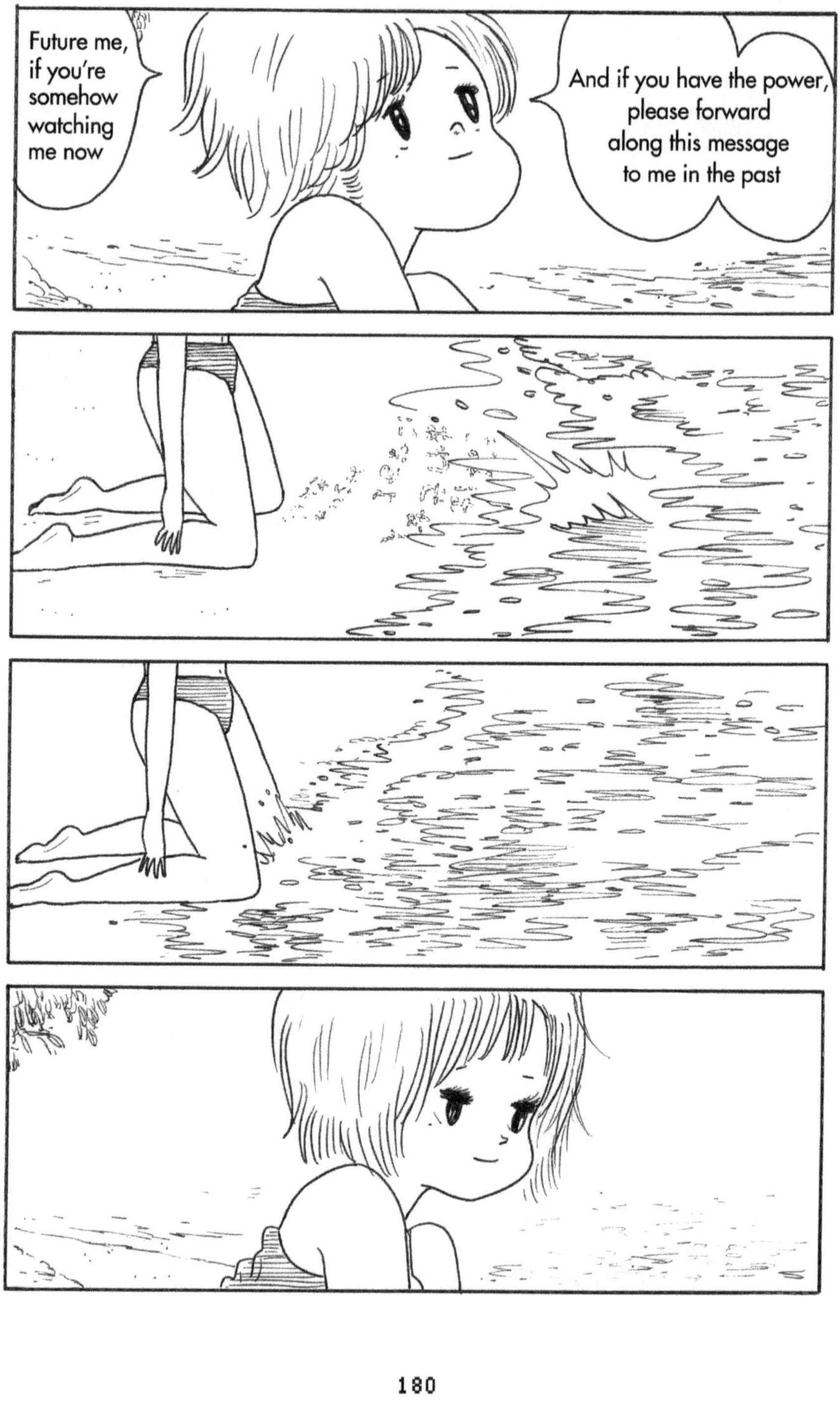
Future me, if you're somehow watching me now
And if you have the power, please forward along this message to me in the past

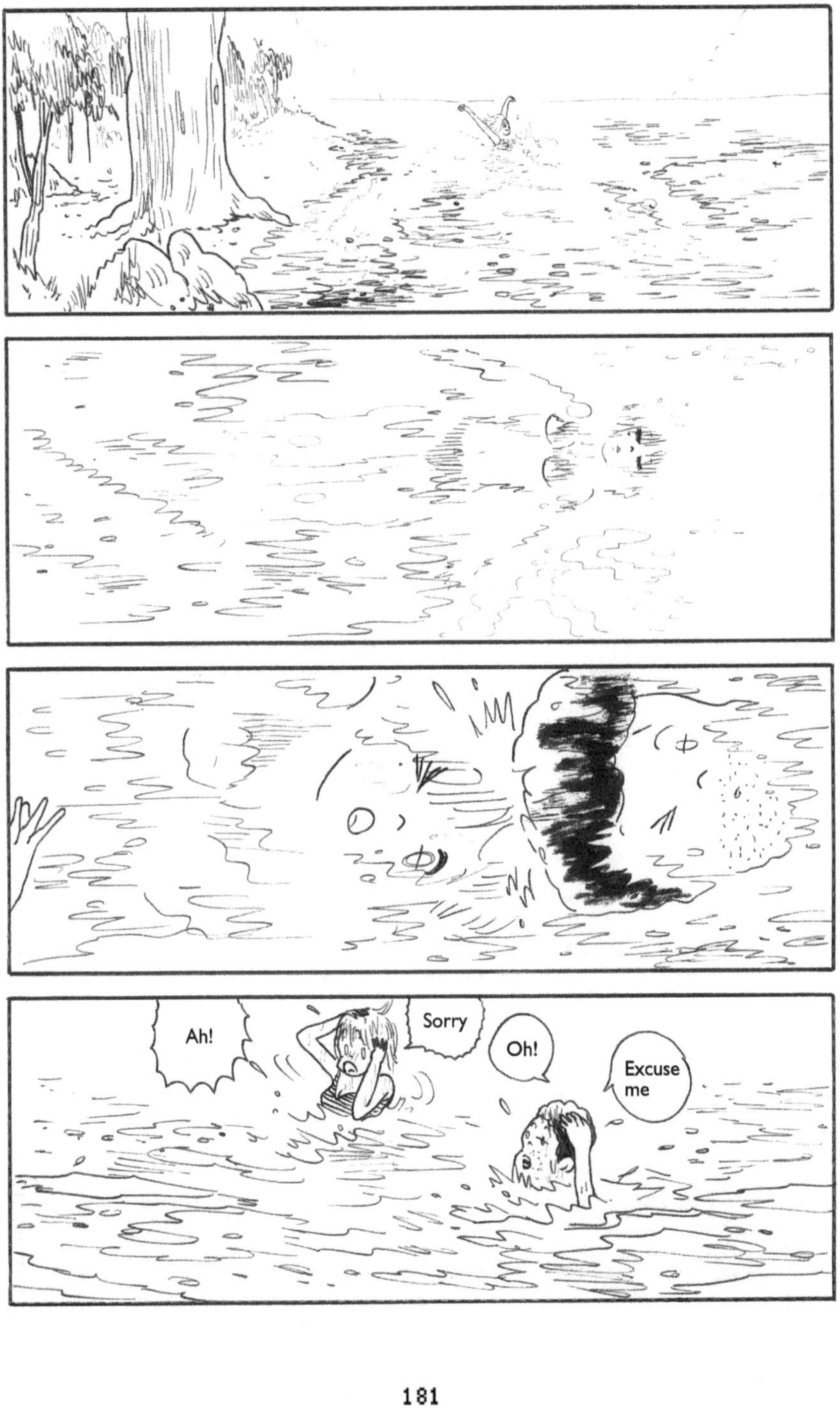
Ah!
Sorry
Oh!
Excuse me

WOOOSH　ザザァァ

You'll also be happy

From the future you

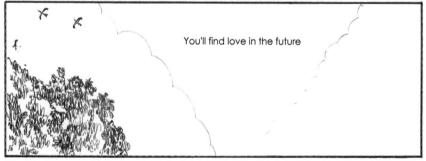

You'll find love in the future

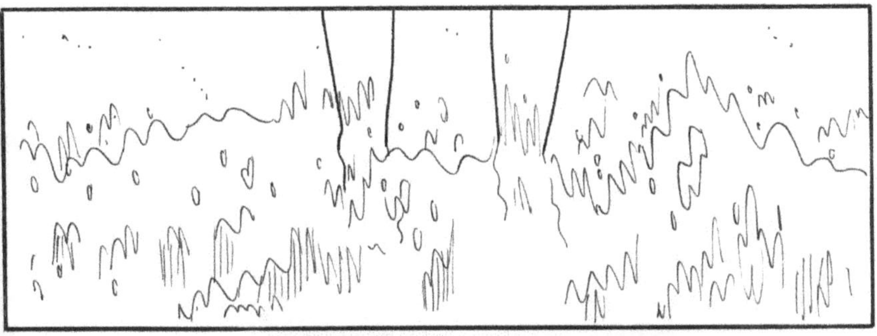

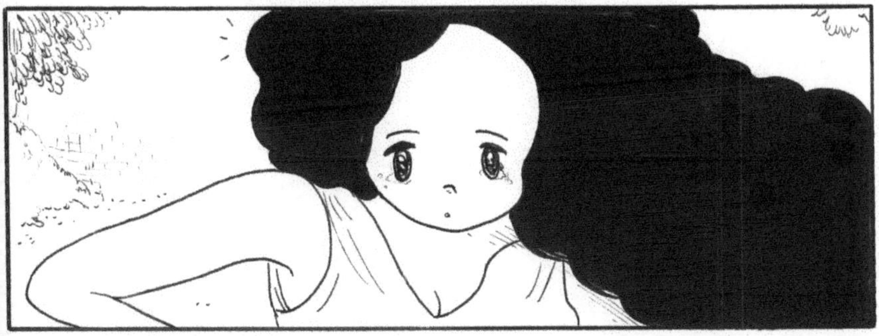

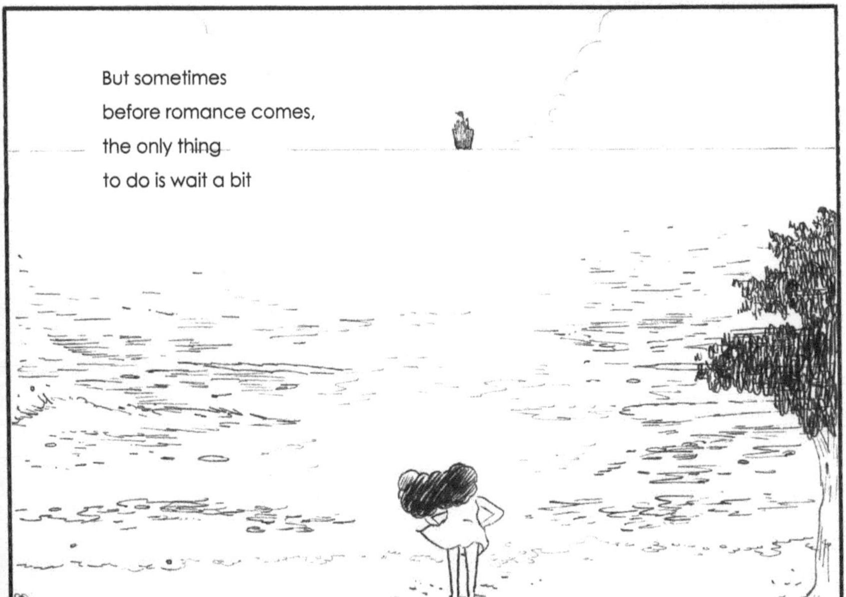
But sometimes
before romance comes,
the only thing
to do is wait a bit

Afterword

It doesn't seem like a coincidence that Wisut and I managed to become friends, overcoming difference in nationality, age, and gender. When I first encountered his work, I knew at a glance that he experienced the same things as me when, for instance, looking up at the night sky.

Before meeting Wisut, I thought it'd be impossible for such a dreamer, such a good person to exist in the world. But I've gotten to know Wisut and we've become friends. We learn much from each other because we have different weaknesses and strengths. When one of my weaknesses is exposed, Wisut reassures me with conviction that everything will be fine. My doubt melts away.

I once felt down because of someone's negativity directed towards me. I spoke with Wisut about matters and he reassured me by saying, "the only person who can get inside you is you. You're the person in control here."

Aside from having different strengths, Wisut and I share much in common. Like me, Wisut's sketches of the world take an allegorical shape. And as with my own work, he also doesn't obsess over miniscule details. Wisut instead creates an aesthetic that is his own, without having to compromise. Once readers finish this book I'm sure they'll be glad they've experienced all the feelings in their lives of which the text reminds them, because it is as if magic coats the pages of this book.

By Banana Yoshimoto

Translator's Note

I hope you've enjoyed reading Wisut Ponnimit's first English translation. Outside of Japan, it's hard to imagine just how acclaimed and multitalented he is. The first time I saw his fans funnel into a Tokyo art gallery for an anime screening with his live music and narration, I was surprised to find myself seated next to a woman resembling the author Banana Yoshimoto. Before us, in a white t-shirt and old jeans, Wisut gently perched his hands above a piano. Soon drawings of a boy cleaning an elementary school began to swirl on the gallery walls. The artist started playing a solo musical accompaniment and performed the voices for all of his characters live, in Japanese. Wisut's characters — fashion models, shy children, lifelong elevator riders — found themselves in love, philosophizing about the universe. Occasionally, Wisut took a break between animations to translate poetry or to cover the Velvet Underground on acoustic guitar.

For those who haven't had the pleasure of encountering Wisut around Tokyo, I suggest squirreling away the airfare or train cost for a visit. In the meantime, you can find some of his animations online. In his animations, as in this book, Wisut blurs genre lines. Perhaps for this reason, Japanese bookstore clerks seem to struggle in deciding on where to place Wisut's publications: I've seen his works stocked as manga, self-help, and even philosophy. While perhaps not a philosopher in the typical sense, Wisut certainly tries to make sense of the human condition with a buoyant, smart style. In any case, you are probably feeling how I do when I finish Wisut's books, I want to read them again.

By Matthew Chozick

Lightning Source UK Ltd.
Milton Keynes UK
UKHW012033230522
403389UK00004B/1184